PHOENIX RISING

"IS JESUS CALLING YOU OUT?"

Evelyn Bross

Dedication

1. I need to dedicate this book to my Neurosurgeon who did my brain surgeries. He never gave up on me when he realized I had a Severe and Rare type of Epilepsy during this brain surgery. I had told my Neurosurgeon, "If I die on the operating table, you do not give up on me. I will come back to life. Just don't give up on me." My Neurosurgeon told me I only had a "5%' Chance that I would Die during my brain surgery. You need to read to see what happens.

2. I also want to dedicate this book to my dad. Dad never "Laughed" at me, and he helped me Re-Learn some simple things that people take for granted. My dad was the only person who listened to me and answered any questions I had "Truthfully". There is more you will learn of why dad was a very important figure in my life.

3. Then I need to dedicate this book to my sons. They were young teenagers when I had my Four Brain Surgeries in Two Weeks. I know they never understood how serious my brain surgery was. My sons had to teach me things that a "Two-Year-Old" would have to learn. Not only this but both of my sons saved me years later from serious situations that I should have never encountered. You need to read this book to find out what that is.

4. Another dedication goes to the store manager of a restaurant that I worked at prior to having my brain surgeries. She saw me at the restaurant two years after I had my Four Brain Surgeries. She came to me and told me she remembered what a good employee I was before I quit there. She asked me if I would come back to work there two days a week. I told her I just had brain surgery two years ago. I told her how serious my brain surgery was. She said she never knew I had brain surgery. I told her I need to Re-Learn everything all over again. I told her I needed an employee to be with me to teach me everything all over again. She agreed for me to have the assistance if I came back to work. You need to read this book to find out how far I have come working there.

5. I Need to dedicate one more important person who was there for me before, during, and after my brain surgeries. This person took over my "Four" different newspaper companies when my seizures got chronic. He helped me nonstop after I experienced a serious fall after my ranch home caught fire. He was the "Only" person who helped me try to go through the debris to see what is salvageable. None of my relatives would lift a finger to help me and I had a broken ankle (not associated with the fire). He also stayed with me for a short time after I came home from having my four brain surgeries. Read to find out why he never stayed very long with me after I came home from having my four brain surgeries. You need to read this book. I believe it will shock you.

6. I need to Dedicate Barry and the BookFuel Publishing Company for publishing my book. Barry treated my book as if it was his own book being published. Barry Put his "Heart and Soul" into overseeing all the departments working on my book. Departments like the designer, writers, etc. Barry even helped finish up the loose ends to my book. Barry and I stayed in contact throughout my book being published. It was a great blessing to have Barry in charge of my book being published.

7. There is one very important Person that I need to thank deeply for always being there for me through thick and thin. This person's name is Jesus Christ!!!! Jesus never left my side. He was there protecting me with anything and everything that I encountered throughout my entire life. If Jesus wasn't with me, I know that I would never have survived what all I have encountered.

Note: My family was a religious family. I went to church every weekend throughout my childhood life. But when you live behind the "Closed Doors" of this family, you will wonder how a religious family could be like this. Even though there were times I never went to church, I always had Jesus, the Holy Spirit, and God in my LIFE.

Is Jesus Calling You Out?

About the Author

Evelyn Bross was told by a student Neurosurgeon that she has a 3% chance to be where she is today in life. That was before she even shocked herself by advancing even further than that just a few years later. You see Evelyn died as an infant. She came back to life as an Epileptic. Evelyn life was horrific starting as a child. Things never got better for about half a century of her life. Something happened to Evelyn when she was a child. She couldn't remember the details of what happened until over half a century later. Evelyn finds the "Missing Puzzle" that was traumatizing her all her life. Not long afterwards Evelyn found out more information that was withheld from her. Evelyn had to do her own research herself. Evelyn is someone you wish you would have gotten to known. Even though all the odds are against Evelyn, she stands tall because even though nobody would listen or help, she knew that Jesus was listening to her prayers. Jesus, the Holy Spirit, and God are Evelyn's protectors from all the episodes that have happened to her. Evelyn has encountered many Atheist type people in her life. Or is it that these people claimed to believe in Jesus, the Holy Spirit, & God but they do not practice the faith in Jesus, God, and the Holy Spirit regularly? Jesus has some things that he wants her to do in this world. You see, Evelyn experiences have taught her how to help other people who are in the predicaments that she has overcome. Evelyn has a business plan to start up a Re-Learning Center for people with brain damage. The people Evelyn wants to help are the people who have at least a GED to a master's degree in college and then they have brain damage. Many people who have brain damage are put in a facility for the rest of their lives. Evelyn has helped several people who have memory issues. Once she told them what to do, Evelyn would see this person a few months later looking so much better. Oh. Evelyn has even wondered if she can help early-stage Alzheimer's and Demetia with her Re-Learning Center. You will understand why she wonders about this after you read her book. She did give suggestions to someone she met to help her parents who have Dementia. She explained to Evelyn her parents a little bit.

That's when Evelyn knew what she needed to do to help her parent with Dementia. Evelyn saw this woman about two months later and the woman said her parent is improving a little. Then she said she didn't know how smart her parent was before this.

Today Evelyn is working at an Adult Daycare Facility for Adults with physical and mental disabilities. These adults even have a low I.Q. But Evelyn believes that with her personal experiences she has developed that she can helped these clients. What is the outcome of working at this Adult Daycare?

Evelyn is looking for some qualified people to be on her Committee Board to start-up her Re-Learning Center. Evelyn is also looking for a very good Grant Writer. Evelyn has plans on how to do fundraising. The "Lightbulb Brain" is her logo drawn by a person she gave some hints to help her memory. She told Evelyn I will draw your Logo for nothing. She drew this lightbulb Brain for me. My phrase for my Business is "Turn on the Memories".

One more thing. Evelyn is trying to start-up Epileptic Rights. Evelyn knows Jesus does not like what he sees happening. This is where the subtitle Is Jesus Calling You Out? Comes in. When you read her book you will understand why she is determined to help all Epileptics to have Rights.

Contents

Chapter One

The battle for my life started right when I was born.

When I was an infant, I was diagnosed with scarlet fever. Nobody could tell how I fhad fallen victim to this deadly disease, but one thing was sure… the chances of the infant surviving the night were pretty slim.

This was the '60s. Back then, antibiotics were almost non-existent, and hospitals were only locally oriented institutions with fewer than a hundred beds available. There were no modern facilities, and nobody knew how to cure scarlatina. Perhaps that's why nobody could come forward to lend a helping hand when I was struggling on my own.

The house call doctor tried everything in his power to reverse my fate, but to no avail. The infant me was no longer breathing. I was pronounced dead. But the doctor was not ready to accept another defeat from scarlet fever, so he asked my mother to let him try a new technique. The doctor made his point but alerted her at the same time. He informed my family that the technology was not proven, and nothing could be said for sure, but was there anything to lose? I was dead; what else could go wrong? My mother agreed, and the doctor proceeded with what today is known as CPR.

I am sure it must be hard to accept that CPR was not a thing back in the day, but that is how we lived all along. That was the first time the doctor ever performed CPR on an infant. It was a battle between life and death that lasted almost one and a half hours. Nobody knew what would happen in those ninety minutes and how things would unfold. The CPR was too risky since nobody knew its outcomes.

Finally, the CPR worked like a charm, and the doctor brought the brain-dead me back to life. And that's how I was revitalized. But, it was not the end of tragedies in my life. In fact, it was the beginning of all the torments coming my way. Soon enough, my mother had to call the doctor because my infant body would not stop jerking. The doctor made another visit and broke the tragic news. My mother stood there listening to how one part of my brain was signaled before the other, not knowing what this could mean for her daughter. The doctor then informed my mother that her daughter was epileptic and would have to live the rest of her life with this brain disorder.

During those days, epilepsy was shrouded in all sorts of misconceptions and mysteries. People used to frown over epileptic patients. They used to link it with demonic possession, and the seizures were seen as an attack by demons. In this day and age, people would probably laugh, knowing epileptic seizures were considered paranormal activities, but the truth is, people saw it as divine intervention. Believe me; your imagination could hardly come close to the torture of living as an epileptic person during the '60s. One moment, you are dealing with the pain and seizure, and the other, you are labeled as demonic just because your electrical pattern was disrupted.

I still have an intense memory of my childhood, which was never like some ordinary child. I remember taking medicines first thing in the morning before going to school. The church school was just half a block from my residence, and I used to rely on the church bell to remind me of my medicine in the second half of the day. The instant I heard the bell ringing, I went to my mother and said, "It's medicine time." That was a pretty pathetic routine for a child who wanted nothing from the world but love and composure. However, the world is a cruel place, especially for people who are weaker than most, and it was the same for me, or maybe even worse. I was just a kid who loved watching Cinderella. You could say I saw my reflection in her. Not to mention, our lives were so similar that, at times, it felt uncanny. Cinderella and I never got a chance to have a normal childhood. She was isolated from the world and never got the opportunity to make friends, and I was no different. She had two ungenerous elder sisters, and my sisters were no better. However, Cinderella was slightly different from me in one aspect. Her stepmom treated her as an indentured servant; all she received from her was a cold shoulder, but it was different for me. I was not being wounded by a stranger with no blood ties; instead, it was my biological mother who oppressed me. At least Cinderella knew her biological mother would have loved and cherished her if she had been alive, but it was the contrary for me.

Tell me, how can I ever let go of this melancholic feeling when I know my own mother despised me? That's how I started feeling a close connection with Cinderella. I felt as if I was the muse behind her story, as if we both were living the same life but in different dimensions. For all I know, I started believing that my pain is not eternal and that I can live a happy life like Cinderella one day. Deary Me!

It would be better to say that Cinderella became my coping mechanism, and I started using her to escape my reality. In the early years of childhood, all I ever encountered was my mother shouting, yelling, and screaming at me and others for no reason. The whole family yelled, screamed, and fought endlessly. I had to deal with this trauma daily with epilepsy. Occasionally, my mother picked up one side of the table and slammed it down with all her might to show us her power. She would also throw glass dishes across the room. Anybody in the way had to move out of the way or get hit by the glass dishes flying in the air. Mom would also sit in the kitchen chair, make a fist of both hands, and pound the kitchen table, screaming like a petulant child. We siblings had no idea what was happening. We were clueless but terrified. After that, there was not a single day when incidents like this did not flare up.

My mother knew I was sensitive to name-calling, yet she never stopped my siblings from calling me "sissy." It was the only nickname I got at home, and what a shame because it was extremely humiliating. One that I refused to own. It was my mother's cousin's idea to give such a disgusting name to a naïve baby. Though I cannot say much about her intentions, nobody called me Evelyn again from that moment on. Since then, everyone began calling me "Sissy." Nobody knew how badly this name perforated my young and tender soul. I despised this name, but nobody cared.

My siblings believed my real name was "Sissy." My brother was in grade school when he drew a picture of the family. He put their names on each family member and wrote "Sissy" for my name. Upon being scolded by the teacher, my brother said, "That's her name." The teacher called my mother about my questionable name. She unashamedly explained, "That's what we have called her since she was a toddler." The teacher told my mother to tell the siblings my real name. Until then, all my siblings thought my name was Sissy!

The truth is that epileptic people did not have an easy life back then. They were always the center of the public's mockery and snide comments and were religiously ridiculed and laughed at. I was one of their targets as well. Not only my classmates but even my family members used to give me all kinds of derogatory names. They called me 'Devilish,' 'Evil,' 'Wicked,' etc., hoping that I would not retaliate since I had epilepsy. But what made these children, let alone my family, think that people with epilepsy can't fight? Oh, it's because if we fight, we are demonic. If we don't, we will have to endure this torment until our last breath.

I was an outcast at my school. From a distance, so many students of my age appeared to surround me, but I was permanently alienated, and trust me, it was a torment. Not a single day passed when I went to school without a gloomy face. Students formed alliances to tease me by giving me several demeaning names. The sad part was that even my home was not a safe place for me. My mother and siblings treated me no better than the bullies at school. Returning home from school was like going through another episode of torture. I was just a kid who had nobody and nowhere to go. All I ever asked for was to be treated like everyone, but no place would welcome me without holding prejudices against me. I was left holding back my tears and letting them flow when alone. Like any ordinary child, I yearned to go out with school friends and do girls' stuff, but my little dream could never come true. This is when I learned to play records on the record player and started singing along to songs. I made singing and playing records my coping mechanism that shielded my heart from the cruelty of this world and poured tranquility into my life.

I still can't forget the day when I had a seizure while I was still surrounded by students in my school. Even before the seizures, students used to call me all sorts of disheartening names, but now they had encountered my weakness. How bad could my life get?

The school principal called my mother, but she never answered the phone. The principal told me, "Your mom's not home." I said to him, "She goes to my aunt's house." The principal advised me that I should call my aunt's house and see if my mother was there. I did as told and found my mother at my aunt's place. However, since it was me who called and not the principal, my mother never believed that I had a seizure. She called me a liar and a deceiver. The principal got on the phone and told her what I had been through, but my mother said she wouldn't come to pick me up. I had to stay in school, which resulted in me having several more seizures. I was already embarrassed by all that had happened, and my mother's reaction toward my condition made me want to flee on the spot.

When my mother came to pick me up, the principal took me to the car and told her I had been struggling with seizures throughout the day. That is when she took me to get the booster shot to stop the continuous seizures. I needed the booster shot on occasion until I started different medications that stopped the seizures in fourth grade. I still remember there was no guilt in my mother's eyes, and not for a second was she worried about me. Trust me; she would have never believed me if it weren't for my principal.

I was allowed to make friends in my neighborhood until I turned nine. That is when everything started going downhill. Though I was nowhere to be blamed for whatever happened between my mother and father, I was still forced to sacrifice my childhood solely for my mother's doing. I was isolated from the world, and everything a normal child would do—have friends… best friends, go places, and do things with them—became a sin for me. I never had a friend in all my twelve years of school!

I was never allowed to ride a bike or learn to swim. My mother's excuse was you might have a seizure. Once, I told my mother, "Mamma, what if I fell in the water someday and drowned?" But my mother was in no way ready to budge from her decree and said carelessly, "You can just stay away from the water then." Even though I had never had a seizure since fourth grade, epilepsy was always the excuse she gave me to keep me from doing anything or going to any place. I was seizure-free up until after my high school graduation. My last seizure was in fourth grade, but that didn't matter to my mother.

Every day, I felt suffocated, living like a prisoner. However, to add to my loneliness, my mother gave me indoor games. Then again, I was a loner and had nobody to play these games with. What was I supposed to do with them?

When I was in high school, I remember a few students approaching me to do drugs with them. It was the time when drugs were becoming a norm among youngsters to socialize, and naturally, I felt the urge to be included, so I asked them, "How does it make you feel?" The moment they shared what that drug did to their brain, I stepped back and refused their offer. I vividly remember how curious the students became about my refusal of drugs, as if nobody could ever say no to this divine thing. I told them that the so-called sensational feeling they get from drugs is close to what I feel as an epileptic patient. I further added, "I will take your brain, and you can have my epileptic brain in exchange. Then, you can enjoy the seizures and have the same feeling without getting high. On the other hand, I will have your brain, and I won't do drugs. I would be more than glad to say 'NO' to drugs as long as I get to live with a healthy brain, unlike you all who pay to feel the same way as an epileptic patient."

Another incident similar to this one took place a few years later when I was 19. My relatives offered me a can of beer and told me to drink it. At first, I took a sip, but instantly, I spat it back out. I bluntly told them, "It tastes horrible." However, they kept insisting, saying, "Come on, drink some more. After a few cans of beer, you'll grow on it." But for me, a hard NO means NO. So I told them loud and clear, "No way. I'm not forcing myself to like something to be in a clan." Since then, I never took a sip of beer again.

Ironically, people who do drugs even mock epileptic patients, creating obstacles in our way to getting medical treatment. For junkies, it is easier to crawl into their hideouts to do drugs whenever they want, living an experience similar to that of epileptics. Nobody would see them in their pitiful state on the streets, but epileptic people don't have such privileges because a seizure cannot be predicted. An epileptic person could be walking a crowded street when a seizure occurs. They could be crossing the street and go into a seizure. But a person doing drugs doesn't cross the street while under the influence. You see, drug addicts have a choice to be wherever they want to be to get high. They have a choice to hide in times of vulnerability, but this is not the case for us.

Perhaps that's the reason why they like this feeling because they have not encountered the biases and prejudices attached to epilepsy. But I have been a victim of these biases all my life, and I know what it is like to be associated with people who willingly do drugs. Whenever someone gets a seizure in a public place, people frown at them as if they have sinned. People approach them with presuppositions and call them junkies even when they struggle due to their condition. Sadly, this is the faith of a person with epilepsy in this contemporary world, where people choose to treat us derisively as if we don't deserve any love.

At this point, I would like to share a harrowing incident that I encountered ten years ago while commuting on a city bus. At one of the bus stops, there was a 15-year-old girl lying unconscious on the ground. There were two drivers (on-duty and off-duty) on the bus. Instantly, both of them got off the bus to check on the girl. Suddenly, everything became chaotic, and the drivers rushed to check her pulse and breathing. Everybody freaked out, not knowing why the girl could not wake up. She was breathing, but she couldn't move at all. They were shaking, pinching, and slapping her, hoping she would come alive miraculously until I shouted at the top of my lungs that the girl had epilepsy. I made it clear that it takes longer for epileptics to come out of a seizure when on their back and that a team of professionals should be contacted immediately. On the arrival of the rescue team, I told them the girl was most likely to be epileptic, but to my surprise, they still didn't tackle the situation very professionally.

They asked me her name. I said, "I don't know. Look in her school bag and call her school. They will know."

Once the two bus drivers got back on the bus, I told the off-duty driver what I said earlier... that the girl was epileptic. He replied, "No. These kids nowadays are doing drugs."

Thankfully, the on-duty driver told him, "No. She's epileptic. They got her records."

I can't explain how grateful I felt that the on-duty bus driver was there to support my argument.

You see, prior to the moment when I stated that the girl was most likely to be epileptic, they all were seeing her as just a drug addict. This incident opened my eyes, and I realized people were more aware of drugs but had little to no knowledge about the world's most prominent neurological disorder i.e., epilepsy.

Why do epileptic patients have to prove themselves even in a state where they are fighting for their lives? You see, in modern times, it is easier for drug addicts to make friends and acquaintances than for epileptic patients. People are more welcoming and tolerant toward them than they are toward us. As much as this sounds imbecile, this is the reality of our world, and the sad part is that it is not changing any time soon. Decades back, in school, I was treated like some possessed creature. People always maintained their "safe distance" from me as if I would harm them, but it was quite the opposite. Even though I never hurt anyone, I was still subjected to verbal or physical abuse time and time again. So epileptics have gone from being cast as demonic spirits in the past to being drug users today. When are epileptics going to have rights?

My mother treated my youngest brother and me with the same cruelty. She isolated us from the world and forced us to agree with whatever fabrications she came up with. We were young, and all we knew was that our mother was coming up with figments of her vile imagination. Our young minds could not comprehend why she was lying. As a kid, I tried to confront her with a positive attitude, thinking it would not always lead to conflicts, but I was wrong. Whenever I confronted her, she started hurling insults and threats to scare me. Gradually, we siblings grew habitual of my mother's lies, and sadly, my mother's habit of lying ended up consuming my siblings too. They grew up to be pathological liars.

I was the first girl in my family to graduate with my classmates. My two older sisters never graduated from high school. I worked while going to high school. My job was half a block from the house. I also developed the habit of buying my own school supplies and clothes. This small independence of mine, my mother hated so much. She told me I had to quit my job because I had become too independent. She said, "I don't buy your school stuff anymore." I confronted her and said, "I'm not quitting work! You want your kids to be independent." Working got me away from the toxic life I lived at home. But Mom constantly called my job when the restaurant where I worked closed and yelled, "Get home NOW!" I would say, "No! I'm sitting here with the co-workers talking." When I finally came home, my mother would start yelling and screaming at me.

I still had the job after graduating, and I was planning to have a life by getting my own apartment and becoming independent. However, my mother told me I could not afford to move out. She said I had to live at home until I got married!

Living with my mother was no less than a nightmare. It was the major cause of my agonizing life. My mother completely shut the world out for my youngest brother and me. We never got a chance to live a normal childhood and became victims of our mother's constant abuse, which is exactly what my mother tried to inflict on my baby sister. As a result, my baby sister, who was still a toddler, was saying the "F" word consistently. My brother and I made up the word "Cake-Pie." We went to our baby sister and told her there's this one word you never want to say. It's the worst word you could ever say. Then we told her never to say the word "Cake-Pie." Well, the sister went around saying "Cake-Pie" to everyone. Nobody understood what she was saying. We told them we were sick of her saying the "F" word all the time. So we told her "Cake-Pie" is the worst word you could say.

My mother wanted my baby sister to be a loner, too, but in no way my brother and I would have allowed history to repeat itself. Back then, we were young and could not stand up for ourselves, but we could certainly provide our sister with a happy and healthy childhood now, and we did. We became our sister's shield and made her live her life fully. It was a promise to ourselves that we would never let our mother destroy our youngest sister and protect her under all circumstances.

There are moments when I wonder why no adult (except for my aunt on several occasions) ever tried protecting my brother and me from the tormenting life she carved for us. Growing up, I believed my siblings and I could create an unbreakable bond, but that did not turn out well either. For people, having a beautiful, healthy family is common, but life is not the same for everyone. Having one normal dinner with my family is a dream I know can never come true.

When we all used to celebrate Christmas together, I remember it was the only time my siblings got me anything. I was happy to receive their love in the shape of presents from my Secret Santa. But, it did not last long. All my siblings started getting married gradually and moved out of the house. Subsequently, they stopped getting presents for me on the occasion of Christmas too.

At first, I tried to understand their situation. "What if they are going through a rough patch?" But no, that was not the case.

The bitter truth was that my siblings wanted to detach themselves from me, so they stopped getting me Christmas presents. Even then, I continued getting presents for them, thinking I might be able to mend our relationship, but all my attempts were futile, and once again, I was cornered and isolated like the young

Evelyn, but this time it was my own siblings who left me all alone in the middle of nowhere.

"There are many forms of betrayal, but one hurts the most… betrayed by the family."

-Anonymous

Chapter Two

A chilling recollection resurfaces as I sit on my comfort chair today, writing about a grotesque incident that I encountered at the age of my innocence… back when I had just started the sixth grade. It is a disturbing reminder of the inherent evilness of a depraved man and the corruption of his mind that I desperately want to banish from my memory. However, the sad part is that I bear the weight of his filthiness to this day. But today, I summoned the courage to confront a gruesome memory of the time when I was just a kid who was still learning to cope with epilepsy and its effects. I hope that by narrating the gut-wrenching incident, I find solace, understanding, or perhaps a sliver of redemption amidst the shadows of the past.

My mind struggles to recall if, on that scarring day, the flowers were blossoming or if autumn's hue was around the corner. Whatever season it was, the weather was utterly pleasant outside, and cherry on top... I was home alone. I felt that nothing could go wrong—at least while my mother was out.

In the bygone days of the early 1970s, it was not common for girls to wear pants, and the idea of women wearing pants was not accepted. It was a distant thought and seen as something far away from the accepted standards of grace and elegance. It was a time when girls used to adorn in dresses even in the comfort of their homes, and so was the case for me.

The silence of the empty house settled around me like a comfortable cloak, granting me the freedom to roam, relax, and explore unhindered. The house had embraced newfound solitude, and its familiar walls radiated a liberating sensation.

I remember being on cloud nine since I was not surrounded by someone who would monitor my every single movement or restrict my breathing. For once, I was on my own. I could not tell how liberated I felt until I heard the unfamiliar knock on the door. Then again, it was the early '70s when random visitations were not considered harmful. Besides that, the innocence of someone as young as a sixth-grader would never be able to comprehend the danger I was about to experience.

So, my natural response was to inform the man at the door who delivers propane gas tanks to our house that Mom wasn't home. But then he insisted on coming in to check the propane gas tank. As a kid who still had unwavering faith in the inherent goodness of elders, I willingly opened the door and allowed him to cross the threshold. Little did I know that this one decision of mine would alter the course of my perception of humankind and would leave me shattered.

At first, everything was seemingly normal. He came inside, waiting for my Mom to come home to see if we needed propane gas tanks. But then, gradually, when he made sure there was nobody lingering around, he took his chance. An alarming sight unfolded before me as his dirty, grimy, and oily hand suddenly grabbed my chest. His disgusting touch shocked me, disrupting the sense of security I had naively embraced. With the automatic reflex of self-preservation, I started resisting his unsettling grip. Fear was stirring in me as I summoned every ounce of strength to push him away, desperately seeking distance from the encroaching threat. In the dreading moment, I started running away from him, searching for a place where I could hide. The chase began between a predator and prey as I sought refuge from him.

But then, this unhinged dance halted for a brief moment as he took his time to pat the dog. He then gazed at me and, in a spiteful tone, said, "Look here, this dog is nice." I stood on the opposite side of the dog, where I thought the dog would protect me. As a kid, I looked for respite in his existence. However, this respite was short-lived. Soon, I found myself in danger. This disgusting guy, whom my family was familiar with, not only petted the dog but also put his greasy, oily hands under my dress, and his greasy, oily fingers started playing with my privates. I yelled, "No," as I jerked away. I started running away from him in the opposite direction.

Now, my dress was all covered in oil and grime. My underwear was black and oily from him putting his filthy fingers under my dress. And you know what was traumatizing? This disgusting guy in his forties was laughing and chasing me around the house after he had molested me. I would be on one side of the hallway, and he would chase me from the other. It was a cat-and-mouse chase where he would try to grab me by any means. This encounter continued for at least five minutes until he said he would return when my mother was home.

The incident left me overwhelmed as the tears streamed down my face. In my despair, I had none to rely on. I wanted to be comforted, but an epileptic person was already subjected to all sorts of biases, and given the situation, I was not ready to take another mental damage. But then I could not let the incident be hidden for too long, so I picked up the house phone and reached out to my aunt for comfort and guidance. I was crying, recounting the unsettling event through sobs. My words were incoherent and stifled, but I still had a lot to utter. Sensing my anguish, my aunt got furious and asked me to instantly inform my mother, who she felt would be concerned about my well-being. She assured me the matter would not be neglected; instead, the predator would bear the severe consequences. My aunt behaved more like my mother, and even during this whole incident, she was the one who was most concerned about the state in which I was. However, she was not my biological mother, and this matter had to be dealt with by someone related to me by blood.

It brings back memories of my aunt going to a grade school art fair. In art class, the teacher told everyone to carve a picture and then use a roller of paint. Afterward, press a piece of art paper over it, and you will have a picture. I carved a 'butterfly' with 'flowers.' At the bottom, I put these words: "The world has changed since then." The art teacher liked my picture and said he was going to put it up at the art fair. I was excited that I had accomplished something really cool and that the teacher was going to showcase it at the art fair. I went home and told my mother about it. Mom showed no interest in my accomplishment. I told her to come to the art fair and see my picture. She told me, "No! I'm not going to the art fair." I asked her to drop me off at the art fair. Mom coldly replied, "I'm not taking you there either." I then asked if somebody else could. She simply said, "No." I knew my aunt would be at the art fair because she had kids my age. So the next day, I called my aunt and asked her if she got to see my drawing. My aunt told me, "Yes," and praised me for how beautiful the picture was. She told me that the art teacher must have liked my carved picture of a butterfly with flowers very much because he had framed it just like a picture frame. Why didn't my mother care? I can't seem to come up with an answer.

Let's get back to the time when my aunt tried to comfort me and told me to share everything with my mother when she got home. At the same time, Mom came in while I was still on the phone with my aunt. She took the phone from me, and then my aunt continued telling her what had happened. Seeing my dirty, greasy dress, Mom said she would take care of it and instantly called the cops. They came in and saw my greasy, dirty dress. I told the cops the guy put his hands under my dress and played with my privates. The cops had me change so they could take my dress and underwear for evidence to charge the predator for child molestation. After all, they were a poignant piece of evidence and were held in custody to preserve the truth. The cops then told my mother to take me to the hospital to see if I was still a virgin, and

Mom did exactly what they asked her to do. She took me to the hospital. The doctor put a tool inside me to see if my hymen was intact. I screamed in pain. It was painful to have the instrument inside me. Finally, the doctor told my mother that I was still a virgin.

Despite my tender age, a fierce fire ignited within me, fueling rage through my veins, demanding that justice be served and that this man face the consequences for his unspeakable and abhorrent deed. It was a burning desire to make sure that no one, not him or anyone else, would walk the streets free from the weight of their sins, especially the sins committed against those who are vulnerable in the eyes of the world.

At that time, I found myself in a defenseless position where I longed to be protected. But, it seemed that my mother had other plans. Though I yearned to prove my strength and fight for myself, her path deviated from mine. Initially, it was expected that this despicable man would get ten years of imprisonment, which certainly was nothing in front of his heinous crime, but I still felt content, thinking that he would be put behind bars.

However, out of nowhere, the man and his wife started pleading with my mother to withdraw the charges against him. Surprisingly, my mother, who never showed any trait of saintly nature, suddenly decided to drop the charges, fearing that it would tarnish our family's reputation. The irony lies in the fact that she never consulted me about it. I was the one who was molested... I was the one who was robbed of innocence at such an early age, yet my opinion did not matter.

On the day of the trial, I was happy to visit the court and testify about what the child molester did to me. I felt I was finally getting a chance to have people on my side. But then my mother told me, "You are going to school today." I told her, "No. Today is court day." That's when my mother told me, "No. You are not going to court. I dropped the charges on him." I was in disbelief and started getting upset, but my mother told me to shut up. She said, "You are going to school today. I'm not going to see him going to prison for ten years for what he did to you." After she said this to me, Mom called the cops and told them that she was dropping the charges of the guy molesting me. The cop asked her, "Are you sure?" My Mom replied, "Yes." The cop could not wrap his head around what he had just heard and said, "We would hold the dress and underwear for evidence for the next two years in case you decided to change your mind and press charges."

I was in utter disbelief upon hearing the news. A mother, who should have chased down the culprit, made the incomprehensible decision to let the man who had molested her daughter walk away without facing the consequences. Despite having solid evidence and the court on our side, my mother prioritized preserving her own reputation over seeking justice. Not knowing what to do next, I went straight to school that day. I still remember how heavy my heart felt throughout the time, struggling with the painful question of why such a terrible ordeal had befallen me. My mother stopped me from getting justice. Am I just a *nobody?*

The trauma took a toll on my mental health, which got pretty evident to my family members. The weight of the experience profoundly impacted my mental well-being; on top of that, my family overlooked my pain and denied me the support I desperately needed. After what transpired, I became very sensitive, whether I was at home or school (or anywhere else). I would cry over anything I did wrong, any name-calling, etc.

In the midst of this turmoil, my mother suggested I seek therapy. For the first time, I felt she cared for me, but in the car at the parking lot of the psychiatrist's office, my mother told me viciously, "Don't you tell the doctor anything of what that guy did to you. I'm not going to let you ruin the family's reputation for what the child molester did to you. *Remember, he's not a stranger.* He comes to the house a few times a month to change the propane gas tanks." At that moment, it became evident that preserving the family's reputation held greater importance to my mother than acknowledging justice for me.

But the whole purpose of seeking a psychiatrist was to find an outlet to share my trauma and receive the guidance necessary for recovery. But there was no way I could vent anything related to the day I was molested since my mother had accompanied me. The psychiatrist asked me many questions, and you have no idea how desperately I wanted to tell him about being molested, but I couldn't. At the end of the session, he took me out to the waiting room, where my mother was waiting for me. The doctor told her, "There's nothing wrong with her. She's going through her Pre-Teen stage."

I went through a traumatic experience that I desperately wanted to share with someone. I wanted to be heard and be sympathized with, but unfortunately, I was always surrounded by people who held biased views toward individuals with epilepsy, so I never got the opportunity to express myself, and until this day, my voice remained unheard.

I wanted to scream and yell, but my internal struggle remained internal as the doctor concluded my state as mid-adolescence. That was the end of my one-time therapy, where my unresolved trauma remained unresolved, and I continued fighting my internal battle quietly.

Two years passed, and my mother never pressed charges against the man who molested me. The police called to verify if Mom was going to press charges against him. But she told the cops, "No." The cops asked again to make sure she wasn't going to press charges, but her answer remained the same. The cop said, "Okay, then your daughter's dress and underwear will be thrown away. The paperwork for this case will also be tossed out. You won't be able to press charges after that." My mother told the cops, "It is okay with me." You won't believe it, but that beast of a man still came around to change the propane gas tanks after molesting me and scarring me for life. You have no idea the trauma I had whenever he came around. This man went to his grave without paying the consequences for his actions. Am I just an object who isn't supposed to have any justice?

"After all, when a stone is dropped into a pond, the water continues quivering even after the stone has sunk to the bottom."

-Arthur Golden

Chapter Three

After spending years feeling trapped inside the house, my heart desired to break free from the pretty cage built by none other than my biological mother. Moving out was not an option for me since I was still a teenager in high school. Nonetheless, this did not halt my search for freedom. For the nonce, I started working as a cleaner for an elderly woman in my early teens. Working with older adults could get a little strenuous for most people, but surprisingly, my work was just up to scratch. The elderly woman was in love with my habit of placing things right back where they used to be so she did not have to go through any hassle. The elderly woman praised my work in front of my mother, who was surprised that I managed to do a good job. The elderly woman was going to tell her elderly friends about the great job I did for her. She said she would recommend them to have me clean for them. Unfortunately, it never came to be after the praise I received.

After a little while, I found another way to spend less time in captivity and took on a new role where I had to watch the neighborhood kids. Being a teenage caretaker poured vitality into my life once again. I was in complete charge of the children, from cleaning their house to playing with them. I felt as if I would be released from confinement. But my mother came down to the neighbors' house to check on me all evening and night until the children's parents returned, and I was back home. How could I forget that my mother was not the type of person who would want to see my heart contended?

Despite my countless attempts to stop my mother from controlling my life, she snatched the thread of hope from my hand and made me lose yet another job. It was understandable that no parent would want to hand over their children to a caretaker constantly being watched and intervened by her mother. I was a teenager, hired to look after these kids, yet here I was being supervised by my mother; funny, isn't it? But even when I was in thrall to my mother, I knew one thing: no one but I could lead me to my independence. I told myself that I had stayed under house arrest long enough, and now I refuse to live a hollow, meaningless life. That's when I became more than determined to get away from the toxic environment at my home and got hired somewhere.

I wanted to run far away from my house, but there was no way for me to find relief. I started walking downtown, browsing the stores, thinking perhaps my solace would lie there. But again, my mother had this habit of keeping a watch on me constantly. She would drive around town looking for me ceaselessly until she found me. Once she saw me, she would honk the car horn nonstop until I went to her. If I didn't come to the car, she would slowly drive down the street, honking the horn and yelling at me, "Get over here right now. I want to talk to you." There was no way I could hide from her, even briefly. She would unearth every place in our small town to track me down and honk at me. Every time I heard the sound of my mother's car, I knew a series of questions would bombard me. She always attacked me with questions like, "What are you doing?" "Where are you going?" "When are you coming home?" "You get home right now," and "You get in this car right now." I got tired of her tracing me down, so one day, when I went downtown to escape her, I started walking on other streets. I would walk up a flight or two of stairs or up a hilly street. When my mother found me on the street nearby, I started walking up steep hills or another flight of steps in a different area where she would not look for me. However, when I got home, a series of questions were thrown at me in a yelling voice. You can only think what it is like to be watched by someone interminably, and that's not the end. You will also have to report to them about your every move. Trust me; it is sheer torture! Even when I graduated from high school, I had to follow my mother's strict guidelines specifically designed for me while my other siblings were on the loose.

I heard from two of my fellow high school students that a restaurant nearby was hiring a dishwasher. I instantly realized this was my chance to get a little hold of my life, if not entirely. It was a golden opportunity for me since the place was half a block away from my house, so I applied there immediately without giving it another thought. Amazingly enough, they hired me in an instant.

I would not lie… the place was one of a kind. Everybody was dolled up, with men in suits and women in pretty gowns. All the tables were set in strict accordance with the table guidelines. They were adorned with white tablecloths and napkins, and candles were lit on each one of them, providing the room with aesthetic dim lighting. Before visiting this place, I had no inkling about the table-setting guidelines, but the place taught me why the knife should stay in the middle and why spoons should always be on its right. This place was a hot spot on the weekends, and we had to take reservations to accommodate the customers. Sometimes, we had to put customers on the waiting list in case somebody would cancel their reservations, which was less likely. There were days when customers would walk in to see if there was any room for them to dine there.

During the weekends, we had two designated dishwashers that would help with salads, desserts, and dishes. But during the week, there was only one dishwasher. I worked on the weekends only during the school year because my grades were important to me, and I wanted to graduate with my class. But, during the summer break, I worked full time. The owners realized I could manage everything from dishes, salads, desserts, helping the cook, making coffee, etc., on my own. At times, on the swamped weekend, I would be the only dishwasher at the restaurant. I had to wash dishes, make salads and desserts, make coffee, etc. The crew and owners witnessed how I kept up with everything on my own. They appreciated my work and told me it takes three people to do the work I did by myself. They complimented me on how fast I was and how I never slacked on anything. Of course, they provided me with helping hands by the end of the shift or if they needed something right away.

Sometimes, while we chopped vegetables for pasties, the chef used to teach us how to make them. Moreover, my job included cleaning the refrigerator and keeping everything organized at the restaurant, which, by the way, was badly ruined by slackers in my absence.

But honestly, this was the happiest and most joyful place where the chef, who also happened to be the partnership owner (his co-partner was the bartender and managed the dining room), used to sing cheerfully around the restaurant. The audience loved listening to him sing "Oh Danny Boy." I vividly remember all the employees going out on weekends and singing songs to show their gratitude, and you have to believe me when I say this was one of the kindest things I have witnessed so far in my life.

The restaurant also had an exceptionally good pianist. He was in charge of tickling the ivories throughout the day until the restaurant's doors were finally shut. Both of my managers were in love with the idea of dedicating songs to customers. They were light-hearted people who made a beautiful gay couple at a time when gay marriage was unthinkable. Perhaps that is why this place had such a high number of gay employees, or maybe no place other than this would hire gay people since gay rights were still taboo at that time. However, growing up under a gay manager was beneficial for me. It helped me eliminate the stereotypes attached to them and made me discern the challenges they face.

Back in high school, I was asked about my favorite singer. Without giving it much thought, I told them I'm an "Elton John" fan. The shock on their faces made me realize how people's perceptions change based on someone's choice of living. They were baffled and asked me, "Why him? He's gay. None of us like his music because he's gay." But it wasn't a big deal for me. I clearly told them, "It's his music that I like."

Moving on, this high-class restaurant was now becoming my safe place. It was my escape from reality. This place had the vibes that made me forget my household's harrowing memories. At this place, I learned what a real Sunday brunch was like. I worked here on weekends during my high school years. But during the school breaks, I worked as a full-timer. Working at this high-class restaurant was like therapy for me. I actually was around normalcy.

At first, I started working here because I was running away from my house, but things were changing now. I was looking forward to working every day with my colleagues since I finally got to develop healthy relationships with them.

At this place, I met the kindest chef who used to get us leftover pasties. At times, when the food was insufficient, the chef used to make everything from scratch so that everyone could eat. We all used to sit at the back of the dining room, where everybody would laugh and tittle-tattle about things. It was a haven of sorts where my reality was not chasing me.

I remember, after closing, we all used to sit in the back dining room. And looking at all the smiling faces, I desperately wished to have a life where I could laugh and enjoy without restrictions. But even this place was not free from my mother's obsession. On one occasion, my mother called the restaurant right at closing hours, and my boss rushed to me, informing me how she was yelling on the phone. The moment I placed the receiver against my ear, she started yelling again, "Why aren't you home yet?" Her enraged voice was loud enough for everyone to hear. I was habitual of her yelling, but this time, I was not the only one affected by her behavior. While I was explaining the situation to my mother, I felt mortified. Yet, my mother never cared about my reputation; she only wanted me to be home since it was a matter of her decree that should not go unnoticed.

My bosses were quick enough to understand the gravity of the situation and decided to take matters into their own hands. They talked to my mother and ensured I would be home soon. My bosses were reliable and very much like my parents to me. They treated me like their daughter, given that they helped my mother calm down even when she was going bonkers. They knew the meaning of private space, while my mother failed to understand that, all along, I was not running from my home but from her. She would harass me to be accompanied by someone when I came home from work at night, which was hardly half a block away from home. Almost every time my mother tried holding me back, I used the restaurant as an excuse to escape from her self-made brig.

But the day I graduated from high school, I took an oath to live my life on my terms. As my initial step, I borrowed money and purchased a car to ensure I didn't have to tag along with anyone. But, I was delusional in thinking that I could get independence this way, and the reality soon hit me hard. Even when I graduated high school and had my own ride, I was still getting bombarded with thousands of questions. I was past my legal age. At nineteen, I was still not free to drive around or visit a disco on my own without my older sister accompanying me to it.

Every day was becoming a torment for me, and every restriction of my mother was suffocating me to death. One evening, a friend I made at the high-class restaurant where I worked asked me to go out with her. This friend of mine came from a high-class family. We went out to eat at an elegant restaurant in a different town. The dining tables had white tablecloths and napkins (just like the high-end restaurant we worked at). All the customers around us were dressed up elegantly. It was as if I was getting the "life" I dreamed of. After dining, we went dancing. It was after midnight before heading back to our homes. This was the happiest time of my life. I was so lost in my happy moment that I forgot about when my mother once antagonized my friend's family when we were just kids.

My worst nightmare came to life when I received a call from my friend the next day. She told me how my mother had called them twenty-one times in a row while she and I were out. Her obsessive behavior had irked my friends' family. After a brief, uncomfortable silence, she declared she could no longer stay friends with me. It was not the first time this had happened to me, but I still felt my heart sinking. My mother could not bear to see I was making some progress in life; she shattered my dreams and ended my friendship. She always wanted me to be sidelined by the world, and yet again, she won.

Once, I saw a 'Help Wanted' ad in the newspaper. It was a job position for a dispatcher at the Sheriff's Department. The application had questions related to epilepsy; my honest mistake was that I answered them truthfully. But then, who could have thought a place like this would be biased against an epileptic person? I gave my application to the dispatcher. He gave it to the Sheriff right away. The dispatcher came back to me and said the Sheriff wanted to interview me right now. It was evident that the Sheriff liked my application. He basically hired me, but he saw on the bottom of the application that I said "Yes" to epilepsy. I was a perfect candidate for the job, with two years of employment experience while I was attending high school. It showed I was a responsible person who graduated from high school with hands-on work experience, making me not only book-smart but street-smart, too.

However, my seizures, which I haven't had in a long time, snatched my chances of getting a stable job. The Sheriff rejected my application by saying, "I cannot hire you. You have epilepsy." Once again, my hope was crushed. I was desperate to run away from my mother's imprisonment, but with every passing day, it was getting harder to find a way out.

But one thing was clear: living under the same shed as my mother meant I would forever stay confined in this dungeon. I wanted to move out immediately, but I had no way out. My mother would not let go of her puppet this easily. On several occasions, I tried convincing her, but she outright said 'No.' I was even planning to find an apartment and get away from the dysfunctional home life I had to be around, but my mother told me, "You're not moving out! You can't afford it." I told her, "I can pay my bills. I'm working." She said, "No!! You're not moving out of the house until you get married!!"

My mother felt that I was not capable of taking care of myself. She made it clear that only marriage could free me from this seemingly eternal life of mental and emotional torture. Marriage was the only key to my emancipation.

At first, it did not seem like a bad idea. I mean, what could possibly go wrong? My life was already pretty much doomed. I believed I had my fair share of complications and decided to search for my male counterpart, who would be my knight in shining armor and who I believed was my uncle's stepson. I was enticed by the fact that by marrying him, I could travel hundreds (if not 1,000) miles away from my compulsive, controlling mother. My uncle's stepson was a military man who seemed reliable at first. Besides that, he was the first to ask me for marriage, and naturally, my

35

answer to his proposal was yes. It was a golden chance to move out.

But before I could marry him, my seizures returned. I was taken aback since I hadn't had seizures in a long time, and my soon-to-be husband had no idea about my condition.

With the seizures' sudden return, I went to the doctor, thinking that my insurance would cover it. Though I had medical insurance from State Farm, they refused to pay any medical bills or medication. The agent said that my epilepsy was diagnosed prior to receiving health insurance. I was told blatantly that they would neither pay for the doctor's bill nor the medication I needed for my recurring epilepsy. And now, I couldn't get any medical help for my recurring epilepsy.

I had never felt this hopeless before in my life. I had no money but needed medical care to treat my epilepsy. I was completely stuck. This was when I realized I could be treated at a military hospital if I married this man. I could see a neurologist, receive my medications for seizures, and have any tests needed to be done (blood work, EEG, CT scan, or MRI). And I did get treated at the military hospital, but at what cost?

"You tell them - you tell them there's a cost... Every decision we make in life, there's always a cost."

-Brad Meltzer

Chapter Four

While I was a teenager, my uncle and his new wife brought his stepson to my parent's house to meet us. I thought I could finally make a friend without my mom stopping me like she did all these years because he was my uncle's stepson and was in the military. As time passed, we started talking to each other. Then, I got his address to write to him while he was away at his military base. It felt good to have no restrictions with this guy. He would call and talk to me about once a week. After a few years of dating, he proposed to me. I remember how my mom said I couldn't move out of the house until I got married. So when he proposed to me, I got excited and said yes right away. "I will marry you," I said. I thought I would be able to travel and have life finally. Life with him would be much better than the toxic life I had to live so far, or so I wondered.

I was a virgin when I married him. I believed in saving myself for the guy that I married. I believed in staying married.

My heart believed that through marriage, I could finally claim the independence and freedom I had always yearned for. I thought I was no longer bound to the sheltered life I had endured since the day I was born, and with the impression that I was finally on my own, my heart desired to explore new places and experience the beauty of different parts of the country. However, quickly enough, my dreams of liberation gave way to a reality I had never anticipated.

After the wedding, my husband, a military man, got posted in the Midwest temporarily. We settled into a small cottage home, a residential place that I believed to be our own. Those first six weeks of marriage were pure bliss. We spent quality time together, exploring and savoring the joy of being newlyweds. After six weeks of being married, my husband was stationed to move to the South. And as soon as we relocated, everything started to fall apart like a house of cards.

It all began when he started asserting his ownership over my belongings, or to be precise, the car that signified my freedom. This was the same car I had bought to celebrate my journey toward liberation. To me, it held more significance than just being a means of transportation. It was not only about its materialistic value; it represented my freedom and the path I was paving. My husband started pressuring me by saying that my car was now his property, and soon enough, I found employment. The job was six miles away. At that time, we were living out on the county highway. I knew it was time to tell my husband I found a job. I need my car to get to work. But in return, he told me, "No. The car is mine to go to work." I told him that our neighbor works at the military base at the same job as you. You take a ride with him to work. He refused right away and said, "No, I'm not bumming a ride with anybody." He then mentioned again that the car was his and he would use it to go to work. This was when I realized he was claiming my car as "his car." I surely wasn't going to let go to work stop me because my car was being taken away from me, so I walked six miles to work and six miles back home five days a week. What I didn't realize then was that my husband was trying to control my life entirely. It wasn't the car that he had snatched from me, but my right to stay liberated.

I walked six miles to work and six miles back home on a two-lane highway. There were no sidewalks. I walked on the lumpy grass five days a week to stay off the road. When I became pregnant, my husband still wouldn't let me have my car to drive to work. I still had to walk six miles to work and six miles back five days a week until I took a leave of absence at eight and a half months pregnant. I endured all types of weather, be it braving rainstorms, scorching heat, or freezing cold, throughout my eight and a half months of pregnancy. After giving birth, I went back to work around six weeks later. I found a babysitter half a mile away, so I walked my baby to the babysitter and then walked another six miles to work. After work, I walked six miles to the babysitter and then another half a mile to get home. My husband didn't really show he cared about our child or me. He would hang out with guys he worked with and always came home drunk (especially when he got paid). He demanded that supper be ready when he came home. The food got cold often because he would stay away until later to be with the guys. There was a time when I even made a candlelight dinner for us. This brought back good memories of the time when I worked at that elegant restaurant when I was in high school. Well, the candle burned for hours without my husband coming home.

Finally, I gave up on waiting. I blew the candle out and threw the food I made for him in the garbage.

I had no iron board or iron, and my husband demanded I iron his military clothes. I told him I had no iron or iron board. He didn't care less. I had to figure out how to iron his military clothes. I figured I would put a bath towel on the table and heat up the cast iron on the stove burner—that's all I could do.

While I was still trying to process my spouse's changed behavior, I was hit by something that made me see all the subtle red flags he was leaving behind. One day, when he returned home, he proudly proclaimed that he had traded my car in for a van with a window out. He transferred the title to my car without my consent. He had taken away my reliable car, replacing it with a ramshackle van that needed repairs.

I had to go to the laundromat. Many times, there was a line of people waiting to do laundry. I had to wait to get a washer, let alone a dryer. It would take me longer to finish the laundry and get home because of the crowd at the laundromat. Once I got back home a little late, my husband started yelling at me, accusing me of seeing somebody while I was out doing laundry. I told him no. I had to wait for the washers and dryers to be available for me to use. He wouldn't believe the truth that I told him. That's when he told me, "From now on, you are not allowed to go to the laundromat to do the laundry. You will have to clean the clothes out by hand at the house and air dry them at home." I was pregnant, but from that day forward, I had to scrub all clothes, linen, and undergarments out by hand in the bathtub and then let them air dry.

The situation started taking a turn for the worse when my husband's violence started taking an apparent turn. The new him would no longer try to hide the abuse behind his words; instead, he was becoming more open about his animalistic ways of living, as if he had become braver and feared none. His weekend ritual was to come home drunk and throw furniture around while expecting me to have food on the table. Every time I heard his footsteps coming our way, I clenched my fist in fear. Now, he was no longer my husband but a reminder of terror. He was becoming increasingly violent as the dates of his overseas deployment approached because he didn't want to go. However, it wasn't half bad news for me. I was glad that, for a brief period, the shadow of fear and terror would move away from me. With this thought, I moved in with my parents.

As the days grew closer to my husband's surprise return to the States for a two-week leave, my Mom told me, "I'm not supposed to let you know, but your husband is coming home for a two-week leave from overseas." She said he wanted me to keep it a secret from you. My mother thought it would be better if I knew in advance.

My heart sank at the revelation, for I knew I wasn't meant to know about his return. A thought suddenly crossed my mind that going on the birth control pill while he was home would only make him believe that I had been messing around. I never took birth control since my husband went overseas because I believed in my marriage vows. Going on birth control while he was here would only make him believe that I had been messing around in his absence.

Our son got sick when my husband was home. We took him to the hospital and spent a lot of time caring for him while he was awake. But when he slept, we spent time alone as a couple. I told him if we did anything, I would become pregnant again. I told him I hadn't taken birth control because I believed in my marriage vows. Before he took the plane to go back overseas, I told him I was pregnant. He didn't believe he could get me pregnant in two weeks of short leave.

I went to the doctor, and my pregnancy was confirmed. Yet doubts clouded my husband's mind and that of those closest to him. His mother and sisters were filled with suspicion, accusing me of unfaithfulness. They denied the possibility that my husband could be the father of my unborn baby, arguing that our time together had been far too brief. Their voices echoed with disbelief, dismissing any notion of truth in my words. It was a battle, pitting my honesty against their skepticism.

The doctor then gave me a due date for my baby that aligned perfectly with my husband's homecoming. He went back nine months from that due date and realized that was the time he was home. It was a bittersweet revelation: the medical professionals supported my claims, yet their endorsement failed to sway the disbelievers. My husband said, "The doctors are framing me. They want me to be the dad of this kid." There was almost nothing I could do to make my husband or his family believe otherwise.

When my husband returned from overseas, we moved west into military housing. At that time, I was six months pregnant. Once, our one-and-a-half-year-old son and I were sitting at the coffee table having breakfast. My husband was at the kitchen table eating. He was looking at a city road map to find a street. He told me to come over here. I want you to show me where this street is on the map. I told him I'd come over after I finished breakfast. He said I didn't tell you to come later; I told you to come now. I'll count to ten, and you better be over here. He then started counting. I refused to jump to his demands once again. He got to ten, but I didn't obey his command. He suddenly flipped the kitchen chair back and came to me furious. He told me when I tell you to come, you come. If I tell you to jump off the cliff, you jump off the cliff. I told him no, I will not. He then pushed me down on the couch. I got up. He pushed me down again, and I got up. He then slapped my face, so I hit him back. That's when he took both of his fists and started punching me in the face. Our one-year-old said, "Daddy, don't hurt Mommy." My husband told our son to shut up, you brat. My husband then went across the room, picked up a forty lbs. military bag, and threw it at our one-year-old son. My baby fell to the floor and started crying. I picked up my baby and took him into the bedroom. I checked his body for any injuries. Gladly, there weren't any.

Luckily, my son had no visual injuries, but he was crying badly. I held him close and kissed him, saying I love you. My face was hurting badly, and I was six months pregnant. A little later, my husband came into the bedroom and said that he wasn't sorry for what he did to me or the baby. I was scared to report the beating because the military officials said we would be evicted if there were any issues. The last thing I needed was to be evicted while pregnant and with a baby. I declared if this happened ever again, I would call the military police.

After the beating, I couldn't even put a spoon in my mouth to feed the baby in my stomach. He beat me so badly that my jaws were locked. I tried hard to force any type of Jell-O or other liquids to go in my mouth to feed my baby in my stomach. As I said, I was scared to call the military police because we had just moved in, and I was pregnant with a year-old baby. This was the time when Domestic Violence wasn't a law yet. It was about twelve years later that Domestic Abuse became law.

Whenever my husband received his military check, he spent several hundred dollars on going out, drinking, and eating by himself and on gas. Even though he made enough to pay the bills (rent-free because it's military housing), I got a small amount of money to buy groceries for two weeks. I would write down what meals to prepare for the next fourteen days (e.g., roast beef, pork chops, meatloaf, etc.). Then, I would look in the cupboards, freezer, and refrigerator and see what food is left over (e.g., hamburgers, eggs, spaghetti noodles, etc.). Then I wrote how much hamburger, eggs, cereal, cheese, etc. I needed to purchase. Next, I estimated the price of the eggs, roast beef, hamburger, etc. I then added the price of all the groceries. If the total to purchase these items was higher than my money, I would change some of the meals (e.g., cancel a roast beef and replace it with french toast). Once I got the estimated price in the price range of the money I had, I went shopping and bought those groceries.

When I gave birth to my second baby, I realized I was cutting on groceries even more to buy baby formula. I got yelled at for not having the groceries in the house. So, two weeks after I had a C-section to give birth to my baby, I had to find work. I had to find a babysitter to watch my two babies while I went to work. This was the only way that I could purchase the baby formula to feed my newborn baby (not including the diapers). One day, when I went to work, I saw I was no longer on the work schedule. I asked my boss why. He said, "You had just had a C-section. You need to stay home and take it easy." I told him I could not stay home. There's no money for me to buy baby formula for my newborn. My baby cannot go to work to make money to buy his baby formula. I must work. He was dumbfounded because my husband was in the military. I told my boss that my husband spends hundreds of dollars every paycheck on himself to go drinking, eating out, etc. My boss adjusted me back to the work schedule but told me to be careful at work.

Finally, after a few months, my mother-in-law saw my newborn baby. She smiled and told my husband, "Son, this is your baby. He looks just like you when you were a baby." Finally, after being accused of cheating on my husband, it was proven to be a lie. My husband and his family were flabbergasted because he was only home for two weeks before returning overseas. The claim that my husband couldn't have gotten me pregnant in the two weeks that he came home proved I was never lying. But I had to put up with the accusations for over a year before the truth came out.

When I made supper for the four of us, I always made sure that I fed my two babies (six months old and two years old) first. My husband told me to sit down and eat supper. I told him not until after I fed the babies. That's when my husband told me, "If we ever get divorced, you will have to have the kids. I worked for this food. My money bought this food. I eat first. Whatever is left over is what the kids eat." I was shocked by his statement, or was I? I remember having to go back to work two weeks after having a C-section so I could purchase baby formula and diapers for my newborn baby. There was no money for baby formula or diapers if I didn't go back to work.

With the passage of time, my husband became meaner, and it was no safer for my babies or me to be around him. This was when I started to go to a hotel room with my babies in this large city. I must try to keep my babies safe.

During one of my stays at a hotel to escape from my husband's violence, I took my babies and me to a grocery market nearby to purchase some food and drink. I met up with a guy who looked like a bouncer. I asked him if he was a bouncer. That's when he told me he was an undercover cop. I felt a sigh of relief to confide in him of my desperate situation with my abusive husband. After hearing about the issues in my marriage, he told me to tell my husband that he wanted to meet him. He gave me his phone number. I went back home when I felt safe returning. I eventually told my husband about this undercover cop I met a few days back. I told him he wanted to come over for dinner. My husband quickly agreed to it.

When the undercover cop met my husband, they talked by themselves. Before the undercover cop left, he told me, "If you ever have issues with your husband, call me. I'll be right over. I kept his phone number with me at all times. I have had to call him several times to come over to protect me and my children from my husband's wrath. He acted as a mediator in settling down my aggressive husband.

One time, to get away from my excruciating married life, I returned to my parents' home with the children for a short time. Somehow, I have always been a woman burdened by the weight of my circumstances. While I was at my parents' house, I received a call from my husband, a troubled soul who had gone AWOL from his military duties. He demanded financial aid in order to return to the military base where he was stationed. Despite knowing our financial circumstances, my husband didn't budge for a second. Not knowing what to do, my mother borrowed money from a third party to help my husband get back to the military base.

After only two weeks, it was time for me to go back. However, the lack of financial resources prevented me from purchasing return air tickets to the West Coast. It was my mother's kindness that saved us, as she provided bus tickets for our journey. But not in my wildest dream could I have predicted that this trip would unfold into yet another tale of hardship.

My journey with the Greyhound bus started out smoothly. It carried us through remote regions. After a little while, the bus driver stopped at a restaurant out of nowhere. The bus driver asked the passengers, "Who believes in here ever after?" Only two people raised their hands. That's when the bus driver said, "You only have ten minutes to get back on the bus. If you're late, you'll be left behind." I had to change my two babies' diapers (six months old and two and a half years old).

I then took the babies with me to go inside the restaurant to get milk for the babies. There was a long line. I was stressed, knowing I only had a total of ten minutes to get back on the bus. When I finally got the milk I needed for the babies, I headed toward the bus outside. The bus was gone. I was out in the middle of nowhere with only this small restaurant to shelter me and my babies.

I went back inside the restaurant and looked around for anyone resembling a Greyhound bus driver. I saw two guys who looked like the bus drivers. I asked them if they were Greyhound bus drivers. They said yes. I felt a sigh of relief. I told them, "My bus has left me behind with my babies. All my stuff is on the bus." The drivers asked me where I was going. I told them my destination. One of the drivers said he was heading there as well. He told me to get on his bus and get off at the next bus stop over sixty miles away. I told him again that my belongings were on the other bus. The driver said, "The driver would take my stuff to the claims department at the next stop. That's where you will have to claim your belongings." The catch to the next bus stop was a staggering sixty miles away, making the journey even more tiring. Nevertheless, I was still grateful for the assistance.

Upon reaching the claims department, a group of concerned passengers from my previous bus came running toward me. They expressed immense relief at my safe arrival with my babies. They told me they yelled at the bus driver during the whole trip of over sixty miles. The bus driver never got a minute of peace from any of us. They said they found out his name and wrote it down for me. They gave me the bus driver's name, who left me stranded with my babies. I took the paper with the driver's name on it.

Curiosity sparked among the passengers as they started inquiring about my destination. Surprisingly, one of them revealed that their journey aligned with mine for a significant portion of the way. The stranger was determined to ensure my safety and that of my babies. He insisted that I remain on the bus with my children, promising to help me by providing any necessities I required at each subsequent stop. When he reached his destination, he told other passengers coming on (many passengers had already reached their destination) what had happened to me. He didn't leave until he found a passenger to continue looking after my safety by getting off the bus to get what I needed for my babies and myself until I reached my destination. The passengers were like a "Mother Hen" for my babies and me for the rest of the trip to my destination.

Eventually, I reached my long-awaited destination, but the trials were far from over. As I stepped out of the bus, I saw my husband waiting to pick me up. This reunion was met by a grim discovery. The car brakes went to the floor, leaving all of us in an unsafe situation. We were in the middle of a large, bustling city with brakes going to the floor. Once again, I was in the midst of chaos, all alone, wondering how to go about the situation at hand of unsafe transportation. I had to find someone to fix the car brakes right away. There was no waiting. This was when I called the undercover cop. His mother answered the phone. I told her I needed her son's help to find a mechanic for the brakes of the car. She told her son. The undercover cop called me and told me of a mechanic who does work at his house. He got me connected with this mechanic to fix the car brakes for cheap. This man came to the rescue for the safety of my children and me. At that moment, filing an official complaint against the Greyhound bus driver for what he did to my children was the last thing on my mind.

During the time I was away, chaos had unfolded within the walls of my home. My husband, who could barely take care of himself, brought a military buddy of his to live in our home, and together, they failed to fulfill their basic responsibilities of picking

50

up the trash. The house had fallen into disarray, with garbage piling up. The garbage from two weeks ago was still in the house, and stacks of dishes in the sink were left as they were two weeks ago— still not washed—with more dishes piled on top of those dishes. My husband and his buddy's clothes were scattered all around the house. When I returned to this scene of utter neglect, I felt my patience hanging by a thread. Deep down, I knew I couldn't take this anymore.

The weight of responsibility fell upon my shoulders as my husband announced that his parents would be moving into our military housing. Our financial situation became dire with him stationed somewhere in the boonies for two weeks. His absence meant that the money he earned went wherever he was, leaving us with little to sustain ourselves until his return. Faced with mounting bills and the pressing need for food, I had no choice but to seek employment again.

At this point, finding a job on the graveyard shift became my lifeline. My in-laws lived with us and stayed with the kids at night until I got home from working the graveyard shift.

As a waitress working through the night, I struggled to stay awake due to the drowsiness caused by the epilepsy medication I took. Upon my return home, his parents would empty the house, leaving me alone with the children while they sought rest elsewhere. Exhaustion consumed me, but I had no way out. My in-laws weren't helping me much, not knowing the hardships that burdened our lives.

Once, after not having slept for at least a day and a half, my tired body succumbed to insomnia and dozed off on the couch while the babies loitered around. When I woke up, a neighbor came over. She told me my oldest son (two years old) made toast and brought it over to her apartment. She brought him back home and told him to stay in the house until his mom woke up. I had the door locked before I fell asleep, but somehow, my son unlocked the door. From that moment on, I took my children to daycare whenever I fell asleep. There was a need for this additional support, and I made the decision to enroll the children in daycare, a choice that required my own financial contribution.

Then, there came a time when my husband stopped contributing even less to the family. However, he came home in a drunken state and now wanted to snatch every penny I had to purchase groceries for the six of us. With the weight of our family's needs heavy on my shoulders, I refused to give him any grocery money. I told him that his parents don't contribute any money toward the groceries. They eat what groceries there are in the house. In a fit of rage, he lashed out, physically assaulting me while his parents were out. Now, I was determined to break free from this cycle of abuse once and for all for my kids' safety as well as mine. I called the military police.

My in-laws arrived back home before the military police arrived. My mother-in-law tried to stop me from making a police report of the abuse. The military police saw how red my face was from the beating and told her, "Don't interfere. She's going to make a report at the police station. I need to know if you are going to watch your grandkids while she goes to the police station to make a report." The mother-in-law agreed to stay with the babies while I went with the police.

The police brought me back home. They told me, "When your husband comes back home, call us. We'll be here to arrest him." My husband came back, claiming he was moving out. I called the military police and told them, "My husband is back, and he's packing up, claiming to move out." Within three minutes, the military police were there and arrested him.

My husband's commanding officer called me the next day and asked me what I wanted to do. I told him, "I need to move out with the babies." That's when the commanding officer told me, "If you want to move away with the babies, you have to pay for your own move. We are here for the military person, not their family."

Once again, I found myself trapped in this dangerous marriage. I couldn't afford to move out with my babies. I am a Christian. I prayed to God to please have my husband be stationed overseas ASAP.

About a week or two later, my husband told me he got papers served on him to go overseas. He didn't understand why he only had three months left in the military. He told me he didn't know if he wanted me and the children to go overseas with him or not. I told him, "It's up to you." However, I kept praying to God to please have him go overseas alone so my children and I would finally be out of the abuse that he was doing to us.

Finally, my husband said that he was going overseas by himself. This way, he would only be overseas for two years. When I was away from him, I said, "Yes. Thank you, God." We packed up and traveled two thousand miles back to my parents' house.

When my husband's airplane got off the ground to go overseas, where he was being stationed, I felt a hundred pounds fall off my shoulders. I never cried when the airplane flew away. My family was stunned to see I wasn't crying over his departure overseas. That's when I told them of the physical and mental abuse my children and I were getting from him. After they heard my reasoning, they understood. That's when I was ready to call the marriage quits. I said, "I don't ever want to have my children or myself go back to him."

After my husband went overseas, I became aware of my husband's deceitful nature and the things he and his comrades had schemed together. You would be surprised to know that one of his companions advised him to claim that his family still resided on the West Coast, as they knew it would result in higher financial support for the children. However, this was merely a fabrication of facts, as my husband was well aware that I had gone back to the Midwest. My children and I never received any financial aid from him. Despite my husband getting extra pay for claiming I was living in the West, my kids and I were struggling immensely because I wasn't receiving any money from him. Not receiving a single cent from him, I had to rely on my parents for support. I had to go to the food pantry for necessities (even baby diapers).

After not receiving any money for months from my husband, I wrote a heartfelt letter to my husband's commanding officer overseas. I pleaded with him about the immense financial need for the children and me. It was only through the intervention of this officer that my husband was compelled to sign the necessary paperwork, providing my children and me with the support that we deserved. My husband later said, "If my commanding officer hadn't been there, I would've never signed those papers." He even claimed that I got sixty thousand dollars from him, which is a blatant lie. I did not get that kind of money. If that amount was sent to someone from him, I don't know who that lucky person was in California. It most certainly wasn't me.

The next thing I got to know about my husband was that he was discharged from the military. I don't know if he was honorably or dishonorably discharged. I didn't know where he went. With my marriage crumbling and my husband not coming around, I found myself stuck in a plight. Since I was married and had no idea where my husband was, I couldn't get the necessary medical aid or food stamps. There I was… trapped in a bureaucratic maze, unable to access vital assistance due to my marital status. Now, the hope only lay in the prospect of divorce, which would grant me access to essential support systems. However, finding a lawyer willing to take on my case without financial compensation proved daunting.

Eventually, a kind-hearted lawyer emerged, offering his services despite the lack of financial gain. Perhaps he was able to recognize my desperate need for freedom from afar. The lawyer said, "I'm only getting you a divorce. I'm not going to fight for child support for you." And by the end of the hearing, I finally found myself liberated from the shackles of a loveless marriage. Though the divorce granted me no benefits from my husband's end, I was finally able to secure food stamps and medical assistance for me and my children. I needed medical care not only for my children but also for my treatment for epilepsy. Before the hearing, I asked my mother-in-law where her son was, but she wouldn't tell me. Once I gave her the divorce papers to give him, she told me, "He doesn't want you to know where he is." Then she told me, "He's in prison."

"In the midst of darkness, light persists."

-Anonymous

Chapter Five

Now that I am a single parent, I realize life has a way of throwing unexpected challenges our way. For me, these challenges came in the form of family dynamics and jobs, responsibilities that demanded more than I initially thought. My first paying job as a single parent was in the *Elegant* restaurant I previously worked at when I was a teenager. There were new owners (husband & wife) now who didn't work in the kitchen or dining area.

I worked evenings (weekdays and weekends) at the *Elegant* restaurant. The dishwasher who worked the day shift (lunch hour) was a guy (mainly in charge of dishes). He left me with an overwhelming mountain of dishes (pots, pans, glasses, plates, silverware, utensils, etc.). Every time I came in for the evening shift, the cook, waiters, and waitresses told me they needed this pot, pan, utensils, etc. They needed glasses, silverware, etc., to either cook with or set the tables before opening up the restaurant. I had to prepare several different salads (coleslaw, beets, lettuce with shredded carrots, cucumbers, radishes, etc.) for the salad bar and backup salads for when the salads at the salad bar ran low out in the dining room. The cook and waiters/waitresses needed these pans, utensils, glasses, silverware, etc., to either cook with or set the tables prior to opening. I also had the waiters and waitresses on me to clean the dishes they needed to set the table prior to opening. I could neither make the salads nor fulfill any other responsibilities I needed to do that were included in my job description. There were times I never had a chance to make backup salads because I had all these dried-on pots, pans, dishes, etc., to take care of. The cook, waiters, and waitresses needed items cleaned A.S.A.P. Such issues never existed with the prior owners when I was a teenager. The restaurant ran smoothly back then. These new owners of the *Elegant* restaurant brought along challenges that should never have existed. Even though I complained to the owners about the noon-hour dishwasher, he replied every time that he had to leave early or we let him leave early because we weren't busy. Little to no appreciation of my extra work made me think, "Do I really want to stay here?"

One day, I struggled to manage the mounting pile of dirty dishes left by the lunch-hour dishwasher. One day, I went to the owner and told him to change the schedule because the dishwasher couldn't handle doing dishes; I told the owner to change the schedule during the week so that I could do dishes during the lunch hour. I will still work the weekends in the evenings. The owner agreed. Things were smooth for a while. But one day, the owner came to me during my lunch hour shift and told me, "You never showed him how to clean out the sinks after closing in the evening. I told him that's a lie! I taught him how to use *Comet* to clean out the sinks at night." This accusation was the boiling point. I took off my apron and told him, "I Quit!" The owner tried to stop me from quitting, but I wasn't listening. I walked out the door and never looked back.

Soon enough, I started working at another kitchen out of town. I came early in the morning to make different types of donuts for the customers. This time, things were different. The atmosphere was more supportive and appreciative. I honed my skills and took pride in my work. Not only did I cook, but I also did dishes when the other cook came later in the morning. One day, I was given the responsibility of preparing a large meal for a group of people all by myself. There were twelve separate orders for this large group. Drawing on my previous experiences, I carefully planned each step, ensuring that all dishes would be ready at the same time. My strategies included making those dishes first that took the most time.

I had come a long way from working in a chaotic kitchen with irrational demands, and now I was at a place where my efforts were being celebrated. I prepared the twelve servings. The waitress told me that the other cook always made one order at a time. The group of customers had never received all their breakfast meals ordered at the same time before this. When the cook finally came in, she was jealous of my ability to conquer this large order (something she could never do).

As a single parent, the struggle to provide for my children weighed heavily on me. The food stamps I received were a lifeline that ensured my children had enough to eat. With no permanent home for my children or me, I received food stamps. I ventured these food stamps into stocking up my parents' kitchen cupboards, refrigerator, and deep freezer by using the strategy I used when I was married and with a limited amount of money for groceries for two weeks. But now I had to budget for a month's supply of food with my food stamps. Not only was I purchasing food for my children and me, but for my parents and anybody else who came to my parents' house.

My mom went with me when I grocery-shopped with my children. I never used the food stamps for pop, chips, cupcakes, donuts, etc. My mom bought those items. My food stamps were for meals (beef, pork, chicken, dairy, four to six cases of canned goods, cereal, etc.), not for snacks. Yet the truth remained hidden that I used my food stamps to jam-pack up the kitchen cupboards, refrigerator, and deep freezer.

My siblings, nieces, and nephews would come to my parents' house and say, "Grandma/Mom, you have a lot of food. I'm hungry. Can I have some of this food?" Even worse was when the siblings or nieces or nephews said, "Grandma/Mom, we need food in our house. We don't have any meat, canned goods, etc." I would get upset because the food wasn't purchased by her. I bought this food for my children and me. But sure enough, Mom would not hesitate and would get bags out to fill them up with groceries for her kids or grandkids. She made them believe that she was the person who bought the groceries in the house. It made me so mad that she had no concern that the food in the house was bought with my food stamps to feed my children and me. However, all I heard from my siblings was that my children and I were the suckerfish leaching off my parents. My family's lack of understanding and acknowledgment of the truth was disheartening, to say the least. I would confront Mom about taking food out of the house that was meant for my kids. Mom would tell me she'll go to the store tomorrow and get some more food. I kept pestering her until she replaced the food she gave away. I used up all my food stamps. I had no more food stamps to purchase more food.

My siblings were very jealous of how my parents spent more time with my children than theirs. They often told me this in front of my mom. This made my siblings turn against me. This so-called unnecessary attention ignited resentment within them that smoldered beneath the surface, but what they really couldn't comprehend was the fact that my children were receiving all this love and care at the cost of my freedom and sanity. They always claimed that I was living off my parents, and their growing discontent stoked up their demands—a call for my children and me to seek our own place to live. In their eyes, our presence felt like an insult, a reminder of the undue and unwarranted attention they believed we received. But I wanted to break free from this confinement so that I could live freely with my children alone.

My son was five years old and wanted to help Grandpa and Grandma with the hammer and saw. My parents yelled at him and said, "No. Get out of here. You are too young. I went in defense and said, "You do not deny my son the right to learn. I don't care if he's five years old!"

A few months later, it was Christmas. My son would turn six years old by then. I went to the department store and looked for a children's tool set. I found a toolbox with a real hammer, saw, pliers, screwdriver, etc. On the tool case, it stated for children six years old and older. AHA! The perfect Christmas present for my son. I went to the lumber yard and got scrap wood they were throwing away. I purchased nails there. On Christmas Day, my son was so excited he got a real tool set with wood and nails. My mom was mad at me until I showed her the toolbox is for children six years and older. After that, she couldn't stop my son from learning to work with tools. My dad took an interest in teaching my son how to use the tools. Before this, my dad was never allowed to have any communication with either one of my sons, talk to them, hug them, etc. My mom tried to stop my dad from teaching my son (his grandson) how to work with tools, but I jumped in and stopped her. I told her to leave them alone. My mom hated Dad and would yell at anybody who socialized with Dad prior to this. Then, not too long afterward, my sons came home crying, saying, "Mom, our friends have dads to do boy stuff with. We don't have a dad." I told my sons they have a dad. They were shocked. I told them that their maternal grandpa was my father. He is your "Grandfather". My sons went running to Grandpa to ask him questions. My mom started going after my sons to stop them from going to their grandpa. I got in front of my mom and stopped her. I told her, "Leave my sons alone. They are going to talk to their grandpa. Their dad is not in their life. They need to know boy stuff." From that day forward, my sons went to their grandpa with any questions or to do things with. My siblings were jealous that my sons were spending time with Grandpa and their kids weren't. But the siblings never stood up to Mom and stopped her from keeping their kids away from their grandpa. But from that day forward, my dad was able to socialize with his other grandkids, let alone socialize with his own kids.

I'm going off track to reveal something important that will be said in one of the upcoming chapters. Like I said in the beginning, something happened to me when I was nine years old; ever since then, my mom told my siblings and everyone she knew that I had a different dad. The dad I call Dad is not my dad. My siblings believed my mom. Ever since then, one of my older sisters told me that when Mom and Dad die, I get half of what they get because "I'm their half-sister." You have no idea how torturous my life was ever since Mom revealed something she couldn't prove. It was just what she said without no proof to back it up. Whenever my children or I said, Dad/Grandpa, my siblings/nieces and nephews would tell my children and me, "That's not your dad/grandpapa. So and so is your dad/grandpa." This has been an ongoing issue ever since the siblings, nieces, and nephews were told I and my children had a different dad/grandpa. Ever since then, whenever they came around and I or my children said Dad/Grandpa, they would always throw in our faces, "He's not your dad/grandpa."

In the chapters to come I will talk about this more. But you must read the whole book to understand why.

My mom realized my siblings had their own houses with their kids, and I didn't have a house of my own for my kids and me. So my mom told the siblings that she and Dad were putting in their Will that after they die, I, Evelyn, will be getting their house. Mom and Dad went to the lawyers' office and did put in their Will that I, Evelyn, will get their house after they both die. My siblings argued with Mom the house should be sold and divided up. Mom said, "No. Evelyn doesn't have her own house for her and her kids." I saw my parents, Will, and it stated that I, Evelyn, will receive their house once they both die. Keep reading to find out what happens.

My kids were playing cowboy and Indian at the house. I told them to stop playing this game. My kids were stunned. My mom started to interfere to tell me to leave them alone. I said no way! Then I told my kids that they had Indian blood in them. My kids were shocked. I told them that their dad has Indian blood in him. I then said, "Go to your paternal grandma." My kids went to their paternal grandma. She told them all about the several types of Indian blood in them. After this, my children grew a bond with their paternal grandma.

My children and I finally moved into my first apartment. The rent was $100 a month. It felt great for us to have our own place away from the chaoticness at my parents' house. I couldn't afford to give my children allowance money, so I signed up to deliver a weekly newspaper. I took my kids once a week to deliver the free newspapers to homes (roughly forty papers). The money would be divided between my two children.

I went for walks with my kids. One day, there were many ducks on the sidewalk near where we lived. My son ran to the house to get some bread so we could feed the ducks. We were feeding the ducks. There was an apartment building nearby with older women on their porches. I heard one woman say, "There goes our Welfare Bread." I was working but not making enough without food stamps. I didn't buy junk food on my food stamps like most people did, so why the ridicule?

My mom called me three times a day, asking me what I was doing, etc. If I went shopping with my kids, I always took them out to eat before we came home. Many times, I would get home in the evening. When I got home with my kids, I would either get a phone call or a car honking outside. I would find out it was my mom. She used to yell at me, "Where were you? I've been looking for you all day. I called you, but you never answered. I drove around town looking for you, but I couldn't find you. I also came over to your house honking the horn, and you never answered my honk." Then she yelled at me again. "You tell me when you go somewhere at all times." This issue was a continuous episode with my mom on a daily basis (three times a day, seven days a week, three-hundred-sixty-five days a year).

I started noticing an issue with my carpet near the electric heater soaking wet. There was an electric outlet on the carpet near the electric heater where the carpet got wet. Then, I started finding mushrooms growing out of the soaked carpet. The landlord wouldn't fix it. The next issue I noticed was the busted sewer line outside. The river was not too far away from the sewer line break. Toilet paper, etc., was bursting out of the ground whenever any of the tenants flushed the toilet, drained the sink, etc. Lo and behold, one more issue. My electricity was going out. I had an electrician come to see why. He found out I only have *one fuse* for my whole apartment (six rooms). When I went into the basement with the electrician, I noticed very large *river rats* in the basement. They were the size of a raccoon. I had had enough. I went to the city and complained. They came and inspected the complex. They saw the brick was deteriorating, etc. The city shut down the apartment complex.

When I moved out of there, I moved with my children to a low-income housing complex. I saw the parking lot was filthy, so I got a broom and dustpan and started cleaning the parking lot. While sweeping the parking lot, I had an unexpected encounter with a neighbor.

The simple act of sweeping the parking lot attracted the attention of a curious neighbor child. He questioned, "What are you doing?" I told him, "I'm cleaning the parking lot. If you help me, I'll take you to McDonald's for ice cream." That led the boy to run to tell the other neighbor kids in the complex about being treated to ice cream at McDonald's. The boy came back with at least ten other children. The other children said, "I want to clean."

I only had one broom, dustpan, and garbage bag. The kids all tried to take the broom and dustpan away from each other. I told them to wait for their turn. For each cement square in the parking lot, there was a different group of kids cleaning. They were fine with this. Once the one cement square was cleaned, the next three children cleaned the other square. Once done, I took my children and my neighbor's children (with their parent's permission) to McDonald's for ice cream. Afterward, at McDonald's, the children asked when we could clean again. I said, "Once a week. We will also clean the playground equipment with soap and water, pick up trash in the yards, and clean the parking lot." I told them I would decorate a character Wilton cake for their birthday. Soon after that, a neighbor girl's birthday was coming up. She came to my house and picked one of the over twenty-character Wilton cake pans I had for her birthday cake. She watched me decorate her *Barbie* cake. She proudly carried the Barbie cake to her house.

I only had one broom and dustpan for the weekly cleaning with the kids. So, I tapped into my resourcefulness, visiting local businesses to garner support for this grassroots initiative. A hardware store provided us with brooms and dustpans, and a pizza place sponsored shirts with the name of our team on them for the kids as a token of appreciation. The bright yellow shirts symbolized their commitment to transforming their community. Every Sunday, these young volunteers, donning their vibrant shirts, gathered to clean and beautify their surroundings.

One Sunday, the apartment manager drove by while the children and I were cleaning the parking lot. She stopped and asked me what we were doing. I told her the children and I are cleaning the parking lot, playground equipment, picking up trash, etc. I then told her that I take the kids to McDonald's for ice cream afterward. The apartment manager told me that she would take my group of kids and me out for pizza. The day we went out for pizza, a few kids had dirty clothes. We told them to change their clothes before we go. The kids came out crying, saying their mom wouldn't let them change their clothes. We couldn't leave those children behind because of the parents, so the kids with dirty clothes came with us. The apartment manager gave the kids money to play games. The kids were loud in excitement (like kids are).

The joy to see the energy and enthusiasm that only children can bring when they sweep, scrub, and pick up litter with pride. Once, an adult neighbor guy was walking in the grass area where the children's play equipment was. He threw garbage on the grass. One of the kids from the cleaning group saw this and ran to this adult man, pointing his finger at the trash, and said, "You pick up this garbage right now. I clean every week before I get my ice cream at McDonald's. I'm not doing any more work than I have to before I get my ice cream at McDonald's." The adult man was left stunned. He looked at the kid, then picked up his garbage and put it in the garbage can. After each cleanup, the promise of ice cream at McDonald's was the cherry on top of their hard work. The children were always wanting to help me out. I received knocks at my door from these children. One child asked if I needed anything done. I told him I had to take the garbage out. He said, "I got it," and took out the garbage. Then, a three-year-old girl knocked at my door crying, saying, "Is there anything I can do?" I told her, "I have to do the dishes; if you want to help me rinse the dishes, you can." She got excited. I put a chair up by the sink and helped her rinse the dishes. Afterward, she said, "Can I have ice cream now?" I opened my freezer and let her pick out a flavored Popsicle. She then left all happy and smiling.

Whenever I came home in my car, the children would come running to my car. They would see if there was anything that needed to be carried into my house. The children wouldn't let me carry anything.

A new fast-food restaurant was opening up very soon. They were taking applications. I applied to this newly-built restaurant. Food restaurant. I worked at fast-food restaurants when I was married, so working for them wouldn't be much of an issue for me. I have had over ten years of restaurant experience by this time. To my amazement, I was hired at this new fast-food restaurant. I now had an outstanding opportunity awaiting me at this place. Having spent a decade working in various roles across the restaurant industry, I developed a keen eye for efficiency and productivity. I worked during the day for a while. Then, one day, the owner of the restaurant asked me if I would work the *closing* shift the next day. He said it's taking too long to close the restaurant at night. I agreed to work the closing shift the next day.

On my first night closing, I drew upon my previous experiences and efficiently executed the tasks at hand. The owner's son was managing the shift the first night of my closing. At a certain time in the evening, I started prepping to close the fast-food restaurant without anybody telling me what to do. The owner's son came to me and asked, "Who told you how to do this?" I told him, "Nobody. I just know how to prep to close and open. I have over ten years of restaurant experience." The owner's son said he was going to tell his dad (the owner) that we closed thirty minutes quicker with me tonight.

The next day, the owner himself approached me. He requested that I document my step-by-step process for closing the restaurant, and I did accordingly. I compiled a *three-page* detailed step-by-step list outlining *how to prep to close the restaurant.* The list stated the times in the order of what to do first, second, third, etc. (e.g., 7:00 p.m. break down prep station to this amount; 7:30 p.m. break down this section, etc.). I gave a three-page guide on how to *prep-to-close* the restaurant to the store owner the next day. The owner looked over my list and then put it in the filing cabinet in the office. He then told me that I could get off earlier tonight because he had my guide list on *how to prep-to-close.* I was leaving early in the evening when the assistant manager asked me, "Where are you going?" I told her the owner told me I could leave early tonight. She told me that I could not leave. She doesn't know how to close the restaurant without me. I told her about my three-page guide on *how to prep-to-close* the restaurant at certain times so that the closing manager knew how to close the restaurant easily.

The manager told me to stay right there until she finds that list. She was determined to find that prep-to-close list I wrote up. After about twenty minutes, she found the list I wrote up. She went by my list step-by-step to tell employees what to do at what time by looking at my three-page prep-to-close list. She continued to look at the list until she knew it by heart without having to read from it.

I received phone calls at work from my mom nearly every day. She would tell me, "You get home right now. The kids are acting up." And in reply, I would tell her, "I can't. I'm working right now." I told her if she can't handle my children, then I will find a different babysitter. My mom said, "No way! Nobody watches these kids but me." The owner of this fast-food restaurant knew my mom called constantly while I was working. He clearly stated, "If your mom doesn't stop calling at work, I would have to let you go." I went home disgusted by my mom's constant *control* over me and my children. I told her if she doesn't stop calling me at work, I'll find a different babysitter. You will no longer be babysitting. Mom said she was the only one who was going to babysit the children. I told her the next time you call, I will be getting a new babysitter. After that, my mom stopped calling.

Now that my children were going to school, one was in kindergarten and the other in second grade, my parents didn't watch my children. I took my children to the daycare center early in the morning before I started work. The daycare had other children who came early and were also attending school. The daycare was just walking distance to the grade school. They walked the children to the school every day. Then, when the children were done with school, the daycare would walk up to pick up the half-a-day kindergarten children. Then, when the children studying from the first grade to fourth grade were done for the day, the daycare employees would go pick those children up. The parents were mostly working when school got out for the day, so they depended on the daycare staff to pick up their children at school.

Back when I was working the prior jobs, I made sure my children went to preschool. I had to pay around $40 a month for each child to go to preschool. I took them to preschool every day and then picked them up a few hours later from there. Preschool was two to three days a week. I wasn't going to deny my children to connect with other children and learn things prior to kindergarten. I didn't care how short of money I was. My children's learning and bonding with other children were more important to me. I remember my one child had all the kids in preschool look up to him. Whatever he did, they followed him. The preschool teachers told me how all the children looked up to my son. Whatever he did, they wanted to do it with him.

A rich family had issues with their child who was in my son's preschool. They saw how all the children looked up to my son, and they asked me if my son could go to their house and play with their son. They told me they wanted their son to be like my son. I was shocked by their request. They were rich and had a fancy home. I was on food stamps, barely making it. But I agreed. My son went over to their house to play with their son a lot. Their son got influenced by my son, and he started acting like my son. It seems that once my son helped their son to become like him, they no longer wanted him over to their house, or was it? Perhaps my mom called their house many times (like she did when I went out with a new friend. She called her mom twenty-one times that night).

As time passed, my role evolved further, and I was promoted to the position of breakfast manager. I prep to open the restaurant as a breakfast manager. I put the money in the registers and made sure the crew had everything ready to open up on time. The owner recognized my unparalleled commitment and the exceptional value I brought to the team. After a while, the owner came to me and said, "The kitchen isn't the same without you. Anybody can be a manager. It's rare to find employees like you. You do work for three people." The owner said he would do anything to get me back in the kitchen as an employee. I told him I needed a certain pay and hours. He agreed to it immediately. In fact, he and his wife did even more than that. They would take me out to get my hair done, face made up, and buy me things like clothes and make-up because they knew I put my children's needs before mine. I made sure my children had new shoes, clothes, coats, winter boots, school supplies, etc. I took them to a beautician to get haircuts, took them out to eat, and so on. I would wear my same old clothes, shoes, etc., because my children came first.

One weekend, the owner's son said while going to our cars, "I'll see you later, Evelyn." My heart sank. I had a bad feeling something was going to happen to him. I tried to wave and yell to get his attention, but he and his college buddies were off. Two days later, the owner's son was dead! Somebody poisoned his drink. From that day forward, I decided I would never hold back my gut feelings (you call them *Mother Intuitions*) to anybody again. After his death, the owner and his family were never the same. The restaurant never ran the same without the owner's son. Things started going south. I tried to stay on, but after nearly one year of this, it didn't matter how good of a job I did anymore. The owner told the managers to find something wrong with my work performance. The managers told me to get a toothbrush and scrub the cracks of the tile in the bathroom. I was stunned. The manager said she finds nothing wrong in my work, but she must find something that I am doing wrong. Not too long after this, I walked out on this job.

Then, when my oldest child finished second grade, the teachers voted for my son to go to *College for Kids* that summer. My son received twenty-six A's in second grade. I had to borrow money from the bank for my oldest child to go to college that summer. The drive to the college was thirty miles away from home. I drove my son every day to the college, and my younger child accompanied us.

I had my children go out for baseball starting in first grade in the summer. They went out for soccer and football a few years later. I also planned to have them learn to swim (something my mom refused me to learn). When I drove the kids to the swimming pool, my mom followed me in her car. She yelled at me, "Don't you dare have those kids take swimming lessons. They will drown." I said, "My kids are going to learn to swim. You refused me to learn. You sure are not going to stop my children from learning to swim." Out of the blue, a swimming instructor (grade school teacher) heard the commotion. She came over and found out my mom was trying to stop my kids from learning to swim. The instructor told my mom, "The children will not drown. We are here teaching them to swim." My mom had a disgusted look on her face and left. With the swimming instructor's help, my children were not denied the opportunity to learn to swim like I was by my mom.

My aunt, who treated me more like her child than my own mom did, worked at the bakery that I started working at. I learned how to make turtle candy, cashiered, and cleaned up there. The owners were mean to their employees. Not only that, but I witnessed them making dough for donuts in the most unsanitary manner. I saw *bugs* crawling around in the dough. I told the owners that they needed to throw this dough out. There are bugs in the dough. She told me she was not going to throw away the dough. The bugs will die in the hot grease. Have you ever wondered why there are dark spots in your donuts or other bakery food?

On weekends, there was another cashier working with me. The owners came to me, accusing me of stealing money out of the register. I told them I did not steal any money. I then asked them if the register ever had money missing during the weekdays when

I was alone. The owners answered, "No." I told them if the register isn't short during the week, then I sure am not taking money when somebody is working with me. Later, the woman working with me said, "What if the person needed the money?" Right then and there, I knew she had stolen the money. But after the male owner threatened to blacklist me from working, I quit.

I had more than enough of my mom's control. I decided to find low-income housing once again and finally got into it. One evening, while I was in my apartment, I was talking to a neighbor on the phone. I had my eyes closed while talking to her. I kept seeing these three numbers (ex. 742) with my eyes closed. I would open and rub my eyes. I would then close my eyes again. I kept seeing those three numbers again (742) when I had my eyes closed. I hung up the phone quickly and went to the local gas station. I asked when the daily three-pick lottery was being drawn. The cashier said in ten minutes. I told the cashier 742 anyway. That means 742 can be out of order, but all those numbers must come up to win. I got home quickly and turned on the TV. The lottery drawing was live on TV. every night. I watched the numbers being drawn. The first number was a "4". I waited impatiently for the next ball to come out. The next ball was a "7". Now, my heart is starting to beat. I waited anxiously for the last number to be drawn. The last number drawn was "2". I was stunned! I actually won the pick-three lottery drawing. I only won $50 because it was out of order.

In 1989, I heard on the radio that Nashville people were coming to the area on this date. They were coming to listen to people audition singing. I had always loved to sing. I always had the records, cassette tapes, or the radio playing.

During this time, I was delivering a weekly paper. I met up with some customers at a local bar when I went there to deliver the newspaper. I told them that Nashville people were coming to listen to anybody who wanted to audition. I told them I plan on auditioning. A guy at the bar told me he would let me borrow his microphone to practice singing. I went to a music store and got a cassette tape of a certain song that I was going to sing. The tape had only the background music of the song (no vocals), so I used this cassette tape to practice singing with the microphone I had borrowed.

On the night that the Nashville people were in the area, I went there with my cassette tape. After everybody was done auditioning, the Nashville people told everybody, "We are only taping you singing. We are taking everybody's auditioning singing back to Nashville Recording Studios. If they like your singing, they will contact you."

Well, one week later, I received a phone call from a Nashville Recording Studio. They said, "Evelyn, this is... Recording Studio from Nashville. We heard your singing. We never heard anybody sing like you before." Then they asked me if I knew *Reba McEntire*. I told them I didn't know her. They told me they were working with Reba and that she was going to be famous someday. They said, "You can be up there with Reba, but you would need $2,000 to get into the recording studio." I told them I didn't have the money. They mentioned they would help me, but I said I would talk to my mom. She would help me.

I went to my mom and told her about Nashville calling me. I asked her for her help to go to Nashville. Mom told me, "No. You have kids." I told her that the kids would go with me. Mom said, "You're not going anywhere. You're staying right here!" Nashville was going to help me. They gave me their phone number, but I threw it away after what my mom said to me. This is something that doesn't usually come anybody's way (let alone mine). My family couldn't care less about my success and improving my children's lives as well. After all, who's there that really cares?

NOTE: _My dad's siblings had a band. They (five of them) were playing the band every weekend. My brother had a band when he was still in high school. Why would mom say 'No' to me?_

Now that my once-in-a-lifetime chance to go to Nashville and start a career as a singer was thwarted by none other than my own mom, I decided to go to college. I left the bakery job after they threatened to blacklist me from getting employment. I contacted the food stamp office and told them that I wanted to go to college, but I couldn't work while going to college because I was threatened by the bakery owner to be blacklisted. I told them I'll never go back there again. The food stamp office told me it was fine that I don't work while going to college after the episode with the bakery. I went to the community college to sign up for a course. The college asked me what I wanted to opt for. I looked at all the majors I could go for. I told them I wanted to go to college to be an auto mechanic. The college person started laughing at me. He told me, "No woman has ever taken a mechanics class. That is a *man's* job. You wouldn't be able to lift up an engine." I told him I was going for an auto mechanic. He insisted that I find a different major to take. Once again, I was denied what I wanted to do, so I found a different major to the staff's satisfaction.

Now that my children were both in grade school and I was going to college (with epilepsy), there was no way I could work with all these responsibilities on me. But lo and behold, I received a phone call from the food stamp office. They told me that the bakery called them and told them that they wanted me back to work. I told them, "No way. They threatened to blacklist me." The food stamp office told me, "You have no choice. If you don't work part-time, you will not receive any food stamps or medical assistance for you or your children." I was distraught. I tried to use what little financial aid I had to pay my rent and necessities for my children and me. It was more than I could handle.

I went to a counselor service in my town. The counselor requested that I fill out a questionnaire. I asked how I was supposed to answer these questions. She told me, "Just any way." I asked if it was meant for episodes that happened in my life or if it should be answered in a different way. She refused to answer. So I answered the questions about the episodes that have happened in my life (e.g., Do you feel safe in a park? I think of the times my children and I spent in the park, and I answered 'yes.' Then, a bit down, the question comes up again: "Do you feel safe in the park? I think of the time that I got beat up by relatives and answered 'no.')

After I finished the questionnaire, the counselor claimed that I was *bipolar.* I told her that is not true. She wanted to put me on medicine or worse, so I left.

Well, after a few weeks without any food stamps, medical assistance, or money, I went to the counselor's office at the college, crying. He asked if I was seeing a counselor. I said I was. He and another person at the college took me to the counselor's office. The college counselor and the counselor who made me fill out that questionnaire went inside alone. They called me back into the office and told me I had a choice. Either I sign myself into a *mental institution,* or they would have me *court-ordered* to be put in a mental institution. I told them I was not crazy. They told me, "You have to make a choice. Either way, you're going to the mental institution."

I signed the papers to go into the mental institution. When I got there, the psychiatrist saw me. I told him all that was going on in my life. I told him about the bakery, college, and food stamp office. The doctor said, "What the counselor's office states is different than what you say." He said that he needed a third party to tell him what was going on. So the doctor called my mom. He then came back in and told me that my mom said the same thing I had to say about what had happened. The psychiatrist said, "You don't belong here. You're not bipolar. You're going through financial stress." He further told me, "It's late Friday. It's too late to get you out of the mental hospital today. You'll have to stay the weekend and get out on Monday."

There I was… put in the mental hospital for financial stress. The doctor told me that I had to see a counselor back home. I said, "I refuse to go back. I will not see the person who had me confined here." He agreed to my statement and noted that I would never see this counselor again.

I had drama on top of drama going on in my life. In just a few months, not only did I miss out on going to Nashville to be a singer, but I missed out on going to college to be an auto mechanic. I was not even thirty years old, and I had been through so much so far with epilepsy.

NOTE: *Nobody knew how to treat epileptics in the past, so Epileptics got put in "Mental Institutions." These mental institutions meant for Epileptics are shutdown today & nobody (not even medical students) can go inside these shutdown mental institutions anymore. How badly did these mental institutions treat Epileptics?*

I was told this by someone in the medical profession recently.

After getting released from the mental institution, I, along with my children, moved back to my parents' house. Not too long after my children and I moved back in with my parents, my ex-mother-in-law came to me and told me my ex was out of prison. I was somewhat scared for my children. My ex-mother-in-law told me he was living with her and her husband. She said if the kids came over to her house, she would make sure he was not alone with the kids. I would take the kids over to my ex-mother-in-law's house. I would stay with the kids until we all left to go back home. I wouldn't let them go over alone after that. Then, my ex-husband started working for a construction company. He got paid cash. He never gave any of his several hundred dollars of money every pay period for child support. Once in a blue moon, he gave me $15. But that was only because his mom made him give me some money ($15). Wait! It gets even worse. My older sister married my ex-husband. Now, my ex-husband was my brother-in-law. My sister was an aunt to my kids, so that made my children's dad their uncle by marriage. Even after this, I still never received any child support. I decided if I would force money from my ex, he would later on tell our sons that he couldn't afford to do anything with them because he was giving me child support money. I wanted my kids to see the truth. Not too long after my sister married my ex-husband, my ex-mother-in-law got lung cancer.

I started working at a fast-food restaurant out of town, a job that I quit after one year. I started up more paper route deliveries. After several months, I found myself working for four different newspaper companies, out of which three of them were motor routes. I was delivering to homes, stores, and machines in two different towns. I also delivered newspapers out on the country roads. In the early morning, I delivered two different newspaper companies (motor routes) to two different towns. It took me four hours in the morning to deliver all the papers. Then, in the late afternoon, I delivered the third newspaper company paper (motor route). I delivered papers to homes, stores, and paper machines in the AM and PM.

I took a ten-minute nap in the late evening. I dreamed that I was in a car wreck. Cars were hitting each side of my car. There was nothing but the steering wheel left. I had glass in my eyes, and I couldn't see. I felt I was dying. Then some people are yelling, "Evelyn, wake up. Evelyn wake up. It's ok." I felt hands hitting both sides of my cheeks. They had their hands on me and started shaking me. They kept saying, "Evelyn, wake up. Evelyn, wake up." I finally awoke. There was nobody around me. I had no marks on my body, and I could see. I knew then I had a dream of what was going to happen. I knew something was wrong with my car, but I didn't know what. I drove my car slowly on my paper routes.

On the third day after my dream, I was on top of a hill delivering newspapers. I had to go down this steep hill. I put my brakes on when I started going down the steep hill. The brake paddle went to the floor. I had no brakes. At the bottom of the hill is a highway. I'm supposed to stop at the stop sign at the bottom of this hill. I started screaming, "Oh my God. Jesus Christ. Help me." I kept screaming for God and Jesus for help. I kept pumping the brakes for air brakes, hopefully. Just ten feet before the stop sign, the car stopped. I started thanking God and Jesus over and over for helping my car come to a stop. Remember, if I went through that stop sign, I would have gone through the highway. Just a quarter of a mile up the highway is a mechanic shop. I prayed to get there safely. The mechanic looked at my brakes. He told me both my *brake hoses* are dry rotted. I lost all my brake fluid. I never finished my motor route until after my brakes were fixed.

My ex-mother-in-law was basically on her deathbed with her cancer. She cried, saying that she wouldn't have a tombstone when she died. She told me nobody would know where she was buried, so they could come and see her at the graveside. I told my ex-mother-in-law not to worry. I'll get you a tombstone when you die. She finally died. I waited a few months for her husband, my ex-husband, his wife (my sister), or his sister to jump in to get her a tombstone. Nobody did. They didn't care. I went to purchase a tombstone for my ex-mother-in-law. She finally had a tombstone at her graveside because I purchased it with my hard-earned money. Well, when my mom and siblings found out that I bought my ex-mother-in-law a tombstone, they all yelled at me, saying: Why did you get her a tombstone? It's not your responsibility, etc. I responded back, "Bull... She is my children's grandmother. If my kids want to go see her at the graveside, they will know where she is buried!"

I also had to collect money from the stores and machines biweekly. I would have to use the blank accounting paper the newspaper company gave me to write down each store's account. I had to figure out how many papers they never sold so they get credit for them (ex, ten weekly papers not sold, then I take ten times forty-two cents (credit for each paper). That makes their bill $4.20, which was credited to their bill. If their bill is thirty papers (delivered) times forty-two cents each paper. That is a $12.60 bill before the $4.20 credit. That makes the store's bill $8.40 for the papers sold. Each store had a different amount of bill. I had over twenty-four stores and paper machines. I had to do this every two weeks. The stores received a carbon copy of the bill. The other copy I had to give to the newspaper company with the money to them.

Meanwhile, I was looking for ways to move out of my parent's house. I was making enough money to move out now. I prayed to God to please help me find a house for my children and me. Please, God, not an apartment but a house for my children and me. Let the house be a newer home with a laundry room, dishwasher, a garage, and a nice yard. I didn't know if God could help me find a house to rent, but I prayed anyway. Since I delivered papers to homes and stores out of town, I asked around the out-of-towners if they knew of a house for rent. They said no, but they took my name and phone number. Then I had a ten-minute nap. While I was asleep, I had a dream that I was walking when I heard a guy say, "Come here." I looked at him. He then said I want to show you this house. The guy looked just like Colonel Sanders from KFC. I went toward this man dressed all in white, and he gave me a grand tour of this ranch home. He showed me the whole house with a garage. He asked, "How do you like it?" I told him, "I love it." He told me the amount for the rent. I then responded, "I'll take it. I'll take it." Then I woke up from my dream. My dreams have usually come true in the past. I was hoping this dream would come true as well.

I went about delivering papers, taking care of my kids, etc. Three weeks later, I received a phone call at my parents' house. The woman had heard that I was looking to rent a house. She told me the address of the house in the other town. There were no cell phones to direct you to an address back then. I finally found the house one-fourth a mile out of the town I lived in. When I found the address, I pulled into the driveway. To my surprise, when I looked at the house, it was identical to the one I had seen in my dream three weeks ago. I stood in amazement. I knew this was the house the man in white had shown me in my dream. The landlord said, "Come in. I'll show you the house." I already knew what the house looked like before I went in because I had seen all of it in my dream. Sure enough, I went inside the ranch home. The entrance to the living room, dining room, kitchen, laundry room, etc., was exactly the same as the one I had toured in my dream.

This ranch home was built thirty years ago. It sat on a double lot and came with an electric garage door opener. It had a full

Basement, central air, etc. The rent was under $500 a month. I signed the paperwork with the landlord, and she gave me the house keys and the electric garage door opener. I now had to go hunting for nice used furniture, kitchenware, etc.

The real question is, what lies ahead in this beautiful thirty-year-old double-lot ranch home out in the country for my children and me?

"There are people who make things happen.
Those who watch what happens, and those who wonder what happens."

- Unknown Author

Chapter Six

I was determined to make it feel like home when I moved into my new place. I scoured the newspaper for things to fill it with and came across an ad for a 60-year-old dining room set that instantly piqued my interest. It was a vintage white buffet accompanied by six elegant chairs and a dining table that could fit comfortably underneath the chandeliers in my dining room. I fell in love with the old-world charm of the set. I also found a treasure trove of gently used furniture for my middle room and bedroom. My dad, bless his heart, was the only family member willing to help me with the move, mainly because he had a truck. He had always been my idol, but especially that day, he became my hero, and together, we transformed my new house into a cozy and comfortable abode—a place worth living.

My kids chose to live in the full basement. It had several rooms with a "full" bathroom and had furnace vents for heat or central air for flow in the basement. My kids were excited about our new "house." One day, while I was taking a shower, I heard my children screaming, "Mom!" I got out of the shower and got dressed quickly. I went to them to find out there was a snake in the basement by the hot water tank. The outside door was next to the hot water tank. I called law enforcement to help get the snake out of the house. I didn't know what type of snake it was, but it was large enough (I believed) to be a "rattlesnake." The officers came. They were "scared" to catch the snake at first. You should have seen them jerking away from the snake. They got a box and put the box on top of the snake, trapping it inside the box. Once the snake was trapped in the box, the officers looked closer at what type of snake it was. The officers told me it was just a large garden snake. They took the snake outside and into the fields across the country road.

But all in all, my kids loved living in the basement with a door leading outside. I believe they felt like they were in their own little world down there. My dad (is he?) came to help me tame a wild rose bush, even though the landlord was not in favor of the idea. But as any gardener knows, sometimes you have to trim to make roses flourish. I didn't stop with the roses; I dug up 12 different patches of grass, shaping them into circles, squares, and other geometric designs. Then, I went to the store and filled these spaces with seasonal flowers, creating a spyglass of colors and scents. One of my flower gardens even had a theme—Snow White and the Seven Dwarfs.

I planted fruit trees, lined the walkways with light rocks and Lilac trees, and even added Lombard trees on each side of the property for a touch of elegance. Our yard soon became the talk of the neighborhood. People would drive slowly by to admire the beauty they had never seen in the yard before. My neighbor's daughter even came over to snap pictures of my stunning flower gardens.

Every spring, the landlord arranged for her brother to bring a tractor to plow a section of the backyard for me to have a garden in the summertime. I took full advantage of it and planted over 50 tomato plants, sharing the bountiful harvest with my customers on my newspaper routes and family. Since I moved into this beautiful ranch home, I felt my "independence." Having the newspaper motor routes was awesome. I was my own boss. I could treat my customers how I believe "Customer Service" should be treated (with great respect). It didn't matter if my customers were "rich or poor"; I treated them the same. One of my customers lived in a rundown home that they own. They were elderly. They owned their home, but the house was in bad shape from the outside. When I gave them some tomatoes, their eyes lit up with excitement. They thanked me for the tomatoes. They told me they were lacking money for food. That was when I decided to bring them more tomatoes after I finished my newspaper delivery. They welcomed me into their small one-story home. That was when I realized how bad off they were. Their flooring was weak, with pieces of tile missing. Their wallpaper was peeling off with cracks in the wall, etc. I saw they had a "shower curtain" in the kitchen. I asked them, "Why do you have a shower curtain in the kitchen?" They told me that was where their bathroom was. I was shocked. It was a small area for a bathroom, so I asked where their other bathroom was. They said that it was their only bathroom. They took me to the kitchen and opened the shower curtain. To my surprise, there was only a toilet and sink. I asked them if they had a shower or bathtub somewhere. They told me no. They heated up water and cleaned themselves... It's a shocker how the community didn't come together to help them out. They were elderly, but wait and see how this community really is toward their citizens in dire need on their own.

Somewhere during this time, my ex-father-in-law died. He had not only several biological kids but siblings, nieces, and nephews still alive, but none of them would see that he got a tombstone at his graveside. It only took a few months of seeing his graveside without a tombstone buried next to my ex-mother-in-law before I went and purchased him a tombstone too. Of course, I got the "Third Degree" from my mom and siblings again: "Why did you buy him a tombstone? It's not your responsibility to get him a tombstone," etc.

I had to drive to a different town to pick up the newspapers to start delivering. I have come across many different situations. The most common issue was that I smelled a natural gas leak. You see, I have a very sensitive nose to smell. If the smell of gas was strong, I would pull my car over and check where the natural gas leak was coming from. When I had determined the area of the smell, I would call the natural gas company about the gas leak. The leaks I found were either at a gas meter, in the yard, or on the sidewalk or street. Many times, I would see the Natural Gas Co. truck checking out the leak. They often had to dig up the ground and fix the gas leak (be it at a resident's property or in the street). But sometimes, it would be a resident's gas meter that needed tightening up. If there is a natural gas leak from the gas meter to the street, the Natural Gas Co. is responsible for the repair (not the resident or the city).

The only time a resident or city property has a gas leak that they are responsible for is when it's the gas meter line going into the property.

Another encounter I experienced while delivering the newspapers was when I was delivering the a.m. papers in the early morning while it was still dark out. One of my customers always wanted her newspaper in the mailbox. One morning, when I put the newspaper in the mailbox, I felt a lot of mail in the mailbox. I looked around to see where to put the newspaper. That's when I noticed a bag on the ground with about five newspapers still wrapped around with a rubber band.

I went to the post office after the newspaper delivery was done and asked them if my one customer put a stop on her mail. They told me no. That's when I called the police. I asked them to do a welfare check on my customer. I explained why and gave them her address. In the afternoon, I called the police department back to see what they found out about my customer welfare check. That's when a police officer told me on the phone that when they got there, she was dead on the floor. The officer said that the apartment had a bad smell of death in the air, and the person had been dead for at least five days because of natural causes. This customer was in her senior year. She had a relative who lived in town, but this relative never checked on her.

A different issue I noticed was one of my customers' spouses had most of his leg removed from gangrene. He was in a wheelchair all the time. His wife told me he was getting real grouchy. Remember, my customers are treated equally no matter who needs help. I was talking to his wife for a while and asked if I could see him. I had known this customer for a few decades. I remember him going to the restaurant for coffee with his buddies all the time. Now, he was in a wheelchair with one leg gone to gangrene. While talking, he said his body hurt. I asked if I could give him a backrub. They agreed. The backrub I did for him relaxed him. I told them I would come once a week after I was done delivering my newspapers and give him a backrub. Of course, every week, they were excited to see me. They both had me to talk to besides my giving him a backrub. This continued until, one day, nobody was outside on the porch. I knocked on the door, but no answer. I decided to see if everything was okay with them during my afternoon newspaper deliveries. I finally saw the wife. She told me tearfully that he died yesterday. She told me he was all excited for tomorrow to come because I would be there to give him a backrub. She kept telling me how much he was looking forward to the backrub from me tomorrow. I gave her a hug and said I was sorry. I still kept in touch with her to see how she was holding up after her husband died.

Then, one more incident of many I have experienced is when I was driving on the highway coming to town to deliver newspapers. It was winter time, and they forecasted one foot of snow to come down overnight. There were flurries in the air while I was driving. I saw an older guy on the highway waving me down. I stopped to see what was wrong. He told me he needed to get to the shelter two towns away by a certain time, or he would be out in the blizzard. I decided that my newspaper delivery would be on hold while I helped this guy in need of shelter. The guy smelled bad, but I never said anything. He told me that people had stopped to help him, but when they smelled how bad he smelled, they wouldn't let him stay in the car. I told him it was no big deal and that he was fine. I finally made it to the town he needed to be in. I stopped at a store and bought him a sandwich and a cup of coffee. I then gave him a few dollars for himself and dropped him off at the shelter. He told me, "God bless you, child." I then went back to delivering the newspapers.

At Christmas time, I had my kids help me make over 240 mini bows to make wreath cakes for my customers on the newspaper routes. I would cut out over 240 mini-round cardboard plates and cover them with foil. A few weeks before Christmas, I would bake the over 240 mini cakes and decorate them with green frosting (Wilton Frosting). I then placed a mini bow that my sons made up for me and placed a red bow on the mini round shape cake. I now had a cake that looked like a wreath. I would then wrap each wreath cake in plastic wrap and then put them in a sandwich bag to seal them. I wrote over 240 Christmas cards for my customers. When I delivered the Christmas wreath cakes with the Christmas cards to my customers, I always put a piece of foil on the ground and then I put the Christmas wreath cake and card on top of the foil with their newspaper next to it. Then, if my customers would give me a Christmas tip, I would stash it away until a few days before Christmas. I would then count the tip money. I have found that the tip money I saved up was enough to buy one-fourth of a cow and a half of a pig at the meat market. The type of meat I received from the cow and pig was beef roast, pork roast, steak, spare ribs, hamburger, sausage, pork chops, etc. This meat would fill my deep freezer. Since I purchased this meat with my Christmas tip money, I started wondering why people didn't do the same thing when they received their income tax return. The tax return is extra money. Why waste the money on wants instead of being secured with meals for you and your family?

In the spring, I would purchase more seasonal plants, dirt, and wood chips to blossom up my 12 flower gardens. My dad would come over with a few lawnmowers for him and my children to cut the lawn. My dad was like a father image to my kids. While outside watering my plants, I heard a quenching of the tree leaves. I looked to see a huge bonfire on the other side of my property from the neighbor. He had a bonfire near the trees on the property of the house I was renting. I yelled at him to stop the fire now. I called the fire department. When the fire department came, the fire was smaller. The firemen said, "Oh. It's just him. He makes those bonfires all the time." The firemen didn't do anything about it. They left. I told the neighbor, "The next time you have a fire near my trees and make the leaves burn up, I'll take a picture of it."

I had to collect the newspaper returns from the stores and machines every two weeks. I had to write up the billing statement for each store account (24 stores and machines). Well, on one occasion, I was at the gas station when I heard an argument between a customer and a gas attendant. The customer only had a checkbook to pay for his gas. I went to this customer to talk to him. He explained that he was trying to get home. He lived over 150 miles away, and he was running out of gas. He said they wouldn't take his check. He added that he had no cash on him, and the money was in the account in the bank. Since I had cash on me from collecting from the stores, I told him he could write the check out to me, and I would give him the cash. He kept promising the check was good. The gas attendant was hesitant to let him get gas (thinking he was using a check). I told the attendant he wrote me a check, and I gave him the cash. The guy thanked me over and over again.

But there is one drama that never changed with my independence of delivering the newspapers; my mom would be driving around town. One day, she found me delivering a newspaper. She stopped and honked her horn over and over until I went over to her car. She would give me the "Third Degree." She asked questions like, "When will you be done? Where are you going after this? Come to my house afterward...." It became a pattern with Mom. She figured out what time I would be at this one residence place. She would park her car in the street, waiting for me to come to deliver the newspaper. Once again, she would honk her horn until I went over to her. She gave me the "Third Degree" again. I decided to change my routine of who I delivered to first. Now, my mom doesn't know my routine anymore. But when I would deliver my newspaper to this one customer, they would come to me and tell me my mom stopped by there. "She wants you to call her," "She needs you to get to her house right away," or "Your mom wants you to stop by her house." This became an issue nonstop with my mom.

Then came the challenge of managing the kids. I had a job delivering papers in the early mornings, and while I tried to call them to get ready for school while I was on the paper routes, I would often return home to an empty house. It turned out they had skipped school to hang out with friends, having their adventures while I was working hard, but what could you expect from these pure angels who were yet to be exposed to the cruelty of the world?

I was elated to have made the place look so beautiful. But life does not always go as planned. I was receiving my fair share of highs in life, and now, it was time to encounter some lows. In a very subtle manner, life threw a curve ball at me. You might have guessed it by now, but my epilepsy started acting up, and trust me, it was a frightening experience. I remember one day while delivering papers, I encountered a dizzy spell. I decided to tackle a treacherous hillside with no guardrails, and it didn't end well.

I lost control of my van, and it tumbled off the cliff, doing summer jolts in the air and landing on the street below. The van did another flip backward. It then crashed into a garage door, and the garage door landed on top of the van. The woman who had seen the accident assumed the worst, but to her surprise, I was miraculously okay. The ambulance arrived, and I was taken to the ER for eight long hours of tests. EEGs and CAT scans revealed no epilepsy issues, but I knew something wasn't right. I pressed for an MRI, but the medical staff hesitated. Eventually, they released me, but I was left unable to drive.

My newspaper business was my livelihood, and I was in charge of it. When I thought I had nothing to lose, I found myself facing some unexpected obstacles, including the jealousy of my own family. My sister, who was married to my ex (now divorced him), couldn't help but be envious of my beautiful ranch home. She had her life with her new boyfriend but couldn't fathom the idea that I, a single parent battling with epilepsy, had such a beautiful ranch home. So, now that I needed someone to drive to deliver my newspapers, my sister approached the ultimatum. She told me that she would deliver my newspapers on one condition: "You and your kids must move out of the ranch home and leave everything behind." I was adamant. There was no way I would agree to that. So, I posted a "Help Wanted" ad to find someone to handle my paper routes while I got medical treatment.

Throughout this period, I continued to seek answers for my worsening epilepsy. I consulted with five different doctors, all of whom dismissed my concerns. Despite continuous requests for an MRI, they refused to order an MRI. They told me that my EEG and CAT scan were normal. They would not order an MRI. They claimed my blackouts weren't caused by epilepsy. One of the neurology doctors told me my dizzy spells were caused by my family. This doctor told me to move away from my family. How? I needed help with my medical condition, which I knew was caused by my epilepsy. Frustrated and desperate, I contacted a University Hospital that was two hours away. They hesitated but ultimately agreed to see me without a referral. At the University hospital, a neurologist finally ordered an MRI of my brain, which revealed all the damage to my brain. He told me he was shocked that the EEG and the CAT scan were normal, but the MRI showed all the damage to my brain. The neurologist at the University Hospital explained that my epilepsy was exceptionally severe and required immediate attention. He recommended brain surgery or a change in medication. The neurologist at the University Hospital told me to go back to my neurology doctor in my hometown area and decide to either change the medication or have brain surgery. Now I knew my diagnosis, so without any further ado, I spoke to my neurology doctor's nurse back home. When I told her I went to the University Hospital and saw a neurologist there who did an MRI, which showed severe brain damage caused by epilepsy, he told me to come back to my neurology doctor and decide to either try new medication or have brain surgery. The nurse replied to me, "You went to see a neurologist at the University Hospital behind our back 'without' our permission. We will no longer see you now. You will have to go back to the neurologist doctor at the University Hospital for further treatment." I had to call the neurology department at the University Hospital and plead with them to continue seeing me as my neurology nurse told me they would no longer see me since I came to you guys without their permission. The receptionist contacted the doctor I saw. He agreed to continue seeing me to treat my epilepsy.

I had no choice but to endure the long trips to the University Hospital for tests and evaluations. Eventually, after multiple examinations and consultations, they were thinking that brain surgery was necessary, but the neurosurgeons would need to meet together to decide for sure if they believed brain surgery was a need. My mom was driving me the long two-hour drive to the University Hospital on a two-way highway. She would take her hands off the steering wheel and shake her hands. She told me her hands were getting numb. One time, she had her hands off the steering wheel, and the car went into the other lane of traffic. I yelled at her to get her hands on the steering wheel. It was no longer safe for her to drive me the two-hour drive to the University Hospital. When I got home, I made some phone calls to see if there was anyone who would drive me to the University Hospital. I finally talked to a lady who said the handicap vehicle in town might be able to. I made the phone call to the handicap vehicle office and explained my circumstances. They said they would take me to the University Hospital for my appointments and back. Now I have a secure way to get to the University Hospital safely to go to my appointments (brain surgery still not a yes).

While waiting for the neurosurgeon's decision to either do brain surgery or not, I decided to go on a blind date. My kids went to a teen dance prior to my blind date. While I was getting ready for my date, I heard somebody open the basement door downstairs. I said, "Who's downstairs?" Nobody answered, and then I heard the basement door shut. I live in a population under 1,000 and was out in the country a little bit. I never thought anything of it. I figured my kids' friends had come to see if they were home. Then my blind date came, and we went out to see the movie "Con Air." In the movie "Con Air," there is a song that was sung by Trisha Yearwood, "How Do I Live." After the movie, we went out to eat, and then he brought me home.

Upon my return from a blind date, a catastrophe greeted me on the threshold of my house that once used to be the prettiest in the whole alley. The house, my haven, was enveloped in flames. The fire had taken everything—the dreams, the meticulously tended gardens, and the memories were now nothing but ashes spread everywhere on the floor. My mother, along with my children sitting at the picnic table, waited desperately for my return. In a grieving state, I inquired her about the unfortunate incident. In a quivering state, she told me the house had caught fire within fifteen minutes of my departure.

After all of the drama of seeing the house I was renting catch fire, my kids went back with my mom, and I stayed in the car with my blind date. You see, the guy who was delivering my newspapers came to my house every morning to pick me up so I could help him on the paper route. It must have been about 3:30 am when the guy showed up to pick me up to deliver the newspapers. He saw the house had caught fire. He panicked, thinking I was inside the house that burnt. I got out of my blind date's car and told him, "The kids and I are ok. We were gone when the house caught fire." I saw a sigh of relief on his face when he saw me.

After the newspaper deliveries, we went to my parents' house and picked up the kids to go to the "Burnt House." My kids went into the basement to see what was salvageable. I played the radio just to hear the song "How Do I Live" by Trisha Yearwood on the radio. This song was played in the movie "Con Air" I went to see just last night to come home to a burned home. It tore me up. My son came up the stairs to see me crying. He had something in his hand. He told me, "Mom, look at this. The cross of Jesus never burnt, and it was in the basement." That cross of Jesus was in the TV room upstairs. That cross was important to me before the fire. My son said he took the cross of Jesus downstairs with him a while ago. He told me that the cross of Jesus (nailed to the cross) was under the window in the basement where the flames went pouring out of the basement. My son said he found the cross of Jesus on the floor surrounded by "rubbish." He then said, "Mom. It's ok. Jesus made sure we weren't home during the fire." After that, when I heard the song "How Do I Live" on the radio, I listened to the words of the song. Some of the words, "You're my world, my heart, my soul. There would be no world left for me; you're everything good in my life," etc. That's when this song became a song to sing to Jesus. From that day forward, I kept that cross near me at all times. Then when the song "How Do I Live" was played on the radio again, I took time out to hold the cross of Jesus singing this song. I purchased the CD of this song and a CD player. This song lifted my spirits while dealing with so much trauma in my life.

The only person helping me with the house fire was the guy who was delivering my newspapers. No family or community would lift a finger to help me. I asked for help, but it fell on deaf ears. I finally called one of my newspaper companies. I told them about the fire and that I needed help. I lost everything. The newspaper company put it in the paper. I received a phone call from "American Red Cross." The woman asked me if I was still able to live in the house. I told her no. She told me that she was never notified that my children and I were without housing because of the fire. She set a date to come see the burnt home. Well, there was heavy rainfall one night. The next morning, I helped the guy deliver the newspapers. One of the customers' driveways was gravel and dirt and a little hilly. The gravel washed away, and the dirt became muddy. It was early in the morning when I walked on this driveway. The muddy driveway caused me to lose my footing. I fell and broke my foot badly. I had to go to the hospital, where they admitted me. I needed to have ankle surgery. The orthopedic surgeon had to put a plate and six screws in my ankle. I had to stay in the hospital for at least five days. I had to call the lady at the Red Cross to cancel the appointment to see the burnt home. She waited until I got out of the hospital to see it. After this lady at the Red Cross saw the burnt home, she was furious. She said the fire department or the police department should have called her ASAP for me to get help from her. She said she could have gotten my kids and me a place to live, food, clothes, etc, but because it was over two weeks since the fire, all she could do now was give me three fifty-dollar gift cards for Walmart.

I went to a church and spoke loudly, "I had a house fire. My kids and I lost everything. All the blankets or clothes that were salvageable have smoke damage. I have a broken foot with six screws and a plate in my ankle, and nobody cares." That's when two to three people came to me with a total of $140 between all of them. With the money, I bought a used washer and dryer, laundry soap, and softener. I also got housing for my kids and me.

The only time anybody other than the guy who was delivering my papers helped with the burnt home was the last load. That's when my dad came to help. The only way I could get into the house was when the landlord would unlock the door so we could go in to try to salvage what we could. I had no time to keep my broken foot elevated. I needed to deal with the burnt home and move into an apartment. Oh, and I had four different types of seizures, taking over 20 seizure pills a day and having five seizures a week on top of all of this drama. Did my "neighbor" who made those huge bonfires near my rented property set my rented home "on fire"?

The washer and dryer were in the basement. I tossed the dirty and smokey clothes down the steps, but I had to carry the clean clothes up the stairs. This was when I noticed that I couldn't carry the laundry basket up the steps. Blood would rush to my face. It felt like the circulation to my face was shut off. My kids had to carry the laundry up the stairs. Then I tried to mop the floor. I couldn't mop very long before blood would be rushing to my face, and it felt like circulation was being shut off in my face. I had to stop and put my face down on the kitchen table. After the circulation to my face returned, I would continue mopping until the blood rushed to my face again. It took me at least three to four times to take a break before I would be done mopping the floor.

I couldn't afford to buy my kids school clothes because the house fire was in the summer. I needed to find housing and supply different beds, etc., for the apartment, leaving only $400 after I paid everybody to do my newspaper routes. My mom called me and yelled at me. She told me, "You go buy your kids brand new school clothes for school!" I told her, "No, they have clothes that were brought at the yard sale. I can't afford to buy them new clothes for school." My mom kept arguing with me to buy my kids new school clothes. Finally, my mom told me, "Fine. I'll buy the kids new school clothes. I am going to go tell all your siblings what an 'unfit mother' you are." She then hung up the phone. I had my siblings and others argue with me for not buying my kids brand new clothes for school. The fire was only two months before the new school year began. Absolutely nobody could care less that my home burnt down, I had broken my foot, and I was having five seizures a week, taking over 20 seizure pills a day.

Finally, I received a phone call from the University Hospital. The team of neurosurgeons had agreed to do my brain surgery. I was to come in at the beginning of the New Year to be admitted. They said they were not sure which side of my brain was causing the seizures because both sides of my brain had brain damage. So, they told me that when I came in, they would have to drill six holes in my skull and put wires in them to detect which side of my brain was causing the epileptic seizures.

Well, before I went into the hospital, there was a woman in her early twenties who drove drunk one night. She crashed her car, and she became paralyzed. The local newspaper had news about this woman driving drunk and becoming paralyzed from driving drunk and crashing her car. Every week, there was more news about her in the hospital and her treatments. This woman was a young person with no kids. She lived with her parents. It will be a shocker to you (I believe) that all six churches in this town got together to raise money to build this drunk driver a brand-new handicap home. This community later even purchased her a brand-new automobile, a "handicap accessible van." It gets even worse how conceited these churches and the community became.

Well, the handicapped van came to pick me up to go to the University Hospital to have my four brain surgeries. He came around 3 a.m. to take me to the hospital. I made sure to take the wooden cross of Jesus that was in the house fire with me to the hospital and took the CD Player and CD tape of "How Do I Live" by Trisha to the hospital with me. We arrived at the hospital at 5:30 am. The entrance to the main hospital was dark and there was nobody around. I asked the driver if he would help me get my belongings inside the hospital. He told me, "No." He was only supposed to drive me to the hospital and nothing else. I told him, "I can't. Blood rushes to my face." That's when he told me to get a wheelchair, put my stuff on it, and push the wheelchair in. He drove off once my stuff was in the wheelchair, but I really needed help. There was nobody, so I tried to push the wheelchair with my stuff on it. I could only do about five steps before blood would rush to my face, and I would have to find a place to sit to stop the blood rushing to it. Once the blood rushing to my face was better, I pushed the wheelchair some more until blood rushed to my face again. This continued about seven to eight times before I made it to the registration department.

There was a long line of people waiting to get registered. I couldn't handle standing very long with my blood rushing to my face. I finally got waited on at the registration. They had a lot of paperwork for me to fill out. I couldn't do that with the blood rushing to my face, but I had nobody to help me. I finally finished the paperwork. I asked for registration to get somebody to come help me get to the hospital room I was supposed to go to. Registration said there was nobody this early in the morning; I had to get upstairs to my room by myself. I begged them to call the floor I was going to and let a nurse know that I needed help. The registration department still refused. Again, I had to push the wheelchair for so long and then take a break because of blood rushing to my face. I finally got on the elevator. I was clinging to the elevator wall, ready to collapse. The elevator door opened, and I was not able to hold myself up much longer. A nurse saw how bad off I was and stopped. She took the stuff off the wheelchair to let me sit in the wheelchair. This nurse got other help, and they got me in my room ASAP!

The neurosurgeon had planned for me to undergo a total of four different types of brain surgeries. The first involved an angiogram to bypass my heart and shut off one side of my brain temporarily. They took images and then repeated the process for the other side of my brain. The second brain surgery, however, occurred several days later. I had to have all my hair shaved off my head to do this surgery. Then, when the surgery started, I had to be put under while they drilled six different holes from the bottom of the skull bone of my head up to the top of my head. Those holes were used to insert wires into my brain to monitor any seizures that I may have. They had to do this because I had scar tissue on both sides (left and right) of my brain.

When I came to, the neurosurgeon asked me frantically, "Where is your family?" I told him, "This is nothing new. They aren't coming." That's when the neurosurgeon told me that I had lost two pints of blood during the brain surgery. I asked him if he had two pints of blood put in me. He told me yes, someone from the hospital donated two pints of blood for me. When I got back into my hospital room, those wires put in my skull were plugged into the monitor on the wall to detect any seizures that I would have. One week later, my neurosurgeon came to me and told me that I hadn't had any seizures yet. He said if I didn't have any seizures in the next three days, he would have to cancel the brain surgery because he didn't know which side of my brain was causing the seizures.

I was determined not to leave the hospital without having the brain surgery. I knew if I didn't have the brain surgery soon, I would die. So, when the nurse brought in my seizure medication for me to take, I refused to take it. She kept saying, "You have to take the seizure medicine," but I kept refusing. The nurse left, and the neurosurgeon came in. He told me if I didn't take my seizure medication, I would have seizures. I told the doctor, "You want me to have seizures. If I take the seizure medication, I won't have a seizure because I'm not active enough to have a seizure." The doctor agreed but was scared I would have a bad seizure. I still wasn't having seizures the next day, so I went one step further. I stood at the side of my hospital bed and stood still, moving my feet like I was jogging. The nurse saw me do this and told me to stop because I might get the wires out of my head. I told her I knew what I was doing. I couldn't stay still. I had to get blood rushing to have a seizure. Sure enough, I had three mini seizures. Now, the Neurosurgeon knows what side of the brain needs to be operated on.

I've been in the hospital for over two weeks now. I have never received any "get well" cards, flowers, visits, or phone calls from anybody. I spent most of my time doing a seek-a-word game and playing my CD tape of Trisha Yearwood's song "How Do I Live." I held onto the Cross of Jesus with me all my life while playing this song, but I had the Cross of Jesus on me at all times in the hospital bed. I know Jesus "Won't Lead Me Astray." About two nights before my brain surgery, I had a dream that I was in the car with my "dead" ex-mother-in-law and her "dead" husband. We were just driving around enjoying ourselves. It was relaxing being in the car with them driving me around. They were "dead" and they came to see me, something my own family (alive) would not do (come see me). Did Jesus call them from their "grave" to be there for me for my last two brain surgeries? Did they come to see me because I purchased both of them a tombstone after they died? I had a roommate who was having brain surgery also. Her table was full of vases of flowers and "get well cards." She had visitors every day and received phone calls every day. Her visitors saw that my table was empty (no flowers or get-well cards), they never saw anybody come to see me, and my phone never rang. That's when my roommate's visitors came over to talk to me, so I had company.

Before my last two brain surgeries, the neurosurgeon had me try to put a first-grade puzzle together. I couldn't put any of the pieces in the right spot. I couldn't put a first-grade puzzle together, and I was in my late 30s. On the day of the last two brain surgeries, my parents, my sister, and her boyfriend were out in the waiting room. I never saw them before the brain surgery.

Prior to the surgery starting, the medical staff had to shave all my hair off my head once again; I couldn't have any hair on my head during the brain surgery. Then, I got into the surgery room; I saw my neurosurgeon. The surgeon was young. That relieved me, and I told him that. He asked me why. I told him, "Because you are young, not an older surgeon. I know you will have steady hands while you do my brain surgery." The surgeon told me he had only been a brain surgeon for a few years. I told him, "That means you know the newest way of doing surgery." I added, "If I die on the operating table, you don't give up on me. You keep working on me until I come back to life. I died when I was six months old. I was dead for one and a half hours before the doctor brought me back to life by CPR (a new technique not proven yet)." The surgeon told me I only had a 5% chance I would die during the brain surgery. I told him, "If I die, you do not go out there and talk to my family about it. You stay here and work on me until I come back to life." I also told him I had the Cross of Jesus on my chest here in the operating room. I knew Jesus wouldn't leave me. He told me that it was fine; I held the Cross of Jesus.

The operating staff shot novocaine in many different areas, from the bottom of my skull to the top of my head, to numb my head. I had to stay awake for the brain surgery. Once my head was numb enough, the neurosurgeon started drilling the top of my head, my forehead across my forehead down the left side of my face-behind, and my ear-sawed my jawbone in half. After that, the surgeon used a dentist's water hose to spray the bone dust away from my brain. That hurt. I told the surgeon to put the hose up against my brain instead of far away. It felt like spraying a car at a carwash with the spray hose far away from the car. Then, the surgeon touched the nerves in my brain. He asked me how it felt when he touched this nerve. Finally, he found the right nerve to get to my brain and take it out. He was going to just take out the dead brain, but then I had an epileptic seizure during the operation. That's when the surgeon saw the live brain was causing my seizures. That's when he knew he had to remove 100% of my front left temporal lobe brain (including removing my memory). Well, what I predicted happened on the operating table. I was basically brain-dead on the operating table. The Neurosurgeon had to stop the brain surgery to figure out what happened. He saw that the airways that bring oxygen to my brain were clogged. He had to unclog the airway in my brain so that I could get oxygen to my brain.

The surgery was over six hours long, but I wasn't done yet. I had to go into a different room and be put under to remove the wires that had been drilled into my skull about two weeks earlier. When I finally came to, I was tied down so they could wrap bandages on my head to cover up the brain surgeries I had. I felt like I was going to throw up. I tried to tell the ER staff that I had to get to my side; I had to throw up. They refused. They said that in five minutes, they would be done. I told them that I would be dead in five minutes if I didn't get to throw up. I kept forcing myself to get to my side. I got to my side just enough, and I started throwing up a lot. The staff noticed I was badly off, so they unstrapped me so I could get all the puke up. That room was full of puke on the floor. This was not just a mere surgery but a life-or-death battle, and I had to emerge through this with a fighting spirit.

Now I was in my hospital room. The surgeon only let my parents and sister see me for a few minutes. After that, my neurosurgeon came to me and told me about my brain surgery. He told me he tried to tell my family what a close call it was with my brain surgery, but he said my mom told him she didn't want to hear about my brain surgery. All your mom wanted to know was if you were dead or alive. He told me none of my family wanted to know how serious my brain surgery was. My neurosurgeon told me afterward that I had a "rare type" of epilepsy. He said he was only going to take out the dead brain, but because I had an epileptic seizure during the brain surgery, he said he saw that my "live brain" was causing my seizure. That's when he realized he had to remove 100% of my front left temporal lobe brain. He said he kept the part of the "Fight or Flight" piece in my brain. He said that it is a must to keep in. After this, the neurosurgeon told me, "Evelyn, your rare type of epilepsy is caused by your 'brain infection.'" He told me I wouldn't have epileptic seizures from my left brain anymore, but I still had brain damage on the right side of my brain, which could cause epilepsy. He said if my epilepsy flared up on my right brain, there was no more brain surgery that he could do. He said he took the "maximum amount" of the brain out of me (100% left front temporal lobe brain and the brain behind my left eyeball).

I died at six months old from Scarlet Fever. I came back to life one and a half hours later with a new technique not proven yet (CPR). After I came back to life, I started having epileptic seizures. Did the Scarlet Fever cause my "brain infection"?

That was the only time I saw my parents and sister. Now, I was back in the hospital room with my eyes nearly closed due to the swelling from the brain surgery. I couldn't wear my eyeglasses unless I had the left stem taken off because the side of my head

113

was swollen. I never received any get-well cards, flowers, visits, or phone calls, either, ever since my last two brain surgeries. My roommate was ready to leave the hospital that day. Her family came to take her home. She brought a vase of flowers over to me. I asked her, "What is this?" She told me that she had tons of flowers, and I didn't even have one. She said, "This vase of flowers is for you." I told her she didn't have to. "It's your flowers." She insisted that I take the vase of flowers. She and the people taking her home told me goodbye. Now, I was alone once again, but I was holding onto the Cross of Jesus and playing the song "How do I Live." I couldn't do my "Seek A Word" puzzle anymore. My eyes jumped up and down a line, and I had a double vision since I had the last two brain surgeries.

I had no cable, no phone calls, and no visits from my family during my hospital stay. I endured those four brain surgeries while being alienated by the world, hoping for a better future. My neurosurgeon told me that I would be sent to a very large city five hours away from him for rehabilitation. He said since I lived in a different state than here, my state insurance wouldn't allow me to be rehabilitated here. He told me my state insurance insisted that I get rehabilitated back in my state in a very large city (at least a population of 2 million people). I told my surgeon there was no way I would be five hours away from him in case something happened to me. The doctors there didn't do my brain surgery. They would just be guessing what to do if something flared up. The surgeon told me if I didn't go to that city to be rehabilitated, I would have to go home. He said I couldn't stay in this state to be rehabilitated unless I moved to this state. I couldn't move, and I refused to be five hours away from my brain surgeon, so five days after my last two brain surgeries, I was discharged from the hospital. My surgeon did a few tests before I left. One of them involved him making me try to put a first-grade puzzle together. With a little difficulty, I was able to put the first-grade puzzle together. My surgeon told me that I "wouldn't" improve much more in "ten years," but he wanted to continue seeing me afterward to see what improvements I had made. But why would my state insurance pay for my brain surgery to be done out of state but refuse to be rehabilitated in the area where I had my brain surgery? What if I had difficulties after brain surgery? My brain surgeon would be five hours away from my rehabilitation center. Would you be rehabilitated five hours away from your brain surgeon after brain surgery?

On the fifth day prior to being released from the hospital, the nurses took the bandages off my head. The brain surgeon checked out my scars to see if there were any issues with the stitches, swelling, etc., before being discharged to go home. My neurosurgeon talked to my mom and aunt prior to me being discharged to them. My head was all swollen up, and I had stitches from the top of my head, my forehead-across my forehead-down the side of my head (jawbone sawed in half). My eyes were nearly closed, and I had the left stem of my eyeglasses taken off so I could wear my glasses. When I got in the car with my aunt and mom, they told me, "We don't want to hear anything about your brain surgery. Our open-heart surgery was worse than your brain surgery. I asked my aunt for her daughters' phone numbers. My aunt told me, "I'm not going to give you my daughters' phone numbers. You leave my daughters alone. They have their own lives to live." Then my mom jumped in and told me, "Don't you call your siblings. They have their own lives to live."

I asked them to stop at a convenience store so I could get coffee. I went inside to get coffee. A customer saw my scarred head with one of my stems off my glasses. This guy laughed at me. He pointed his finger at me and said, "It looks like you got into a catfight."

I said sarcastically, "Yeah. The doctor beat me up. I had brain surgery."

The customer stopped laughing and said, "I'm sorry."

I finally got to my house and saw these kids in my house. I didn't know them. I asked these kids, "Who are you?"

They said, "We are your kids."

I then asked them, "What are your names?" My kids had to tell me their names. It took me some time to remember my kids, let alone their names.

Not even an hour later, when I got to my house, I got a phone call. One of the newspaper companies was on the phone. The boss informed me that I hadn't collected from the stores or machines for over a month. I told him I could not collect. I just got home from the hospital after having brain surgery. I said, "I told you you would have to collect because I was having brain surgery."

My boss told me he didn't want to hear any excuses. He told me he was not going to do any collecting. He then told me that I must get out there today and collect from the over 20 stores and machines "Today."

I told him I couldn't. "I can't read, write, say my a,b,c, count, write my numbers, add, or subtract. My eyes jump up and down the line, also."

My boss told me, "No excuses; you get out there tomorrow and collect from the 24 stores and machines."

Despite my struggles after brain surgery, I had nobody I could turn to. I went and got old copies of the billing statements from the stores in the past. I didn't know how to write the alphabet letters, so I drew the letters, not knowing what the letters were, let alone what they read. Then, I drew the numbers, not knowing what the numbers were. I used a calculator. I looked at the calculator for the numbers. The guy doing my paper routes tried to help me write the billing statements. Now, remember this is only five days after I had all of my left front temporal lobe brain removed from brain surgery. I also had the six wires that were drilled into my skull removed. They put "plugs" in these holes to block the permanent "holes" in my skull.

Well, the next day, the guy doing my paper routes drove me around to the over 20 stores (in two different towns) to collect from them. *What will I encounter trying to do the collections from all of these stores? What will people think of me with a shaved head with tons of stitches in my head and one stem of my glasses taken off?*

"The Holy Spirit empowers us to do the impossible and accomplish great things for God's Kingdom."

- Unknown Author

Chapter Seven

It had only been five days since my last two brain surgeries. I didn't have any hand or eye coordination. I couldn't figure out how to hold a pen to write (draw the letters) with. My son had to teach me how to hold a pen, which felt like a foreign object. I couldn't grasp putting the pen between my fingers and holding it to write (draw) with. My son stayed with me until he taught me how to hold a pen. It wasn't easy holding a pen, let alone moving the pen to draw letters with. You see, I couldn't read, let alone know my alphabet. I drew what I saw (letters or numbers). However, I was determined to conquer this in order to write over 20 billing statements for the stores and machines. After my son and the guy delivering my paper routes helped me out so I could try writing up the billing statements, I conquered it. Now it was time for the harder part: collecting from over 20 stores and machines the next day.

Six days after my last two brain surgeries, the guy who was delivering my newspapers drove me to the over 20 stores I needed to collect from. My head was shaved with many, many stitches (from the top of my head, down my forehead, across my forehead, and down the left side of my face with my jawbone sawed in half). My eyes were nearly shut, and the left side of my head was all swollen. I had to have the stem off my glasses on the left side due to the swelling. The first reaction to anybody who saw me at the stores was, "Your 'stem' is off your glasses." They never asked me, "Do you need help? Can I get you anything? Why are you out collecting after "brain surgery?" Etc. They had "no concern" for my health or well-being.

After the store gave me the newspaper dates of the newspapers they didn't sell, I found a place to sit down if I could. Most of the stores never had any place for me to sit and do the paperwork. Now, I had to separate each date for the last fourteen days (I had 28 days or two billing statements for each store to do). The guy with me helped me separate the dates. Then, he helped me try to count. I couldn't, so he showed me how to do numeral numbers. So, for each return, I put four (IIII) numeral numbers. But if I kept doing it that way, I would mess up. The guy told me that after I put four IIII, I should then put a line across the four numeral numbers to make five. Then I had to use the calculator. The guy helped teach me how to press 5, then a +. I had to count 14 days (12 for weekly and two for Sundays). So, for each numeral number adding five, I put 5. But if the numeral only had two numeral numbers, I put 1+1 on the calculator. After that hard struggle, I then had the guy help me figure out how to take the total of returns and multiply it by .34 cents. I then had to do the Sunday return using numeral numbers and then times it by 1.32. After that, add the daily and Sunday return credit together. After that, I had to take the charge and deduct the credit to come up with what they owed the newspaper company. You need to know that this was really hard on my brain. I was having headaches doing this. I had to take breaks and go back to it. I really needed to be home and resting my head after having four brain surgeries in two weeks. When I went to collect another time, the store manager told me that I overcharged them. I added the credit to the bill instead of deducting the credit to the bill. I told him, "I'm sorry. I just had brain surgery. I shouldn't even be collecting from any stores." I told him to deduct that amount from his billing statement the next time I collected. He understood and deducted the difference.

While I was in the hospital having brain surgery, I had my mom be in charge of my checking account (checkbooks). About a week after I got out of the hospital, I demanded my checkbook back. My mom was writing what amount each check was, but not writing down the "deposits" from the checks. I was lost where my checking account was. I started receiving phone calls from stores. They told me that my checks bounced when I wrote them. I told them I had the money in the bank. I finally got to the bank. They told me that they were charging me between $35-$50 for each bounced check. I explained I had brain surgery. I asked them to help me. Everybody at the bank "refused" to help me with my checking account. The bank fee for bounced checks was over $1,000. I had no money to pay for that. About 80% of the total amount of my paychecks went to everyone who delivered my newspapers. Not only did the guy get paid, but my "mom and two kids" received money for delivering a weekly free newspaper. I had to find help. I knew a lawyer and told him my situation. I explained that my mom was in charge of my checking account while I had brain surgery. I also told him that my mom never wrote down any deposits she put in the checking account. I told him how I was paying everybody to do my paper routes. The lawyer agreed to go to the bank with me and talk to the bank officer. About thirty minutes later, my lawyer came out and told me that they would refund me any bounce fees they took from me besides any other bounce fees off my checking account. After that, I went to a different bank. Curious: Did my mom take out extra money for herself when she had control of my checking account for over a month? Remember, I could not read or write. This meant that I could not read my mail. I would go to my neighbors, my kids, and my mom and ask them to read my mail to me. They looked at me like I was stupid and said, "I'm not going to read your mail. It's your mail, not mine. You read it." They would then walk away and ignore my plea for help. I was effectively on my own with no family or friends to lean on. Nobody believed me, nor did they care, so my mail started piling up (not opened).

My hand and eye coordination were severely off balance. I tried to feed myself some cereal (with a spoon), but I couldn't. The spoon of cereal went to my cheek instead of my mouth. I figured out I had to put my left-hand sticking outwards at the side of my mouth and try to feed myself. When I put my left hand at the side of my mouth before I put a spoon of cereal in my mouth, the spoon always went to my left-hand. I had glided the spoon (while still touching my left hand) into my mouth. I continued to do this every time I ate anything. The same goes for whenever I tried to drink something (hot or cold), for whenever I would try to put a drink to my mouth (be it milk, water, or a cup of hot coffee), the drink would go to my cheek instead. If it were a cup of hot coffee, I would feel the hot coffee spill on my face and down my chest.

After I experienced hot coffee touching my chest, I had to do the same technique: place my left-hand on the side of my mouth. The drink would go toward my left-hand, and I had to guide the cup of coffee or a cold drink into my mouth to be able to drink it.

Ever since I came home from the hospital, I kept the Cross of Jesus and the song "How Do I Live" by Trisha Yearwood near me. I played the song over and over again. My kids were getting tired of hearing this song played all the time. They didn't understand how important that song and the cross of Jesus were to me. I held the Cross of Jesus on my chest during my "brain surgery." I didn't know how to speak or say sentences, but music has words and sentences in their songs. So, playing that song was not only spiritually uplifting to me but helped me learn to speak. Because I never had any communication (socially) with people (other than my kids and the guy doing my paper routes, I started speaking in "Melody" (like singing). I played music constantly. Songs have sentences, which is how I learned to speak and say sentences. After nearly six months, when I went to my parents' house, I spoke in "Melody." My siblings, nieces, and nephews were smirking and laughing at me. They asked me, "Why are you talking like that?" I tried to explain to them that I learned to speak while listening to music. Nobody was ever around me (except my kids and the guy doing my newspapers) to learn how to speak any other way. Now, I must learn how to speak without "Melody" in my voice.

I had the guy who was delivering my newspapers and his brother stay with my kids and me. I just had four brain surgeries in two weeks. I needed them. They took me wherever I needed to go. My neighbors started complaining to the manager of my low-income housing about the guys staying with me. They were not causing any trouble with anybody. The manager told me that I had to pay over $400 more for them to stay with me. I told the manager I just had brain surgery with no rehabilitation and that the guys were like caregivers to me; I needed them. The manager refused to listen to my medical needs. He said, "No, if's, and's, or but's. You have to pay over $400 more per month if they stay with you." Nobody could comprehend the extent of my difficulties. Even simple tasks like reading and writing were difficult for me. Now, how was I going to manage without them here?

I told my kids, "Since I had my brain surgery, I have the knowledge of a two-year-old. I need you guys to teach me to read, write, say my a,b,c, etc." My kids told me they didn't want to hear it. They said, "You are our mom." I had a two-year-old toy in my house. It was a round ball that had holes to put a square in a square, a circle in a circle, a triangle in a triangle, etc. I didn't know how to do it. I tried to put a circle in a square hole. It wouldn't work. I told my son, "I can't get this circle in this square hole." (I didn't know what a square, circle, triangle, etc. was). My son had to come and show me that the shapes had to match to go inside the ball.

I needed to learn my ABCs, 1, 2, 3, etc. But how? No adults seemed to care. I was outside and saw the neighbor kids. I asked the little kids (eight years old and younger) to say their ABCs. The kids were excited to say their ABCs to me. I would have them repeat the alphabet, but this time, I would say the ABCs with them. I had them write the letters of the alphabet for me. Even though the kids were teaching me (secretly), they thought I was just playing with them. I would ask them to count to ten for me. They counted to ten with excitement. I asked them to write the numbers "One to Ten." The kids were happy to write their numbers for me. I had no idea how to say or write the alphabet or numbers. I asked the kids what one plus one was. I had the kids use their fingers to count. The kids taught me by putting one finger up on one hand and one finger up on the other hand. I then had them put one finger down at a time and count. I then had the kids help me learn to subtract using their fingers. I asked them to put two fingers up on one hand and one finger up on the other hand. I then asked them to put one finger down on each hand. There is a finger up yet. I asked the kids to put the remaining fingers down and count. They did and said, "One." This is how I learned to add and subtract. Just learning the first ten numbers was hard, let alone how to write the numbers. You have no idea how hard just learning this little bit was for me, with 100% of my front left temporal lobe brain removed due to having a brain infection. But one problem: I only had **five** fingers on each hand, so how was I supposed to learn what 6+2, 7-4, etc. were with only five fingers on each hand? I was by myself, and I figured out how to add and subtract numbers from 6 through 9. But, when it came to larger numbers like 24 minus 11, I had no idea. This was very difficult. I had no idea how to subtract or add larger numbers, and I had to conquer this issue on my own without family or community support. I needed to learn to balance myself, so I had the kids play ring-around-the-rosie with me. I would fall to the ground before we got to the end when we fall. The kids thought I was playing and fell down, too. It took several times playing ring-around-the-rosie with the kids before I could stay standing up to the end part where "We all fall down."

I didn't know what my colors were. I got a box of crayons and asked the kids what color this was. I didn't believe them unless they helped me read the word on the crayon. I also didn't know any parts of my eyes, fingers, toes, etc. I didn't know what a knee, ankle, stomach, hand, face, mouth, ears, etc. was. I would just point to these areas and ask the kids what they saw (pointing to my eye, chin, cheek, etc.).

I had been home for a few months since my brain surgery. I was lying on the couch when I felt something enter my body (from my feet up to the top of my head). I had no idea what it was, but I later learned that the "Holy Spirit" entered my body. A few months after this experience, I took a nap. I dreamt that I was in the "White Puffy Clouds." I looked up, and I saw "Jesus." He was about 100 feet tall. I kept looking at "Jesus," but he never moved. I then awoke. I said, "I want to go back into the clouds with 'Jesus.'" I fell back asleep. I was up in the "white puffy clouds," standing next to "Jesus" again. I kept looking at Jesus. I saw Him shake His Head. "No." I then woke back up.

Several months after my brain surgery, my mom called me. She said, "What are you doing?" I told her I was lying down, resting my head. Mom said sternly, "You get off your lazy 'A...'"

and cook your kids a home-cooked meal. They haven't had a home-cooked meal since you were in the hospital." I tried to tell her I couldn't. She said roughly, "My open heart surgery was worse than your brain surgery. You get up and cook your kids supper." My sister lived two blocks away from me. She made supper for her family, but not once did she invite my kids down to her house to have supper with her and her family.

Now, I didn't know how to use a can opener, use a knife to cut with, etc. I still had no hand or eye coordination. I tried to make meatloaf. When I tried cutting the onions, I would miss the onion and cut my fingers. Trying to peel potatoes was hard. I had no idea how to peel a potato anymore. My kids had to help me peel them. My kids also had to use the can opener to open up a can of vegetables. I had no idea how to make meatloaf anymore. I asked my kids what goes in the meatloaf. I could only do about one-third of the task before I had to lie down again. There was too much pressure on my head. After the pressure in my head went away, I went back to mix the meatloaf until I needed to take a break again. I finally had the meatloaf in the pan and put it in the oven. I had no idea what temperature to put it at. I had to ask what to put the temperature at. After a lot of hard work, I conquered making supper for my kids with no adult help.

Reading and writing posed enormous difficulties for me still. The words and sentences were still foreign to me. I had to learn each individual letter formed together to make a word. Those words are formed into sentences. Those sentences are formed into paragraphs. But so many words were spelled differently. I wrote a note saying (example), "I am going two the store." I got questioned about the "two." I had no idea how to spell "to," "too," "two," "sea," "see," "wear," "where," "bee," "be," etc. These steps needed in order to know how to read and write felt like monumental accomplishments I had to conquer. Since I had the barrier of not being able to read, the mail kept piling up. It had been at least five months now, and the mail still hadn't been opened. I could not read. I started getting phone calls from people. They said they mailed me something, and I was to respond back (debts). I tried to explain to them that I had brain surgery and could not read right now. The phone calls kept coming about bills.

Still, 80% of my income is being given out to the people doing my paper deliveries. The guy did the daily newspaper deliveries. Then, my mom and my kids did the weekly free newspaper delivery, which they also got paid for. Nobody did anything for me out of the kindness of their heart in my time of need, not even my own family. In fact, several months after my brain surgery, my mom came to pick up my kids to deliver the weekly newspaper. My mom "honked" her car horn until I came out to see what she wanted. She told me that I didn't deserve any of the checks. She said that I was not helping deliver the weekly newspaper. She said she was going to call the newspaper company and get my name off the routes and put her name on the routes. I told her no. She told me, "Oh yes, I will." I called my boss at the newspaper company and told him of the threat my mom made to me. He told me that she couldn't take the paper routes away from me unless I gave up the paper routes. My mom, kids, or anybody else wouldn't do anything out of the kindness of their hearts for me.

About six months after my brain surgery, my kids and I went to my parents' house one evening for supper. My mom told me to put the "forks" on the table. I did not know what a knife, fork, or spoon looked like. I picked up a utensil and went to my nephews, who were in the twenty-some years old range. I asked them if this utensil was a fork. They said yes. I turned around to go toward the kitchen when I heard the nephews laughing. I turned around and asked them again if this utensil was a fork. They stopped laughing and said yes. I went to the kitchen and put these utensils on the table. My mom saw the utensils on the table and yelled at me, "I didn't tell you to put the 'spoons' on the tables. I said the 'forks!'" I told Mom I didn't know what a knife, fork, or spoon was. I asked the nephews if they were forks, and they said yes. Mom went to the nephews (in their twenties), yelling at them, "Why did you tell Evelyn that spoons were forks?" The nephews told Mom, "If Evelyn doesn't know what a knife, fork, or spoon is, we are not going to tell her." This is just one example of being made fun of since my brain surgery.

About this same time, all the churches that got together to "raise money" to build the "drunk driver" who drove drunk, crashed her car, and became paralyzed (around the time that my four brain surgeries were being performed) had raised all the funds they needed to build this handicap accessible home for her. She was in her early/middle twenties with no kids and lived with her parents before her driving drunk, crashing her car, and becoming paralyzed. The churches purchased a piece of land in town to build this home for her. The community in the town and surrounding area all came together and volunteered their time to build her this brand-new handicap-accessible home.

I had asked for help from the churches and the community since I came home from brain surgery, but they "refused" to help me. You see since the bank charged me all those fees for the bounced checks right after I came home from brain surgery, I have never been able to pay my bills. Even though the bank refunded me all the fees (over $1,000), I still had all these stores that I wrote a check to still not get paid by the bank. Now, all these stores were charging me fees of about $35 for each bounced check that there was. Because I had to pay the stores, I didn't have the money to pay my rent for at least the last three months. I couldn't even pay my house phone bill either. After I paid everybody doing my newspaper deliveries, I only had $400 left for the month. I needed help from people, but nobody would listen. Not only this, but I still could not read, add, or subtract. The neighbor kids were teaching me the basics of counting to ten and saying my ABCs, but that was all I knew. My mail is still piling up (not being opened or read).

Well, the isolation continued even six months later. Nobody came to see me, help me, etc. Since I had been home (over six months), I still hadn't received any Get Well cards, flowers, or visits from anybody (be it family or anyone else). Not even my customers on my newspaper routes called me to see how I was doing.

Years later (after my mom died), I found out from the newspaper customers that they called my mom and asked her how I was doing. They told me that my mom told them I was doing "OK." When I found this out, I asked them, "Why did you never call me? I would have told you I wasn't ok. That I needed help." The customers told me they didn't want to bother me since I had just had brain surgery.

After seven months of isolation since my brain surgery, I found out that there was a family reunion happening. My kids were invited to the family reunion, but I wasn't (excluded again). I had more than enough isolation, neglect, being made fun of, etc. I decided to get a ride to the family reunion. There were the cousins, aunts, nieces, nephews, siblings, one of my kids, etc., laughing and having fun at the park. But things turned for the worse when I tried to share my "experiences" and "hardships" caused by my mom and others. I didn't get to speak of the neglect and needs I needed before my siblings, nephews, and nieces started attacking me physically and mentally. The family ganged up on me because Mom was having chest pains. I told them to take her away so I could speak. I had serious brain surgery, and absolutely nobody cared. Mom only wanted to know if I was dead or alive after my brain surgery. She couldn't care less about anything else. My one sister took her hands and squeezed both sides of my cheeks. The attack my sister did on me caused both of my cheeks to have "large round bruises" on both of my cheeks. My brother and two nephews (the same ones who told me the spoon was a fork) grabbed me by each wrist and each ankle. They had me up in the air. They swung me back and forth in the air (like playing with a child saying "1, 2, 3," and tossing them on a couch). After they swung me in the air several times, they threw me up in the air and let me go. I fell to the ground.

I was hurting badly from the assault from my siblings and nephews. I went to call the police, but my siblings called the cops on me. The cops came and told the siblings, "This is public property. You can't press charges of trespassing against Evelyn." Then the cops told me to leave them alone. I told them of the assault my family did on me, and I was hurting. I went to the doctor's office and had them dictate the injuries I sustained from the beating I received from my siblings and nephews. The doctor dictated "eleven" different injuries to my body caused by my family's assault. I had to endure these injuries only seven months after my brain surgery.

Not even six weeks after this assault, both of my ankles were swollen up. I could hardly walk on my feet anymore. I went to the orthopedic doctor to be examined. The doctor told me that I had "lipomas" in my ankles. The doctor scheduled me to have surgery on both of my ankles. My ankle surgery was going to be done at the same hospital where I had my brain surgery (two hours away). So, nine months after my four brain surgeries, I was having two ankle surgeries (each ankle) to remove the "lipomas." After the surgery, the surgeon told me that each of the lipomas on my ankles was the size of a "golf ball." I had to stay in the hospital until I was able to bear weight using a walking boot on each foot. When I was discharged from the hospital five days later, I came home walking on a "walking boot" on each foot. When I came into my house, I saw a piece of paper on the end table and read it.

I had just started being able to read easy sentences in the past month. So, reading was still new to me since my brain surgery.

The paper was an "eviction notice!" I was being evicted from my apartment without being told anything about it. What was I supposed to do? I had four brain surgeries in two weeks, and then nine months later, I had two ankle surgeries. I was to stay off my feet and keep them elevated by doctor's orders. How? I was being evicted. They were evicting me because I hadn't been paying my rent. I asked for help from everybody. Nobody could care less about my needs. According to them, I should have been able to read, write, add, and subtract just like I did before my brain surgery. Nobody understood that I couldn't read, so how was I supposed to read my mail? Well, instead of keeping my feet elevated, I got some boxes and tried to pack. I had no idea where I was going to go. I sure knew I would not go live with my mom again. After about ten days of trying to pack, I noticed blood on my bandages to my ankles, where I had ankle surgeries. I knew I needed to go to the E.R. room. I had to wait for my sister (who was married to my ex) to come and take me to the E.R, two hours away. My sister kept insisting on knowing from the doctor if I was going to be staying at the hospital or being discharged. She told the doctor she needed to know because she had to get going. The doctor told her I would be staying. My sister didn't hesitate to dash out of there. The doctor looked at me strangely. I told him this wasn't anything new with my family.

The doctor told me that I had blood clots in both of my ankles and needed to have emergency surgery to remove them. I told the doctor that I was being evicted. He said there was no way that I could move. He wanted to put me in a nursing home to recover from my ankle surgery, but I told him I couldn't. I had to get home; I was being evicted. I told the doctor that there was a county nurse who could come and check on my ankles daily during my recovery. The doctor told me that I was "bedridden" until further notice. He said that I was to stay off my feet completely. The doctor wouldn't let me go home until he had it all set up for the county nurse to come to my house on a daily basis. The county nurse was required by the doctor to dictate what my ankles looked like and report this to my doctor daily. The nurse also had to clean my wounds and change the bandages daily. She also had to help me get dressed, empty my porta potty every day, etc. I told her that I was being evicted. The nurse told me, "There is no way that you can move, Evelyn." I begged for her to help stop the eviction.

While I was bedridden, I called the lawyer who helped me with the bank charging me over $1,000 fees in bounce checks. I told him that I had had "eight surgeries" in "nine months" and I was being evicted. I explained my medical condition at the time.

The lawyer agreed to help stop them from evicting me. I kept getting mail and calls that I was being evicted, and I was still bedridden. I cannot bear any weight on my feet yet.

Well, just a few weeks before Christmas, the doctor discharged me from being bedridden. I still had to take it easy, though. I was to bear little weight and not be on my feet that much. At Christmas time, I stayed home and rested after all the surgeries (eight surgeries) I had undergone in just nine months. My kids were at the house when I took a nap. I woke up from my nap in the early evening, and I didn't see or hear my kids anywhere in the house, so I called my parents' house to see if my kids were over there for Christmas. My mom answered the phone. I asked her if my kids were over there. That's when my Mom started laughing, saying, "Yeah, your kids are over here, and so is everybody else." Then she said in a rude, laughing manner, "I hope you are having a Merry Christmas. HA HA HA." She then hung up the phone on me.

The eviction is still in the courts with my lawyer. What will happen next? I wondered.

"Nobody is always busy. It all depends on what number you are on their Priority List."

- Unknown Author

Chapter Eight

It's coming on a New Year. I still haven't heard much from my attorney. My attorney is dealing with the lawyer evicting me, but how strange it is that the lawyer trying to "evict me" has been a "customer" of mine on my newspaper routes. Oddly, he thinks that once he started putting a "case" against me to be evicted, he stopped the two different newspapers that I was delivering to him. I have given him a decorated cake with a Christmas card every holiday season for at least four years. Either he or his wife would contact me (not the newspaper companies) when they wanted the newspaper either stopped, hold on to, or give the newspaper to one of their neighbors while they would be gone. I would do what they would say. I did this to all my customers on the newspaper routes I had. So now that he's taking a case to evict me, he has the newspapers stopped.

My landlord and these neighbors of mine were my customers on the newspaper routes. But sure enough, once the landlord was starting an Eviction Notice on me, he had all the newspapers stopped to everybody. How cold-hearted. They all knew I had serious brain surgery, but they treated me as if I was a nobody.

I could only read the basic words. I could not read, pronounce, or know words like "communicate," "conquer," "instructions," etc. meant. Also, words with the "Ing" and other types of words with an adding to the word at the end were difficult to understand.

Words like "deal and dealing," "settle and settlement," etc. make the sentence difficult to understand. Also, many words were a metaphor to me – words like "beet" and "beat," "cheap" and "sheep," "windy" and "Wendy," etc.

Back to the eviction. It's still held up in the court. I have two surgeries scheduled in about eight weeks to remove the lipomas on each hip of mine. My hips were hurting due to the lipomas. If I have these surgeries in eight weeks, this will make "ten" surgeries that I will have within 14 months (four brain surgeries, four ankle surgeries, and two hip surgeries to remove lipomas on each hip.

It was the dead of winter. It was terribly cold, with snow and ice either on the sidewalks or the dead grass. I started getting sick. I was spitting up phlegm with a cough. I went to the doctor. He prescribed me an antibiotic.

The antibiotic never helped me. In fact, I got even sicker. I went back to the doctor. He said I had pneumonia. The doctor put me on a different medication. I was recovering slowly from pneumonia when things started to get worse. Then, one day, my sister surprisingly came to see me. She told me Mom had died of heart failure.

After my mom died, a medical team wanted me to have an IQ test done. The next time the medical team saw me, they told me that there was no way I could live alone. "Your IQ score is in the 30 percentile range," they said. They wanted to put me in a facility. I told them, "No way! My IQ is low because I just had brain surgery recently. The neurosurgeon removed all my front left temporal lobe brain due to brain infection. The neurosurgeon even had to remove my memory." I further explained how the neighbor kids taught me to say my ABC, count, etc. I explained to them that my memory being gone was a simile of a cassette tape being erased. You must record the cassette tape to put the music back on the tape. It was the same with the brain surgery I had. I had to learn everything all over again and store the information in another part of my brain. We only use a small percentage of our brain for memory. The medical staff looked stunted. They told me they must find somewhere for me to live. I told them I would live with my dad. My mom had just died, and Dad was alone. I wouldn't move in with Dad if Mom were still alive. The staff said they would talk to my siblings. The medical staff contacted me and said they had talked to my siblings. They agreed that I should live with Dad.

When I entered Dad's house, I realized that my minor teenage kids were not there. I asked my siblings, "Where are my kids?" My siblings told me that they had decided that since Mom died, my kids were no longer allowed on Dad's property. They told me they called the police to get my minor teenage kids off Dad's property. "Your kids are not allowed back on Dad's property. You are only here because you would be in a facility if you didn't come live with Dad." I was shocked! I asked them why. To my astonishment, they came up with a bizarre answer. They told me, "Dad is not your kids' grandpa. Dad isn't your dad, either." They went on to tell me that so and so was my real father and my kids' grandfather. I asked them, "Do you have proof that Dad isn't my Dad and the grandpa to my kids? What Mom said about me having a different father is just hearsay! There is no DNA to prove Dad isn't my real father and the grandpa to my kids."

The siblings retorted, saying bull. "You look just like his daughter." I told them, "So? Big deal. Just because I look like his daughter doesn't mean he is my dad." In fact, I told them, "It's the person who raised and supported me who is my dad. I asked them, "Why didn't you have my minor teenage kids move in with you then?" They told me, "No way. They are our half-nephews, just like you are our half-sister."

I told them that in my parents' will, it stated that "Mom and Dad's house goes to me when they both die. I asked incredulously, "You are forcing my kids to stay away from the house that goes to me when Dad dies?" The siblings refused to listen to anything else I had to say. My kids were out on their own instead of being in high school! I had no idea where my kids went, and my mentality at this time was of a child; my IQ was only in the 30 percentile. If I continued arguing with the siblings, I would most likely end up in a facility and never see my kids. What else could I do? After the siblings left Dad's house, I tried to settle in thinking of my minor teenagers. *Where are they? Are they okay? How do I contact my kids to talk to them?*

My kids finally contacted me and let me know they were living with friends. My kids would come over to see me and "their" grandpa. If any of the relatives came over and saw my kids at Dad's house, they would start threatening them and telling them to leave. I told my siblings, "How would you feel if I was saying this to your kids?" They told me I could not. "Dad is our dad, and he is grandpa to our kids." In my opinion, my siblings had become "wicked and evil"! After my siblings left, my Dad's house felt "peaceful." My siblings came over a lot to make sure everything was fine and that my minor teenagers were not coming over to Dad's house. This continues nonstop.

*** Remember: My siblings told me that if I wanted to live with "their Dad," I must not let my minor teenagers come over. If they did, they threatened me that they would have me go to a facility.**

When my siblings were not around, there was no arguing, yelling, or screaming. My nieces and nephews came over to see their "Grandpa." I would argue with my adult nieces and nephews that if my kids could not come to grandpa's house, neither could they. These adult nieces and nephews would argue back that "Grandpa is our *real* grandpa. Your kids have a different grandpa." I would argue with them that that was not true. There was no proof that he was not my dad or my kids' grandpa. I also told them that the dad/grandpa is the person who raised and took care of your needs. Besides, there was no proof that he was not my dad and the grandpa to our kids. This continues to be a non-stop argument between my siblings and my nieces and nephews.

It didn't take long to be able to trust dad. My father, in his wisdom, started teaching me the basics that I had forgotten. If I

140

didn't know what something was, he would calmly come over and show me. You see, I was essentially starting from scratch all over again. My father became my teacher and mentor. He patiently taught me everything I had forgotten. Relearning the fundamental skills was hard, but I refused to give up on trying until I learned what I needed to learn. A few examples are: I had no idea what a hammer, screwdriver, Phillips screwdriver, pliers, a nail, or a screw was, let alone how to use them. Dad showed me what these tools were and how to use them.

I had no hand or eye coordination yet. Dad was standing by me when I tried to hammer a nail. He saw I was putting the hammer above my head to use it to nail something. He stopped me and told me to have the hammer close to the nail; otherwise, I would hammer my fingers. Dad had me do it gently at first. I kept missing the nail and hitting my fingers. I slowly accomplished hammering the nail. When Dad saw that I succeeded in hammering the nail in, he grinned and chuckled with joy. He then showed me the difference between a screwdriver and a Phillips screwdriver, pliers, saw, etc. Dad also let me practice using these tools until I could do it. Each time I successfully used these tools, he would chuckle with a grin. Whenever Dad successfully taught me something, he was thrilled to let the family (when they would come over) know how he taught me something. With my father's guidance, I successfully overcame many limitations.

Dad got a daily newspaper delivered to his house. I would try to read the newspaper, but I didn't know so many words. I would ask Dad what this word or that word was. He would say the word and explain what it meant. When Dad noticed that I had difficulty with many words and their definitions, he would pull out the dictionary and help me find the words in the dictionary. If the definition had words in it I didn't understand, he would explain that word. My dad became my teacher. I never had a "father-daughter" relationship with him before this. It felt great to finally have this father-daughter relationship. You see, my mom kept me and my siblings away from Dad. She always wanted to be the center of attention.

I cooked supper for Dad every night. I would always ask him what he would want for supper. I wasn't going to make something, and then he wouldn't eat it because he was hungry for something else for supper. I cleaned Dad's house, did the laundry, etc. One day, Dad pulled his pant leg up and started scratching his leg. I noticed his leg was full of open sores. Dad said both his legs were like that. I then decided I had to strip Dad's bedding and spray the mattress and pillows with something. I found some Lysol. While I was washing all of Dad's bedding, I sprayed Lysol on his mattress (on all sides). I then sprayed it on the pillows, cloth recliners, couch, and living room chair. I started doing this on a weekly basis. Dad noticed that the sores on his legs were going away quickly. In about two months, all the open sores were gone on both of Dad's legs. He now has normal skin again.

One day, some relatives came over to Dad's house. One of the relatives told the other relative to go get their phone off the arm of the chair. I was stunned. I asked the relative, "What do you mean by the 'arm' of the chair?" They were stunned that I asked such a question. I told them, "A chair does not have arms. We have arms. A chair is not a human; they do not have arms." They took me to the living room, and they pointed to the arm of the chair and said, "This is the arm." I said, "No way." They started laughing and pointed to a different part of the chair and said, "This is the 'leg' of the chair." I was starting to get upset. I said no way. They then pointed to another area of the chair and said, "This is the 'back' of the chair." I told them, "You are making fun of me, trying to make me believe that a chair is human. Humans have arms, legs, and a back. A chair is not a human." They then went to a couch and told me, "This is a couch. It has arms, legs, and a back." I told them, "That is not a couch; it is a chair. You sit on a chair."

They kept insisting that it was a couch. They then went to a recliner and told me, "This is a recliner." I was getting very upset now. I said, "No, it is not a recliner. It is a chair." They went to a living room chair and a kitchen chair. I said, "They are all chairs that you sit on." That was when the relatives were shocked by what I was saying and said, "What the crap did the surgeon take out of her brain?" Nobody ever cared less about the brain surgery I had two years ago until they witnessed my reaction to "arms, legs, and a back" as part of a chair. Why did they care now? One of those relatives was my nephew, who told me that a "fork is a spoon." So, there was no way I would believe what he had to say to me anymore.

Then, one day, I was glancing through a magazine (ex., Better Homes and Garden). By God's grace, I saw a picture of a chair. The picture of the chair had arrows pointing to parts of the chair. I was stunned to read "arm, leg, and back" in the same parts the relatives tried to tell me. I could not believe the family was not making fun of me for a change.

Because 100% of my front left temporal lobe brain was removed, I no longer knew what was right or wrong. I had forgotten all the city, county, state, and federal laws. I had to learn how to say my ABCs, count, add, write my alphabet, etc. I had to learn how to pronounce the letters of the alphabet. After this, I had to learn to pronounce the words and learn what each word meant before I could try to comprehend what the sentence meant. I told my siblings that I did not know the laws anymore. They snapped back and told me I better learn the laws. How? I needed someone to teach me the laws. So, being at the stage of the mentality of a child (IQ of 30 percentile), I went to an officer. I asked them if they would teach me the laws. They asked me why. I told them since my brain surgery, I had forgotten all the laws. The officer responded with a threat, saying, "I am not going to teach you the laws. If you break the law, you get arrested!"

Not only were all my relatives making fun of me and making threats to me and my kids, but law enforcement was now making threats to me, too. Nobody wants to hear how serious my brain surgery was (having a brain infection). I needed a support system for my minor teenagers and me. I needed someone to step in and be the adult figure in my kids' lives since I could not right now, but nobody would step up to the plate to do it.

The guy who was delivering my newspapers during my brain surgeries now has those newspaper routes in his name. He came over to Dad's house every morning after he was finished with his deliveries. Sometimes, when he went to donate plasma, I would go with him to get out of the house. One time, while he was at the Plasma Center, I went next door to the restaurant I used to work for before I started the newspaper deliveries. While I was sitting in the lobby, a woman I worked with back then approached me. She told me she was the Store Manager now and that she remembered what a good employee I was when she was an employee. She gave me a proposition: she asked if I would be a weekend maintenance person. She explained the maintenance person would filter the oil, change the oil, do restrooms, lobby, parking lot, etc.

I didn't hesitate to inform her about my brain surgery two years ago. She told me she was sorry; she didn't know I had brain surgery. She then said she really needed a maintenance person. I told her because my memory was removed, I would need someone with me about six to twelve times in a row. I had to do it with someone there until I learned how to do it on my own. She responded with understanding and agreed to give me the opportunity and the support I needed to learn the tasks that required repetition.

I went home and informed Dad I had a job offer. "I cannot get to work early in the morning unless you take me," I told him. I promised to give him gas money. Dad agreed to drive me to work in the early morning twice a week. Now, I needed to learn hand and eye coordination in anything new I did. In the initial weeks, I had someone guide me through the process of filtering and changing the oil, ensuring that I learned the essential steps through repeated practice. I proved to be a quick learner, even though it typically took me several attempts to grasp new tasks. However, my determination led me to continue practicing until I achieved proficiency. The key was repetition, and I was willing to put in the effort. Over time, I gained more responsibilities in the restaurant, learning to manage different aspects of the operation. I found myself involved in tasks ranging from learning how to prep food, make salads, and cook and make sandwiches. The store manager showed me how to look at the expiration dates on the food. If any food was expired, she told me to let her know.

Then, during Lent, there were special on fish sandwiches every Friday. The restaurant would get call-in orders of fish sandwiches prior to lunch hour. Some orders ordered over 120 fish sandwiches. Another order would be 68 fish sandwiches, and so on. The store manager had me oversee the non-stop dropping of fish in the deep fryer. The non-stop dropping of fish continued for about four hours. The other employees had to toast the buns, put the sauce on the bun, put the fish on the bun, and wrap the sandwiches non-stop. My life was getting back on track between my dad "putting me under his wing" and the store manager treating me like family. Ever since the beginning of my employment, the employees never made fun of me if I asked a question that they thought I should know.

Dad always picked me up from work afterward. He took me to any store I needed to go to. He also took me to any appointments I had. After a few years, my sister approached me and told me that I needed to get my own car and drive myself to work. Dad was getting too old to take me to work. I told her that I didn't know how to drive anymore since my brain surgery. On top of that, my neurologist would have to fill out the paperwork for the DMV that I was seizure-free and capable of driving without having seizures. She told me to make an appointment to see the neurologist and have him fill out the paperwork. The neurologist was two hours away, and I had to find transportation to get there when I did get the appointment.

I made the appointment with the neurologist. He asked me many questions and did some hand and eye coordination with me. He saw that I had successfully passed the exam. He filled out the DMV form and handed it over to me. Now, I needed to learn to drive. *How do I learn to drive again when I am in my forties?* I called the driver's education teacher from high school and asked him if there was any way he could teach me to drive. I told him I needed to learn to drive again since my brain surgery. He had no answer for me at the time. I called him several more times to get an answer from him. He finally told me that I was no longer in high school; he could not teach someone who was not a high school student. I was now at a dead end. What would I do? There were no classes to teach me the rules of the road, have a teacher with me to learn to drive, etc.

I approached an officer in town. I asked him if I could practice driving before I got my driver's license. The officer told me that I could not drive without a license. I told him I needed to learn to drive again so I could pass the driving test. I told him I had called the driver's education teacher from high school, and he told me he could not teach me to drive since I was no longer in high school. I asked him how I could practice driving before I got my driver's license. The officer told me that I needed to get a "Driver's Permit" from the DMV. He told me, "Once you get the driver's permit, you have to have somebody in the car with you while practicing driving."

I went to the DMV and picked up the Rules of the Road to take home to read it. If I had any questions from the Rules of the Road book, I would ask Dad to explain the answer to me. Once again, my dad was my teacher. Once I understood the rules of the road, I went to the DMV office. When I approached the DMV employee, I told him I needed to get my driver's permit. The DMV employee started laughing at me. He said, "You want a driver's permit instead of a driver's license?" He was still laughing at me when he turned his head back to the other DMV employees and said, "Hey guys, she wants a driver's permit instead of a driver's license." The other employees joined him in laughing at me. They made me feel so low. Why? I had brain surgery. All of my front left temporal lobe brain was removed, including my memory. Why must I be ashamed because I needed to relearn again? After they were done laughing at me, the DMV employee gave me the driver's permit test. There were ten questions to answer. I turned in my test to the DMV employee. I passed the test, and he gave me a Driver's Permit card.

I asked the guy who took over my paper routes if he would help me learn to drive again. I told him I needed to learn "hand and eye coordination" driving first. If I drove on a two-lane highway, I would have no room to make any wrong moves driving. I told him, "Because of this reason, I need you to drive on a four-lane highway and pull over in a safe spot. Once you pull over, I could then get in the driver's seat and start practicing driving." Well, he got on the highway and pulled over at a safe area for me to take over practice driving. The highway speed limit was 65 miles per hour. I could not drive any faster than 35 miles per hour without swerving to the right or left of the lane. I had to learn how to look at the speedometer, rearview mirror, side mirror, etc., while keeping the car in the same lane on the highway. Cars would drive past fast, honking their horns because I was only going 35 miles per hour on a 65 mph speed limit. I couldn't go any faster than 35 mph without swerving to the right or the left of my lane. I could not take a Driver's Education Class to learn to drive. This was the only way I could learn to drive again. Every day I drove on the highway, I improved my hand and eye coordination. I was gradually driving at a higher speed of about five miles more per hour. I finally succeeded in being able to drive 65 miles per hour on the highway with great hand and eye coordination.

Now, I had my friend go somewhere in town where there was hardly any traffic to learn to drive on a two-lane street. I drove very slowly. Once I accomplished driving in town, I had a much scarier dilemma to accomplish: I needed to drive on a two-lane highway. I could not go on either side of the line or I would either be in the other lane of traffic or off the cliff. I drove slowly to begin with, even though the speed limit was 55 mph. Like on the four-lane highway, I had cars behind me honking their horns, yelling, "Go faster!" I had to make sure I had hand and eye coordination looking at the rearview mirror, side mirror, speedometer, etc. Each day, I improved my driving and was able to finally drive to the regular speed limit on a two-lane highway. Now, I needed to learn to parallel park. I needed to learn how to use my blinkers, put it in reverse, and turn the wheel a certain way to parallel park. I needed to practice parallel parking from the driver's side and the passenger's side. I finally accomplished this. Once my friend had taught me everything I needed to learn to drive, I went to the DMV office and took the Driver's Test. This time, the DMV employees didn't laugh at me. I left the DMV office with my Driver's License in my hand. I got help to get a car and have car insurance. I can now drive myself to work and back. I have accomplished so much in four years after I had 100% of my front left temporal lobe brain removed (including my memory). I am gaining my independence back!

Once, when I was driving, I stopped at a convenience store in town. One of the customers who knew me asked me if I was sure I was safe to drive a car. I told him, "Yes. I got a driver's permit and practiced driving before I got my driver's license." He said with a sigh of relief, "I'm glad to hear that." I said sarcastically, "Oh really? The DMV laughed at me for wanting a Driver's Permit instead of a Driver's License." The guy was shocked to hear that. He told me that he was going to go and talk to them at the DMV office. "There was no need for them to laugh at you for wanting to practice driving with a Driver's Permit before getting your driver's license." When I went to the DMV office after that, the DMV employees would deny that they ever laughed at me for wanting a Driver's Permit. Of course, they worked for the State Government. If they would admit to it, they would all lose their jobs for acting unethically.

Now that I am getting more mature, I can defend myself against my family refusing my kids to come over to Dad's house. I stood up to them now and told them that they are MY kids! "My kids (now young adults) are allowed to come over to Dad's house to see their Grandpa and me anytime!" I refused for my siblings to push my children and me around anymore.

Now, I had another dilemma I must overcome. I needed to relearn what I learned in high school. My high school diploma didn't mean anything anymore. I needed to relearn what I learned in high school (English and Math, etc. classes). How? I finally figured out that I could relearn by taking GED classes. I asked around to find out who was the GED teacher in town. I found out, oddly enough, that the sister of the "woman who drove drunk and became paralyzed" was the instructor. All the Churches raised money to build a brand-new handicap-accessible home for this drunk driver who became paralyzed. I called her sister (she was my classmate in school). I asked her if she taught GED classes. She told me, "Yes." I told her I needed to take the GED class. This woman responded, "Evelyn, you have a high school diploma, right?" I told her yes. She proceeded to tell me that since I had a high school diploma, I could not take the GED class. I told her I had brain surgery; they removed 100% of my front left temporal lobe brain. I had to learn everything all over again. She reiterated that I could not take the GED class if I had a high school diploma. What would I do? I did not know how to write cursive anymore since my brain surgery. I no longer knew the things that I was taught in high school. What would I do? I fell between the cracks.

The only way I could learn anything was by continuing to ask Dad questions. Dad had been my teacher this far. So, my next step was to have Dad teach me how to write cursive. I knew how to print my alphabet, but writing my alphabet cursively was unknown to me. I approached Dad and asked him to teach me to write my alphabet cursively. My dad (is he my dad?) was excited to teach me cursive writing. I had to learn how to not break cursive in the words. If I did, it would be like printing with each letter "S E P E R A T E L Y." Slowly but surely, with Dad's help, I learned how to write cursive.

Going to work has always been an escape from my family, who like to make my life rough. One day, when I was driving after work, I was going to go to the grocery store first. Oddly enough, I felt the "Holy Spirit" (like mother intuition) tell me to go home. I was thinking out loud in my car, saying, "No. I'm going to the grocery store first." The Holy Spirit (intuition) kept urging me to "Go home." I was trying to ignore this feeling I had, but I gave in and went home instead. I was parked and was getting out of the car when I heard a girl crying. I looked around, and I saw an eight-year-old girl. Her face was red from crying so hard. I went to her and asked her what was wrong. "She spoke, crying, "My daddy left." She pointed her finger, saying, "He went that way in the car." I saw the girl had a school backpack on, so she must have gotten off the school bus. I looked at my watch. Sure enough, the school bus dropped her off 30 minutes ago. She was outside crying for 30 minutes without any neighbors coming out to see what was wrong with her. I told her, "Good thing I found you. Someone could have kidnapped you." I told her to come to my house and stay on the porch while I called the police. I told her, "The police will help you find your daddy."

The girl was on the porch crying still when I went inside Dad's house and called the police. I told them I had found a missing girl. I have no idea why, but my mother's intuition knew this girl was missing. The dispatch wanted to keep me on the phone. I told them no way. I was going back outside with the girl. I went out on the porch by the girl who was still crying. I hugged her and said it would be ok. "The cops will help you find your daddy." After ten

153

minutes, the cops came. The officer asked the girl what her name was. She said, "I don't know" (while crying). The officer asked her where she lived. The girl again said she didn't know while crying. My sister came over and saw the police and the girl crying on Dad's porch. She asked what was going on. The cops told my sister about the little girl. My sister looked at the girl and knew who she was. My sister told me, "Evelyn, this is so and so's daughter. They are your neighbors." She told me she used to play with the girl's mom when they were kids. I told her I didn't know them; I had no idea where they lived.

The cops called for an ambulance to come to take the girl to the hospital. My sister, in the meantime, kept trying to tell me to go down to the neighbors' house and tell them their daughter was there. I kept saying, "I don't know where they live." My sister knew there was no time to spare, so she dashed down to the neighbors' house. After several minutes, the ambulance came. While the girl was going into the ambulance, my sister ran up yelling, "Here is her aunt!" The woman claimed to be the girl's aunt. The cops asked the girl if that was her aunt. The girl said, "Yes." The aunt dashed back home quickly to get her son. The woman (aunt) and her son went in the ambulance with the girl.

I went to work the next day. When I came home, I saw an envelope with my name on it with a plant next to it. Inside the envelope was a letter. It said, "Thank you for helping our daughter. Her dad had a doctor's appointment to go to yesterday." They stated they notified the school and bus driver to have their daughter dropped off at a different stop so she could go to her grandparents' house after school. Neither the school nor the bus driver made sure their daughter got off at the other stop to go to her grandparents' house, so she came home with nobody there. Then they wrote "Thank you" with their names.

The Holy Spirit (mother intuition) knew someone was in need, and they were guiding me to go home to help this person (little girl) in distress. Just like at the fast food restaurant I worked at. The owner's son was a closing manager. When we went to our cars, the owner's son told me, "I'll see you later, Evelyn." I had a bad feeling come over me when he said that to me. I was ready to respond and tell him, "Be careful. Something is going to happen to you," but the owner's son drove off with his buddies before I could tell him. Then, two days later, he died from poisoning in his drink at college. I always said that if I get a bad feeling or the Holy Spirit (Mother Intuition) urges me to do or say something, I will never hold it in again. I never want it on my shoulders. "If only I got to tell him."

"The Holy Spirit is the gentle whisper that guides us in the right direction."

- Unknown

Chapter Nine

I had been overweight most of my life. My weight gain started when I was about eight or nine years old. I was never allowed to go anywhere or do anything without a relative's supervision. My classmates had friends. They went to their friends' houses to play, have slumber parties, etc. I didn't experience any of that. My older sisters came and went places on their own. They had friends they hung out with in school. I asked Mom if I could go here or there with the kids. My mom told me, "No. You can't do anything until you get as big as your sisters." Being a child at eight or nine years old, I tried to figure out how I could be as "big" as my sisters. I couldn't be as old or in the same grade as them. I kept thinking of a way to be as big as my sisters. One day, I saw my sisters weighing themselves on the scale. I looked to see what they weighed. I then weighed myself. Oh my, I needed to gain over 60 pounds to weigh as much as them. Once I weighed as much as my sisters, I would be as big as them, I thought. So, I started eating extra food. At supper time, I always went for seconds at eight or nine years old. I kept weighing myself on the scale. I saw I was gaining weight.

I was starting to get fat, but if the only way I could do anything like my sisters and be as big as them, I would keep gaining weight until I weighed as much as them. After a struggle with overeating so much, I finally weighed myself on the scale, and the scale read the same weight that my older sisters weighed. I then went to Mom and asked her if I could go to a neighbor's kid's house. Mom told me, "No." I told her, "You told me that once I am as big as my sisters, I can do what they do. I am as big as my sisters because I weigh as much as them." Mom told me, "You still cannot do what your sisters do." My heart was crushed. I purposely gained all that weight to be able to be around kids to play like my sisters did things. I was now extremely overweight.

Now that I lived with my dad, things were changing. My dad told me one day that I needed to lose weight. "It is not healthy for you to be overweight like you are," he had said. I had been wanting to lose weight for a while. It took my dad's words for my willpower to start. I went to God in prayer. I asked Him to please help guide me in what foods I should eat to lose weight. I asked God to please help me with the willpower not to have the cravings for junk food and diet soda. I also asked God to please help me have the willpower to exercise on a regular basis. I told God I had no idea what to eat or drink. I told God I needed His guidance to accomplish this dilemma of my weight problem and asked Him to help me get down to a healthy size of clothes and not have any hanging skin from my weight loss.

I had been wanting to lose weight for a long time, but I had no idea how to go about it. I then went to the grocery store, looking around to see what I should eat. I figured I would start at the fruit and vegetable aisle. Sure enough, every time I looked at a fruit or vegetable, I had the feeling the Holy Spirit was telling me "Yes" and "No" to these foods. After I had my fruit and vegetables chosen with the help of the Holy Spirit guiding me, I went up and down the other aisles. I looked at what the food products contained by looking at the labels. Reading the labels of what the food contained helped me decide if I would purchase it or not. After choosing many items in the grocery aisles, I went to the dairy department. I looked over all the dairy products and what they contained.

I returned to Dad's house and put my new healthy foods away. I weighed myself in the morning before I started eating my new healthy foods. It was still winter outside, so I couldn't go for walks yet, so I went to the department store and purchased an exercise machine. I decided I was going to use the exercise machine 30 minutes a day, three times a week. The first thing I did every morning when I woke up was I weighed myself. Once spring came, I started going for a walk. I took a bottle of water with me to keep myself hydrated. I also wore a watch to keep track of how long I walked. My goal was to walk 90 minutes three times a week. For the first week or two, I would have to stop at a hillside to catch my breath. My body was starting to feel much healthier. I noticed that my clothes were beginning to hang on me. I had to go to the secondhand store to get new, used clothes in a smaller size.

Two and a half months later, I lost over 60 pounds, and I dropped ten sizes in clothes. I decided that I needed to change my looks. I went to the beautician and told them I wanted to change my hair color to blonde. They were hesitant. They said my hair might turn orange. I told them I didn't care. I did not want my dark-colored hair anymore. I had just lost over 60 pounds and ten sizes in clothes; I wanted a new appearance. The beautician colored my hair blonde. She even waxed my eyebrows. I liked the new me. When my siblings, nieces, and nephews came to Dad's house and saw me with blonde hair, they were shocked. They tried to tell me that the blonde hair was not good for me. I told them, "I don't care what you think. This is the new me."

Now that I had a new look, I decided to go to the secondhand store again and get dress pants, tops, knee highs, dress shoes, makeup, jewelry, etc. I could only get a few pairs of clothes because I was still losing weight. I continued to weigh myself every morning, eat healthy foods, and exercise three times a week. In five months, I lost over 110 pounds and dropped 20 sizes in clothes. I was now in size six and eight clothes. Absolutely nobody knew me anymore. I was now being invited to family reunions. The cousins went to my siblings to ask them who I was. When they found out it was me, they were shocked. I looked so much better. When I ate at the reunion, I picked out healthy foods. I even went back for seconds. The relatives told me not to go for seconds; they told me that I would gain weight back. I told them, "It's not how much you eat. It is what you eat that makes you gain weight."

I was still working at the restaurant while I was losing weight and continued working there after I lost weight. Since I lost weight, whenever I went to the store, a guy would want to open the door for me to let me in. I had guys wishing to be gentlemen and open the doors for me now. I would approach people I knew in town and ask them, "Do you know who I am?" They would say things like,

"You look familiar. Are you so and so?" I would tell them, "No." They kept guessing names. I kept saying, "No. I am not so and so." When they gave up guessing who I was, they would say, "OK., Who are you?" I would pull an old picture of me out when I was 20 sizes bigger. Their mouths would drop when they saw my old picture. They would say, "No way. Is that you, Evelyn?" I would proudly tell them, "Yes." They were stunned when I told them I had lost the weight in five and a half months. Then they wanted to know how I did it. I always told them I went to God and prayed for help to guide me in what to eat to lose this weight. Many people thought that I had my stomach stapled or I starved myself. I would always tell them I did no such thing; I lost weight by eating healthy. I even had people want to be my friend after I lost all that weight. I told them, "Why wasn't I good enough to be your friend when I was fat? A friend is with you through thick and thin, not just during good times." So, of course, I refused their friendship.

After losing weight, my oldest brother started "chasing" me around the house. He was trying to grab the "upper part" of my chest. I went through this ordeal when I was 12 years old by an older man who brought propane gas to the house. Why would my oldest brother be trying to molest me? My brother kept laughing at me while he was chasing me around the house. I screamed at him to stop chasing me. Dad heard me screaming and came to see what was going on. That was when my brother stopped trying to molest me.

One day, I took a nap with my purse next to me on the floor; my car keys were inside my purse. When I woke up and was going to go somewhere, I looked for my keys in my purse. My keys were nowhere to be found. I looked all over the house. My keys were still nowhere to be seen. I was very upset. I knew somebody had stolen my car keys, but who? I had to use my spare car keys that I had hidden now. Then, one Sunday, I went to church with my dad. I took Dad out to eat after church. When we got home, I heard somebody in the kitchen. I tiptoed into the kitchen to find my oldest brother with a drawer open in the kitchen. I asked him what he was doing. He turned around quickly with both his hands behind his back, closing the kitchen drawer.

When my brother and my dad started talking and walking away, I opened the drawer in the kitchen that my brother was in. To my surprise, my car keys were in the kitchen drawer. My brother had stolen my car keys! I approached my brother with my car keys in my hand that I had found in the kitchen drawer where my brother was when my dad and I returned from church. I said to my brother, "You stole my car keys." My brother claimed he never had my car keys. I told my brother I opened the kitchen drawer that he was in and found my stolen car keys in there. I told my brother that he had stolen my car keys. I told him that I opened that kitchen drawer at least three times a day. My car keys were never there prior to finding him in the kitchen with the drawer open. My brother kept denying he stole my car keys, but I knew he did.

I was upstairs in the bedroom at Dad's house, singing along to some songs I was playing on the CD player. My sister (who was married to my ex) came over with her new husband to see Dad. I had no idea that my sister and her husband were at Dad's house because I was upstairs playing music and singing along to it. After I was done singing a song, I heard my sister say, "Evelyn. I never knew you could sing like that." I told her that I could always sing to music like that. "You just never paid any attention to my singing before." That was when my sister told me with excitement, "Evelyn, come Karaoke with my husband and me." I told my sister, "No way." Nashville called me and wanted me to come there and audition in their recording studio "twenty years" ago, but Mom wouldn't help me start a new life in Nashville with my children and get to Nashville. I told her Mom had told me I could not go to Nashville because I had kids. I told her I told Mom my children would go with me. Mom refused to help me with $2,000 to get to the recording studio in Nashville. I told her if Nashville didn't get me, nobody did.

***

The restaurant I worked at was corporate-owned. They had several restaurants in this city. The supervisor came to the restaurant one day, talking to the store manager about one of the other restaurants. I was working close to where the supervisor and the store manager were talking. I heard the supervisor tell my store manager she didn't know what to do about this one restaurant. It had "failed inspection three times." The restaurant had only one more chance to pass inspection. If they failed this next inspection, the restaurant would get shut down. I went to the supervisor and told her, "I will go over to that restaurant and get it up to par to pass inspection." Both the supervisor and the store manager were stunned when I said that. The supervisor asked me if I was sure I wanted to do this. I determinedly said yes.

I told them this restaurant had taught me everything all over again since my brain surgery. I knew everything about organizing, co-dating food, cleaning out the walk-in cooler and walk-in freezer, etc. The store manager kept telling me that she wanted me to stay here at her store; she needed me here. I told her the other store was in dire need right now. If they failed inspection, the store would be shut down for good. Finally, I had the supervisor and the store manager agree that I could go to the other restaurant and get it up to par. I told the supervisor I would go there under one condition. She looked at me surprised and said, "What?" I told her that the managers there could not tell me what to do there. The supervisor was really confused now. I told her, "The restaurant failed inspection three times already with the managers in charge. I can't get the restaurant up to par to pass inspection if the managers tell me what to do. They failed the inspection the last three times. Please give me a chance to prove to you that I can get the restaurant to pass inspection without the managers telling me what to do." I told the supervisor, "This is your final inspection."

I went on to tell her that this store (I worked at right now) passed inspections with high scores all the time. Finally, the supervisor agreed that I could go to the restaurant and do all the things that needed to be done to pass inspection "without" the managers telling me what to do. I asked her to go over to this restaurant with me on my first day and tell the managers there that I was there to get the restaurant to pass inspection without them telling me what to do. The supervisor agreed to that.

On my first day at this restaurant, I waited in my car for the supervisor to show up. We went in together, and she approached the managers. She told them, "Evelyn is here to clean up the store. You do not tell her what to do. She knows what needs to be done. We have one more inspection. If this store fails the next inspection, this store shuts down." I went to work cleaning. The cooler by the dressing table was filthy. None of the food was co-dated, and there was expired food in the cooler. I made up extra pans for lettuce, onions, etc. (with co-dates on them) to replace the lettuce onions, etc., when they ran out of them on the dressing table. I let the employees in the kitchen know that I had made up these extra pans of lettuce, onions, etc., to replace when their product got low or empty. I told them, "You put the old product on top of the new product (for example, old lettuce lay on top of the new pan of lettuce)." This was all new to the employees. The managers were opening a bag of lettuce, onions, etc., and placing the latest product on top of the old product without co-dates.

I kept cleaning and organizing for several days when the supervisor came to the store to see what shape the store was in before the inspection. When the supervisor opened the cooler, she saw extra pans of products (lettuce, onions, etc.) with co-dates. She checked out the walk-in cooler, walk-in freezer, the stock room, etc. The supervisor was shocked to see a significant turnaround for the better. She said to the managers, "I can tell that Evelyn is here. You are going to pass inspection with flying colors.

On the day of the inspection, everything was cleaned, organized, co-dated, etc. The restaurant passed inspection with a score of "96" out of 100. However, after this restaurant passed inspection, the managers went back to their "old ways." They refused to allow me to make any more extra pans of lettuce, onions, etc. They said they would open a bag of lettuce and pour it on top of the "old" product. The employees told the managers, "Please let Evelyn do it her way. It is much easier the way she does it than the way you are doing it." The managers told the employees, "No, Evelyn is not doing any more co-dating or cleaning the store." Things kept getting worse from there at this restaurant.

Anything I held for too long, I would get the shakes and drop things. I wasn't just getting the shakes holding stuff at work; I was getting the shakes in anything I held, and I would drop it. It was getting dangerous for me to hold anything like a cup of coffee, a bowl of cereal, etc. The shaking was so bad that if I tried to hold onto a cup of coffee, a bowl of cereal, etc. I would lose my grip, and the coffee or food would spill on me, the floor, the table, etc. I was breaking glassware because I couldn't hold it very long. I had to use a tray to carry my food or drink from point A to point B. It got so bad that I had to have Dad's help carrying a cup of coffee from the coffee pot to the table. Because of this medical issue, I had to quit my job.

I went to the doctor's, but they brushed it off. I approached several different doctors for second and third opinions. None of the doctors would listen to me. I decided to go to the ER, where I had my brain surgery. The ER doctor did not listen to me either. Oddly enough, I received a phone call from the last hospital I went to (where I had brain surgery). I was told I had an appointment with a specialist there the next day. The specialist ordered a test for me to have in a few weeks. The appointment for the test was scheduled for the day after Christmas. The weather forecasted a winter storm on Christmas Day. They predicted one foot of snow to fall on Christmas Day. There was no way I could drive (a two-hour drive) in this storm the day after Christmas. So, I decided to pack up some food, extra clothes, a shovel, blankets, etc., with me and take my journey to who knows where on Christmas Eve.

Before I left, I prayed to God to help me find a "Christian family" to be with on Christmas Day. I had no money for a hotel so I prayed to God and asked Him to please help me find some way for me to be able to have a hotel room for tonight, Christmas Eve. I started taking my journey to drive toward the University Hospital for my appointment the day after Christmas. Snow was beginning to come down. I had been driving for over one hour now. It was dusk out now, and it was Christmas Eve. I started driving toward a small town when I heard the "Holy Spirit" tell me to stop in this town. I listened to the Holy Spirit talking to me, so I stopped in this small town. I didn't see any stores open. I kept driving around town, though. I finally saw a store open. I stopped there and went inside. I asked the cashier if she knew of a church that was having a Christmas Eve service tonight. The woman told me of this one church having a Christmas Eve service in 90 minutes. I asked for directions. She explained where it was at. I decided to find this church before it got dark outside. I finally found the church. I decided to stay near the church, so I didn't lose my way back to it.

People were coming to the church for the Christmas Eve service now. I went inside and looked for the pastor; I finally found him. I told the pastor my circumstances. I told him I lived two hours away from here and had an appointment at the University Hospital the day after Christmas, but there was a forecast of one foot of snow. There was no way I would make my appointment if I didn't come this way on Christmas Eve. I asked the pastor if he could help me get a hotel room since I had no money. I told him I had to stop working because of my severe shakes.

I told the pastor I was seeing the specialist the day after Christmas about my shakes. The pastor asked what my name was. I told him my full name. The pastor told me he worked with people who went to that University Hospital. He said he would call the University Hospital and make sure I had an appointment the day after Christmas. I was dressed up (like I always was since I lost over 110 pounds). I had church people come over and greet me. They knew I was a new person in their church. I explained why I was there on Christmas Eve. After service, the pastor told me he called the University Hospital and found out I had an appointment the day after Christmas. He also told me that he had paid for a room for me at this one hotel. He told me to tell them my name, and I would get the key to my hotel room. I went to the hotel, and I went into my room. I breathed a sigh of relief. The Holy Spirit was watching over me.

The following morning, I woke up in my hotel room. I looked in the mirror, and I couldn't believe how much healthier I looked. I had color in my face. I had had a pale-looking face for many months due to the trauma I had been getting from my family. I was in a town where none of the family knew where I was. I dressed up for church on Christmas Day service. I went to my car, and I saw one foot of snow on the ground outside. I had a towel to brush the snow off my car. Other people in the parking lot at the hotel were using an "ice scraper" to take "one foot of snow" off their cars. They saw how quickly I removed the snow from my car with a bath towel. They then wanted to use a bath towel to remove the snow from their cars. A snowplow came earlier before I came out to clear the snow away from the parking lots (except where there were parked cars). I took the snow shovel out of my car and started shoveling the snow away from my car doors and tires so I could get into my car and go to church on Christmas Day. Other people saw I had a snow shovel, and they asked if they could borrow it so they could clear snow away from their cars, too. I let them use my snow shovel. The people even said they would finish clearing the snow away from my car with my snow shovel. After everybody had shoveled the snow around their cars, I got my snow shovel back, and I went to church.

When I got to church, an older woman approached me. She said she saw me at church last night. She asked me why I was there. I told her I had an appointment at the University Hospital the day after Christmas, and I came early because of the snowstorm. She asked me what I was doing for Christmas. I told her nothing; I was going to stay in my car on Christmas Day. She told me to come with her and her husband. They were going to their daughter's house for Christmas. This lady told me I could stay at their house tonight and leave in the morning to go to the University Hospital. This lady told the pastor I did not need a hotel room tonight; she was letting me stay at her house tonight. I got in my car and followed her and her husband to their house. Then, I got in their car, and we drove to their daughter's house for Christmas. There was no yelling, screaming, or fighting. Everybody got along. The following day, I went to the University Hospital to see the specialist.

This was the first Christian Christmas that I had ever had. I prayed to God to help me find a church that was having a Christmas Eve service. I also asked God to help me get a hotel room to stay in. I also prayed to God to help me find a Christian family to have Christmas with. I asked Him to let me have my first Christian Christmas. In my unknown journey of crisis on Christmas Eve, God filled me with many blessings. He knew all the answers even though I had no idea what was to come out of this journey I had.

I went to the specialist the next day. He did a test on the nerves, starting at my wrist. The test showed that my nerves were dying from my wrist to my elbow. He said that I needed surgery done on my elbow. He scheduled the appointment for my surgery. I went home after the doctor's visit. When I got to Dad's house, my wicked sister called me. She asked me how my Christmas was. I told her I had a great Christmas; I went to church on Christmas Eve and Christmas Day. A woman at church invited me to go with her to her daughter's house for Christmas. I told my sister there was no yelling, screaming, or fighting. This was the first Christian Christmas I ever had. My sister was furious at my Christmas. She told me there was no such thing as no yelling, screaming, or fighting. She wanted to hear me say that I had a rotten Christmas.

I asked the family and others if I could get a ride to the University Hospital for surgery on my elbow. All of my relatives refused to take me to the hospital to have my surgery. I asked some people in town (even church people) if they would drive me to the hospital two hours away to have surgery on my elbow. Everybody "refused" to take me to the hospital so I could have my surgery. I need the surgery done to help me with my nonstop shakes. Since nobody would take me to the hospital to have surgery, I drove myself there. Before I left, I called the woman I met at church on Christmas Day and spent Christmas with her family. I asked her if she would go with me to the hospital to have surgery on my elbow to stop my shaking. I told her it was a same-day surgery, and I could not drive until the next day. I then asked her if I could stay at her house overnight before I drove back home the next day after surgery. The lady agreed to be with me for the surgery and let me spend the night at her house that night.

I had the surgery done. The medical staff wrapped my upper arm to my wrist with an "ACE Wrap" while I was still under. When I came to, I noticed that my arm was wrapped with an ACE Wrap. I told the medical staff that I was allergic to elastic; ACE Wrap is elastic. The medical team told me that I would be fine; I had a bandage wrapped underneath the ACE Wrap. I tried to tell them it didn't matter if there was a bandage under the ACE Wrap. The medical team still wouldn't listen to me. Now, the surgeon came to see me. He told me that I had a shot glass full of excess tissue in my elbow. This excess tissue was causing my shakes. The doctor told me it would take me about one year to recover completely from this surgery with the shakes.

About one week later, I noticed my hand (the side I had elbow surgery) was swollen badly. There was a windstorm (white-out condition) blowing snow all over the place. I didn't want to drive two hours to the University Hospital in this windstorm (white-out), so I called the local doctor's office. I told them my hand had been swollen since my elbow surgery. I told them I knew the ACE Wrap had caused the swelling. The local doctors refused to see me. They told me I needed to go back to where I had the surgery done, which was two hours away. I asked my family and some local people if they would take me to the University Hospital. Everybody refused to take me because of the "white-out conditions."

Well, I had no other choice than to drive in that condition. I encountered many spots on the highway where one lane was covered with 6-12 inches of snow piled up. The driving conditions were so bad that it was like driving in dangerous, foggy conditions. I finally reached the University Hospital ER. I told them the ACE Wrap was causing my hand to swell up severely. I then told them I was allergic to elastic; ACE Wrap was elastic. The medical staff took off the ACE Wrap.

I was waiting for the doctor to come in to see me in the ER room. A doctor (I thought) came in to see me. When he saw me, his mouth dropped, and his eyes popped wide open. He started walking backward and pointed his finger at me in shock. He told me, "You had that brain surgery?" I told him yes. He told me, "No way. I just watched a six-and-a-half-hour video of your brain surgery." This doctor told me he was a medical student studying to become a neurosurgeon. This medical student asked me to spell "dog." I did. He then asked me to spell dog backward. I did. This student doctor then pointed at objects and asked me what they were. I told him what they were. He then asked me what color something was. Of course, I answered. The medical student then told me to remember these three words: "dog, floor, and table." I repeated "dog, floor, and table" right after he said those words.

I had learned a trick to remember three words or longer. The student doctor told me to take 100 minus 7, going backward. I started counting backwards 93; 86; 79; 72; 65; 58; 51; 44; 37; 30; 23. After I got to the number 23, the student doctor told me to stop. He said he could not count that far back just using his brain. The student doctor then asked me, "What are those three words I told you to remember?" I told him the words were Dog, floor, and table. The student doctor asked me if I had a driver's license. I told him, "Yes."

The doctor then told me, "There is no way you are supposed to be where you are today in life. You should have been in a facility not being able to do anything." He then said, "I am going to go back and watch the video of your brain surgery again and see how your neurosurgeon did your brain surgery." Remember, I could only put a first-grade puzzle together after my brain surgery. My neurosurgeon told me that in "ten years," I would not be able to advance much more than that after my brain surgery. My IQ was in the "30 percentile" two years after my brain surgery. Now, I was astonishing the neurosurgeon student with my accomplishments. After this student doctor left, the ER doctor saw me. The swelling in my hand was now gone. The doctor told me they would have to wrap my arm with a bandage wrap and use an arm sling. I then left the ER and drove home in the "white-out" conditions. I got back to Dad's house safely.

Since I was not working, I had gathered a small amount of food stamps. I decided to hide my food stamp card in my car since my brother had stolen my car keys before. One day, I went to the grocery store. I went to retrieve my food stamp card from where I hid it. To my surprise, it wasn't there; it had been stolen! I had absolutely no money because I was not working. I called the food stamp office and told them my food stamp card was stolen. The office did a "Shift Report" of all activity done on my food stamp card. The report showed the date, time, what store, what cashier, what food was bought, and the cost. I noticed my food stamp was used at the local grocery store. I went to the manager and requested to see the video of this date, time, and the cashier who rang up the two food items. I told her somebody had my food stamp card and used it here. The manager looked at the video by herself. Then she came out and told me she could not let me see the video. She told me to go to the police; the police could look at the video.

I went to the police office. One officer was going to go to the grocery store to check it out when the Chief of Police (I went to school with) told the officer not to go to the grocery store. I argued with the Police Chief. He told me to get a new food stamp card. I told him it was a federal crime to steal food stamps. The food stamps come from the federal government. The Chief kept insisting that it was not valid; it was state-funded. I told him bull. The federal government gave the states money for food stamps. Nothing got done.

With no one doing anything about the theft, I went ahead and got a new food stamp card with a new pin. I kept my food stamp card in my purse. Sure enough, my food stamp card was stolen once again. This time, my food stamp card got stolen out of my purse. I went back to the food stamp office to report my food stamp card stolen again. The woman at the food stamp office told me, "Evelyn, do not give your brother your PIN number on your food stamp card." I told her I didn't. Sure enough, the same brother who chased me around the house trying to grab my upper chest and then steal my car keys out of my purse was the person who stole my food stamp card. This brother had his own business and a house to live in, yet he stole my car keys and food stamp card and tried to molest me.

A few months after my elbow surgery, I received a phone call from my brother-in-law. He told me my sister (who was married to my ex) was at the hospital on her deathbed; she was dying of cancer. I had no money to take a two-hour drive to see her at the hospital. I told Dad that his daughter was in the hospital dying. I asked him if he wanted to go see her. Dad said yes. I told him I needed gas money; I had no money for gas. Dad gave me money to put gas in the car. He and I were the first ones to get to the hospital.

My sister was not opening her eyes. She kept screaming with pain. My sister died late that night. I stayed at the hospital after she died. It was late and dark outside. I noticed that the medical staff just put a cover over my sister's body in her room and left her there dead. I kept insisting they call the coroner to pick her up; my sister was not going to stay in the hospital room like a number. The medical staff refused to call the coroner. I decided to go into my dead sister's room and stay with her until the coroner came. The medical staff kept asking me if I was ok. I told them yes. I kept insisting they call the coroner. After sitting in my dead sister's hospital room for several hours, the medical staff called the coroner in my town. After they talked to the coroner, they said they could not come until tomorrow morning, so a local coroner was coming to pick up my dead sister. I stayed in the room until the coroner came to get my sister's body.

After the coroner took my sister away, I went into the lobby and slept. I only had half a tank of gas left. I went to the hospital manager's office that morning and asked if they knew where I could get help to get gas to go back home. I told him I lived two hours away and my sister had died here last night. He asked me my sister's name. I told him. He looked it up. He told me he had a meeting to go to soon, but after the meeting, he said he would take me to a gas station and pay for my gas. He then asked if I had had breakfast. I told him I had no money for food. He took me to the cafeteria and told me he was going to pay for my breakfast. He told me to pick out what I wanted to eat for breakfast. After his meeting, he went with me to get gas. He kept asking if I needed anything else before I made the trip back home. I told him no. I thanked him for his generosity, then drove back to Dad's house.

I went to my sister's wake. My wicked sister told me she wanted us sisters to go to see our dead sister in the parlor and say "Goodbye" to her. I went into the parlor and told my dead sister to watch over me when I moved away. The only reason I hung around was because nobody was talking to you. I then told my dead sister, "Now that you are dead, I am going to be leaving." I told my dead sister to watch over me when I left. My wicked sister told me in a mean voice, "You ruined our sister thing." She started coming after me. I walked away toward the room where all the nieces, nephews, and a few other relatives were. My wicked sister looked like the Grinch. She grabbed my upper arms and would not let go of me. The nieces, nephews, and others in the room stood there laughing at me being assaulted by my wicked sister. Finally, a relative came over and told the evil sister to leave me alone. On the day of the funeral, many relatives didn't know who I was. They hadn't seen me since I lost weight. When this one relative found out who I was, they came over and talked to me. They told me to move far away from my family before they ruined my life. I told them I knew; I planned on moving soon.

About three months after my sister's death, I worked at a temp job. There was a Jewish meat packing plant that needed hundreds of workers there. The job was over one hour away. The temp job had us go on a bus to the job site. I worked around the chickens. I had many different jobs that I did there. One of the jobs included plucking any feathers, neck, etc. that shouldn't be on the chicken after going through the slaughter. Another job I had was cutting the skin off the chicken. Yet another job was fascinating; I worked with the FDA people. They look at the chickens for any diseases. There were three or four different types of diseases that chickens could have. I had the chart book to write down what the FDA said for each chicken that had a disease. If the chickens had diseases, they were taken off the conveyer belt and thrown away.

The FDA liked working with me. They asked me if I would take the job of being an FDA employee at this meat packing plant. I told them no; I planned on moving away soon. Then, one day, one of the temp employees got seriously injured. After that injury, the temp job office canceled any more job offers from this meat packing plant. About two weeks later, I got a call from the temp job office. They told me the meat packing plant only wanted a few of the employees to be hired there. The temp office told me that the Jewish meat packing plant wanted me to work for them. I told them I would, but I planned on moving away from here.

"Live to inspire, and one day people will say, because of you, I didn't give up."

— Unknown

Chapter Ten

One month after the job offer at the Jewish meat packing plant, there was a massive flood in two cities. Both cities had meaning to me. The one city was where I had my brain surgery, four ankle surgeries, and elbow surgery. The other city that was flooded was where I had spent my first Christian Christmas just seven months ago, and it was most affected. This city had over 20,000 citizens who had become "houseless" due to the massive flood. I saw on the local TV news that this city's air was polluted. The news said that the flood was many feet high. It was like "The Sunken City Under the Sea." Many houseless citizens were in school gyms or wherever they could find shelter. The news even stated that homes, restaurants, gas stations, etc., were severely damaged due to the flood, and at least one hospital was also flooded.

I knew I had to try to give to the needy who had nothing due to the severe flood that took over their city. I decided to start packing my car up with my belongings that I would not take with me and drive to town where I had spent my Christmas Eve just seven months ago. The trunk and back seat of my car were packed with my belongings. I knew where the elderly lady and her husband lived, so I decided to go to her house. I would give her my belongings, and in return, she could give them to her daughter in this severely flooded city. I drove to the elderly lady's house to give her my belongings. She told me she wasn't affected by the flood, but her daughter's city was severely affected. She told me her daughter wasn't affected by the flood, but her church people were donating their belongings to the affected citizens. After she told me that, she gave me her daughter's address in that city.

I had no road map, no cell phone, nor any Wi-Fi to get directions. I had never had a desktop or laptop computer, nor did I have a cell phone that had Google Maps. I just drove to the city, hoping I never got into the affected flood area. After getting directions several times to this address and being assured that this area wasn't affected by the massive flood, I found this woman's house. Once I got there, this woman was receiving phone calls asking if I was one of the flood victims. She told them I was there to donate things for her church to give to the citizens who were affected by the massive flood. Before dusk, the woman, her husband, her children, and I carried the things out of my car into their basement.

The next day was Sunday. The woman and her family were going to church. After church, they were going to go help one of their church members who was affected by the massive flood. She said the flooded area was no longer flooded; it was now clean-up time. I told her I would go to church with her. She asked if I wanted to go with them to one of their church members' severely damaged houses to try to save whatever they could for her. She told me this church member could not move back into her house; her house had to be demolished because the massive flood caused severe damage to her home. I told her I wanted to go with her family to their church members' house and help save whatever this church member could save from the flood.

After church, the woman and her family drove to the store to pick up items needed to be in the affected flooded area. On the way there, the woman said the items that were needed were "scarce" to find. When I entered the store, I was shocked by what I saw. It looked like when COVID hit us in 2020 – all the stores were out of everything. However, this was many years before COVID hit us. I had to purchase high rain boots, a special filtered face mask, gloves, a long raincoat, etc. The woman told me that if I did not have these items I needed to wear to be in the affected area, I could not go down there with them. I was lucky to find the items that I needed.

I was in the car with them, driving to this church member's affected home. I was told I had to wear the special face mask before they drove into the flood-affected area. I was "astonished" by what I saw! There were red Xs, black Xs, and Xs of another color on all the affected properties in the flooded area. The woman told me one color X meant "demolish," the other color X meant "needs fixing before they can move in," and the third X meant "savable." She told me that houses that had two different colored Xs meant one part of the property got demolished while the other part was savable.

I saw many garbage trucks picking up damaged furniture, etc. I noticed every block had tons of damaged belongings out for the garbage trucks to pick up. The woman said the garbage men were out 24/7 picking up the trash in the affected flood area.

We drove by many streets that were in the flood zone. I noticed there were gas stations, restaurants, homes, etc., all in the affected flooded area. The woman told me that the gas tanks were completely covered by the flooded water. She said the same thing for the restaurants. The inside of the restaurants was completely covered by the flood water. We finally got to the church member's house. I noticed everything was black and scummy. I saw they were using a tub and a garden hose to clean items. I then noticed a bottle of bleach sitting next to the tub. I asked why they were cleaning outside instead of inside the house in the kitchen sink. They told me they couldn't because the house was completely damaged. When some of the people went inside the house to find more items to clean with the bleach water, I followed. I wanted to see how severe the home really was from the flood. I was stunned by what I saw. The walls, floors, and all the furniture were pure black and scummy. They went into the kitchen, and I noticed the kitchen cupboards were black and scummy. I asked them how high the water in this house was. They told me the flooded water got up to the top step of the second floor. They said the second floor wasn't flooded.

I had brought from home medical gloves, rubber bands, garbage bags, and duct tape with me just in case the citizens I might help would need them. Sure enough, the people there were using Playtex gloves and getting holes in them. I told them I had medical gloves for them to wear. They were told they needed to wear gloves to clean everything with the bleach water. I informed them there were 100 medical gloves in the box. If one of the medical gloves got a hole, they could take it off and put a new pair on. I told them that using the medical gloves would be cheaper than the Playtex gloves because you would have to keep buying new Playtex gloves every time you got a hole in them. After the people's gloves got a hole and they had no more Playtex gloves left, I gave them a pair of medical gloves to wear (with a rubber band around the wrist to keep the glove sealed shut) to clean the things in the bleach water.

After getting everything this church member could claim to take with her into trucks, I drove back home. I knew I needed to find help for these citizens in the affected flood zone. I went home and did some brainstorming of what was really needed for the over 20,000 citizens affected by the massive flood. I wrote down items like bleach, long raincoats, long rain boots, gloves, special face masks, etc. I then thought about when I was affected by my house fire when I went on a blind date. I had absolutely no help from anybody – it seemed like the over 20,000 citizens affected by the massive flood were going through the same thing. Remember that "Jesus Cross" never burned in the house fire? Was it coincidence or the Grace of God that what I went through with my house fire eleven years ago was setting me up to help over 20,000 citizens affected by the flood? Did I go through that so I knew how to help others in a similar way? Since the massive flood happened in the summertime, just like my house fire happened in the summer time,

I knew what families needed in order for their children to have the items they needed for when school started in the fall.

After I wrote up the list of store items, school needs for the children, etc. that this city needed, I went to the next city from my town and talked to somebody who worked for the city. I told them I was in the affected flood area yesterday. I saw what terrible conditions this city was in. I explained to this person what I saw there. The person working for the city said they wanted to help this city, but they did not know what the city needed. I gave her the list of items that were needed ASAP. I explained that the stores were completely bare of the necessities that were needed. *Note: Remember what the stores looked like during COVID? This city was in this same dire need as we were twelve years later during COVID.*

I told this person nearly every school in the city had lost all their basic school supplies. I explained to her that they needed all kinds of school supplies for both the school and the students before their first day of the new school year. I then went on to say that many families were living in the school gyms. Parents needed to find a place for their family to move into. I tried to get this lady to understand that the children did not have a summer vacation this year because they were in school with no home to go to. They were living in the school gyms for the summer. After I was done talking to this person, I went home.

To my surprise, I heard on the radio and TV news later that the city was putting out large donation boxes for people to donate school supplies to this flooded city. I was amazed to see donation boxes in stores filling up with school supplies. I then saw on the TV news that three semi-trucks were loaded with all the necessities needed at the stores in this affected city (ex., bleach, raincoats, rain boots, etc.). I was very relieved to know that this city where I had had my first Christian Christmas just seven months ago was getting the help that they needed.

Did God give me this Christian Christmas knowing that not only was I in dire need on Christmas Eve and Christmas Day, but He knew ahead that this same city would need my help soon after?

About a month later, I had to drive out of town for something. I put the last of my money into the gas tank. While driving back on the highway to Dad's house, I noticed a guy walking along the side of the road carrying a military duffle bag. I just drove past this guy walking on the highway when I had the Holy Spirit speak to me. The Holy Spirit told me, "Pick him up." I looked out my window into the sky and I asked, "Are you sure?" Immediately afterward, I heard a very LOUD "YES" in my car. It made me jolt. I told the Holy Spirit, "I only have a quarter of a tank of gas in my car. I do not have any more money to put gas in my car. There is not much I can do to help this person." I then turned around on the highway and started driving back to this guy walking on the highway. I told the Holy Spirit, "I need your help if you want me to help him. I only have a quarter tank of gas in my car." I then told the Holy Spirit to make sure I was safe with this person.

I saw the guy walking and I pulled my car over just ahead of the hitchhiker. I asked him if he needed a ride. The hitchhiker said, "Yes. I just prayed to God for a ride."

I asked him where he needed to go. He told me he needed to get back home, which was five towns away. He went on to tell me that he had been hitchhiking for five days. He said he had been sleeping out in the grass at night on his journey back to his hometown. He went on to explain that because of the Recession, it was hard to find work. He went down South, where his sister lived, to try to find work there, but no luck. He told me he was going back to his parents' house to live.

I told him I didn't know how far I could take him because I only had a quarter of a tank of gas in my car. The guy told me I could take him as far as I could, and he would start walking again. I asked him how he had been eating and drinking. He told me that semi-drivers had been picking him up and paying for his food and drink. He said the drivers took him as far as they could before he had to get out of the rig. I asked him when he left his sister's place down South. He told me the day (ex., Friday, and today was Wednesday). I said, "You have been hitchhiking for five days now."

I knew that my gas tank must be empty, but I never looked at the gas tank. I continued talking to him about his circumstances.

When I got to this fourth town, I pulled into a convenience store and told him this was as far as I could take you. I had driven through four towns with only a quarter tank of gas to start with. I didn't think I could drive one more town to his parents' house. I gave him some coins to use the pay phone to call his family.

While he was trying to use the pay phone, I went outside the convenience store and saw a guy in construction clothes. I approached him and asked him if he had a cell phone. He told me he did. I told him about this hitchhiker I had picked up four towns away and that he'd been hitchhiking for five days and sleeping in the grass at night. I told him the hitchhiker needed to get to his family's house the next town over, but I had only a quarter of a tank of gas when I picked him up four towns away from here. I told him I did not have any money to get more gas to take him to his parents' house, and I had four towns to get back home with what gas I had left. After that, the hitchhiker came out of the store. He told me the pay phone didn't work. The construction guy told the hitchhiker he could use his phone to call his family, so he did. When he got off the phone, the construction guy asked the hitchhiker what his family said. The hitchhiker said his family would not pick him up. That was when the construction guy asked the hitchhiker why he went down South.

"I am looking for work, so I went down South to my sister's place to find a job with no luck," he answered.

The construction guy asked, "Do you smoke?"

The hitchhiker said, "No."

The construction guy then asked him, "Do you do drugs?"

"No," the Hitchhiker replied.

The next question from the construction guy to the Hitchhiker was, "Do you drink?"

The hitchhiker shrugged, "Occasionally."

After these questions, the construction guy said, "The construction work we do is for the State. You come with me, and I will get you a hotel tonight. You tell me what size clothes you wear and I will get you new clothes while you're in the hotel room taking a shower. Then, when I come back with your new clothes, you will get dressed, and I will take you out to eat tonight. Then, tomorrow morning, I will pick you up at the hotel and take you to work with me. I will talk to my boss about you working with us."

The hitchhiker went with me to my car to get his stuff. I told him to listen to the construction guy. "This is where God wants you to be. Do not go back to your family's house. They wouldn't pick you up, and this construction guy is helping you get on your feet," I said. I told the hitchhiker one more time to listen to the construction guy. "Do not go back to your family's house. You are looking for work. Do not pass up this job opportunity."

The Hitchhiker agreed to what I told him. We embraced and waved each other goodbye. I went back into my car to go back to Dad's house four towns away. I looked at my gas tank to see how much gas I had left. My eyes nearly popped out. My gas tank still read "quarter of a tank of gas." *Still?* I couldn't believe that I had driven through four towns with a quarter of a tank of gas, and four towns later, my gas tank still read a quarter of a tank of gas!!

Note: This reminds me of the Bible of Jesus in Matthew chapter 14, verses 14-21.

"14. And Jesus went forth and saw a great multitude, and was moved with compassion toward them, and he healed their sick.

15. And when it was evening, his disciples came to him, saying, This is a desert place, and the time is now past; send the multitude away, that they may go into the villages, and buy themselves victuals.

16. But Jesus said unto them, They need not depart; give ye them to eat.

17. And they say unto him, We have here but five loaves, and two fishes.

18. He said, Bring them hither to me.

19. And he commanded the multitude to sit down on the grass, and took the five loaves, and the two fishes, and looking up to heaven, he blessed, and brake, and gave the loaves to his disciples, and the disciples to the multitude.

20. And they did all eat, and were filled: and they took up of the fragments that remained twelve baskets full.

21. And they that had eaten were about five thousand men, besides women and children."

These verses are a simile to my gas tank staying at one-fourth of a tank of gas from the time I picked up the hitchhiker to driving him four towns away.

About a month later, I drove to the town where I had dropped off the hitchhiker. Just before I approached the town, there was construction being done on the highway. They had "flaggers" doing the "Stop" and "Slow" sign. When I was driving past the flagger, I took a look at him. The flagger I saw looked just like the hitchhiker I had picked up just a month ago. I felt happy to see that he was now working with a construction company.

***

My children were young adults now. They both moved out of the state and were starting their journey in their lives. My one son had a girlfriend. His relationship grew, and he got married. Of course, I went to his wedding. To my surprise, my ex-husband showed up to "our son's" wedding. My ex-husband married someone else after he and my sister got divorced. My ex-husband's new wife had a small child. He spent time with his new wife's son. He saw that his stepson had an automobile to drive when he was in high school. My ex did everything for his stepson but never had the time of day to come see our sons. My ex was still bar hopping. His money went for him and his new family. He never lifted a finger to be a dad to our sons. So, to see my ex-husband not drunk at our son's wedding was surprising.

My other son moved further away out of the state where his one friend lived. He moved away before his brother got married. My son had worn out shoes, so I went to the store and bought him a new pair of shoes. Then, the day my son left, I bought him a large pizza at the pizza parlor. I couldn't afford much more than buying him a pair of shoes and a large pizza. My kids were only teenagers when I had my brain surgery. They didn't understand how seriously my brain surgery affected me not to be able to be a "parent." However, I am happy to see my sons being adults now and moving on with their lives.

Back at home, living with my dad is getting much harder nowadays. My wicked sister is Power Attorney over Dad. Her husband controls Dad's money. At least every other week, I have either the wicked sister, brother, or their other sibling saying to me, "Evelyn, are you going to be able to live in Dad's house once he dies? You will not be able to afford to pay the bills or keep up with the house." I tell them each time that I will be able to keep up with Dad's house once he dies. My siblings want me to explain to them how I am going to be able to do this. I won't give them details of how I am going to manage the house, but I do tell them that I will not have any rent to pay; I will just have taxes to pay. The siblings throw in things like, "What if the furnace goes out?" Etc. I just tell them that I will be able to manage it.

My wicked siblings will not accept my answers. They want to belittle me as much as they can. They also keep telling me that it's not fair that I get the house; Dad's house should be sold and split between the siblings. I tell them, "Mom told you guys that the house goes to me when she and Dad die. She told you guys you have your own houses to live in, and I do not have one."

This issue has become a nonstop conversation. They want me to be in the same condition I was in after I had my brain surgery, even though I have worked several jobs. My first employer (after brain surgery) gave me the chance to prove myself to them even though I had just had the brain surgery two years ago. I worked with this employer for over 7-8 years before my shakes started acting up.

My wicked sister (Power Attorney for Dad) keeps coming to Dad's house and harassing me over getting the house when Dad dies. One time, the wicked sister asked me again, "What are you going to do with Dad's house when he dies?" I told her that I would sell the house and buy a house somewhere else. Oh, did my wicked sister get mad? She told me, "You are not going to sell Dad's house when he dies. If you are not going to keep Dad's house after he dies, then Dad's house goes to my daughter." She told me her daughter and her two kids didn't have a house to live in. She said her daughter would be moving into Dad's house then. The wicked sister kept harassing me over and over that her daughter was getting Dad's house. I told her, "No. That is *your* daughter. *You* take care of your daughter. You have money, a home, and in the medical field. You have your daughter, and her kids live with you. Dad is 90 years old. He is not responsible for your kids and your grandkids."

After that, the wicked sister went to Dad and told him, "Dad, Evelyn is moving out of your house, and my daughter and her kids will be moving in with you to live."

Dad told the wicked sister, "No. I am not having any kids running around the house. Evelyn stays living with me."

A few weeks later, the wicked sister was back at Dad's house. She came to me and told me, "Evelyn, look at me. I have a nice home, several automobiles, and money in the bank. Look at you, Evelyn. You are a NOBODY. You do not have a BRAIN. If you didn't live with Dad, you would be homeless."

I got in my wicked sister's face and told her, "Who is the person that had epilepsy and had to have brain surgery because of it? Look at you. You couldn't keep your legs crossed until you got married. You got pregnant in high school, and you dropped out of high school because you got pregnant."

She didn't have enough credits to graduate from high school. Here, I had epilepsy, and I still graduated with my classmates. I told my wicked sister that I was the first girl in the family to graduate from high school with their classmates. Oh, did my wicked sister get furious with the truth I just said? She had the Grinch look meanness on her face again. Ever since then, my wicked sister would always go talk to the police chief about me. She even had the gall to tell me ahead of time, "I am going to talk to the police chief about you. I will get you out of Dad's house."

The wicked sister went to the police chief so much that he had two cops come and talk to my dad and ask if he felt safe around me. Dad would tell the cops that everything was fine between him and me. The cops told Dad that my wicked sister was telling them that I was a danger to him. Dad told the cops he was safe around me. He told the cops that the sisters had a "sibling fight." There was nothing more than that going on. The cops left Dad's house after that.

Then, one day, I was home thoroughly cleaning Dad's house when the wicked sister and her husband showed up at his house. They went into the kitchen with Dad, who was 90 years old, and told him, "Dad, you have a choice. You either get rid of Evelyn, or I am selling your house on you." Not too much later, the wicked sister and her husband told Dad, "Let's go out and get something to eat, Dad." They left before lunchtime. It was getting dark outside now, and Dad wasn't back home yet. It was winter time and below-freezing temperatures outside. They forecasted the temperature to be at "two below zero" that night. I was getting worried about him. I had no idea where the wicked sister and her husband took Dad, but now it was getting late. Dad had been gone now for nearly eight hours when I heard a knock at the door.

I opened the door to see a police officer and deputy at the door. I thought they were going to tell me something happened, but instead, I heard these officers say, "Evelyn, your father has put a restraining order on you. You are dangerous for your father to be here with you." I was shocked! I told the officers that it was a lie. "Dad and I get along just fine. It's my sister and her husband that do not get along with me." The officers told me that I had to leave ASAP. They told me that I could not take anything with me. I was to leave everything in Dad's house. I told them I did not have money for food or drink. I did not have a place to stay if I left. The temperature was going to be below zero that night. The officers kept forcing me to leave everything behind.

I left Dad's house with nowhere to go. I called a church person and explained to her what had happened. I asked her if I could sleep there tonight. She said, "No, but you can go to my daughter's house out of state and see if she will let you stay with her." I had barely enough gas to drive out of state to where this woman lived late at night. However, her daughter let me stay with her and her kids. I stayed there for a few nights before my son and his wife let me stay with them until I had the court hearing of the restraining order put against me.

Before the day of the court hearing over the restraining order, one foot of snow fell. My dad shoveled the snow off the sidewalks at his house and a few other areas in town by himself. I was worried about how he was doing.

Dad was 90 years old and living by himself now due to the restraining order. It was only a few days before Christmas when I had to go to court about the restraining order. On the day of the court hearing, my son and a relative went to court with me. My son and the other relative were upset over this ordeal. I went into the courtroom, and my son and the other relative were going to wait for their grandpa outside the courtroom. I thought at least the wicked sister and her husband would be showing up to court with Dad, but to my surprise, Dad came by himself. My son and the other relative talked to Dad before he came into the courtroom. When Dad came into the courtroom, he did not look healthy anymore; he looked frail now.

Now, the judge entered into the courtroom. The judge saw my 90-year-old father by himself, and I was on the other side of the court. The judge asked Dad what he wanted to do about this claim of the restraining order. The judge asked Dad if he wanted me back in his house or not. Finally, Dad said, "Yes, I want Evelyn to come back home."

The judge told Dad, "You are lucky you want your daughter (Evelyn) to come back home with you. If you had told me 'no,' I was going to go back into my office and make a phone call to the nursing home to have you put in there."

I felt a sigh of relief. I was stunned to hear the judge say that he was going to put Dad in the nursing home if he didn't let me move back in.

When I got back into Dad's house, I asked him, "Are you hungry?"

Dad said, "Yes."

I asked him what he wanted to eat. He told me, "Whatever you make me."

I asked him, "When was the last time you had a hamburger?"

Dad said, "The last time you made it for me."

I asked him, "When was the last time you had roast beef?"

He said, "The last time you made it for me."

I finally asked Dad, "What have you been eating since I have been gone?"

Dad told me all he ate was soup and cereal. I was furious! My dad was 90 years old, and none of my siblings saw to it that he had a home-cooked meal in the two weeks I was gone. I asked Dad who had been doing his laundry. He said he was doing it himself.

Now, Dad had never used the washer or dryer in his life. He was the laborer. He held down two jobs to support the family. I asked Dad who helped him shovel the one foot of snow that we had just had; he told me nobody helped him shovel the snow. I was really upset that the family was treating Dad the same way I had been treated all my life by them.

My siblings were furious when they found out that the judge had dismissed the restraining order and allowed me back into Dad's house. You have no idea of the commotion that went on because of that. Well, it was Christmas Eve. My brother came to pick up Dad and take him out of town to a relative's house for Christmas. My brother, furious that I was back at Dad's house, told me that I could not go with him and Dad to the family Christmas. I stayed home and kept the radio and TV off. I did not want to hear anything about Christmas and everybody being jolly. I just played my CDs and cassette music (no Christmas music).

My brother did not bring Dad back home until two days later. When Dad came into the house, I felt a sigh of relief. I heard Dad tell my brother, "I go to this heart doctor." My brother ignored what Dad had to say and went to the bathroom. When he came out of the bathroom, he left Dad's house. I asked Dad what he meant about "going to this heart doctor." Dad told me that he had chest pains all night at the hotel. I asked him if he told my brother. Dad said, "Yes, but he wouldn't listen." I knew right then I was going to make a doctor's appointment for Dad to see right now. I made an appointment with the medical doctor in town in the afternoon.

Now, every 20 minutes, I got a phone call from my brother. He asked me why Dad was going to the doctor. I told him, "It's none of your business." My brother tried to tell me that he was in charge of Dad's medical. I told him bull! "I have been taking care of Dad's medical ever since I moved in after Mom died." My brother called me by the wicked sister's name, and then he corrected himself and said, "Evelyn." I told him, "It's none of your business," hung up the phone, and called Dad's heart doctor.

Dad's heart doctor's nurse told me to take Dad to the Emergency Room now. So, I told Dad I was taking him to the emergency room to be checked out for his heart pains. While I was getting dressed, the wicked sister called me and wanted to know why Dad was going to the doctor's office. I told the wicked sister it was none of her business. She told me she was the Power Attorney over Dad. I told her I didn't care. "It is none of your business." I then hung up the phone and got ready.

I took Dad to the Emergency Room and made sure to let the medical staff know that I had been forced to stay away from Dad for the last two weeks. Dad told me all he had to eat was soup and cereal. Dad did not have a home-cooked meal for two weeks. The doctor ordered a blood test on top of doing the test on his heart. The doctor said Dad's heart was fine. I told the doctor that I needed Dad to stay in the hospital overnight to be evaluated. "He hasn't had a home-cooked meal in two weeks. He has only eaten soup and cereal," I explained to the doctor. After what I told the doctor, he had Dad admitted to the hospital.

Dad was taken to the hospital room. They saw that Dad had gotten wet through his clothes. The nurse had to take his clothes off and clean him up before he went into the hospital bed. The nurse put Dad's wet clothes in a bag and gave them to me, but before he went into the hospital room, the nurse had Dad weighed. She read Dad's weight out loud. I was shocked at what the nurse said Dad's weight was. I asked the nurse what Dad weighed. She told me the weight again. I was astonished. I told the nurse, "NO way. Dad weighs twenty pounds more than that all the time! Dad had lost 20 pounds in the last two weeks since I was forced to leave his house.

I told the nurse that all Dad had to eat in the two weeks was soup and cereal. He needed to be fed so he could gain weight back. Once Dad got into the hospital bed, I talked to him for a little while before I told him I was going home to get him clean clothes to wear for tomorrow. I went home and washed Dad's clothes. Once his clothes were dry, I went back to the hospital with clean clothes for him. I wanted to be there when the doctor came to see Dad in the morning. The nurse saw me coming. She stopped me and told me not to go into Dad's room. I was shocked by what she said. The nurse told me that after I left, my Dad broke down crying. "He said he didn't want to put the restraining order on you. He told us your 'wicked sister' had forced him to sign the restraining order." She continued, "Your father loves you, and he doesn't want to leave."

We finally got your dad calmed down. I told the nurse I would be out in the lobby sleeping tonight. I wanted to be there when the doctor saw Dad in the morning.

The next morning, I went into Dad's hospital room. He had a big smile on his face and said, "Hi, Evelyn." I smiled back and said, "Hi." The nurse came in and told me, "Your dad knows you are his guardian angel." The medical staff were furious about how cruel my family had treated both Dad and me. The doctor came to see Dad. He examined Dad over and told him that his heart was fine. After that, the doctor told Dad he could be discharged. Dad had a smile on his face. He got dressed, and I took him back home.

Things went back to normal between Dad and me, but for the rest of the family, we had become estranged. My siblings wanted me out of Dad's house. Whenever they came over to Dad's house, they asked me, "When are you going to move out?" I told them I would move out when nobody knew. It was nobody's business where I went or when. Then, not even six weeks later, I went to my car to go to the bank. I was walking to my car when two cop cars pulled up and jammed my car in so I couldn't go anywhere. I asked the cop (one being the Police Chief) what was going on. They told me to come with them. I asked them why. I hadn't done anything. The cop and Police Chief kept saying to get in the cop car with them. After refusing to go, the cop and Police Chief told me that they had a court order to have me "evaluated" at the hospital. I was shocked. I told them there was nothing wrong with me; I did not need to be evaluated. The cop and Police Chief said they had a court order to take me to the hospital. I went in the cop car, and they took me to the local hospital.

Both the cop and the Police Chief told the Emergency Room I was there to be evaluated. I was put in the room with the cop and Police Chief, waiting for the doctor to come in. When the doctor came to the room, the cop and Police Chief took the doctor out of the room and talked to her. I heard the doctor say, "Oh my God, no way." They came back into the room. After the doctor told me I was being sent to a mental hospital, the cop and Police Chief said, "Yes!" And the cop and Police Chief gave each other a "high five"! I told the cop and Police Chief that my dad was home alone with pneumonia. He was 90 years old. I needed to be there to take care of him. The cops told me that they would watch over my dad. Now, I was being sent to a mental institution for unknown reasons. I never did anything wrong.

What lies ahead now?

"At any given moment, you have the power to say this is not how my story is going to end."

- *Unknown*

Chapter Eleven

Once I was admitted to the mental hospital, the staff asked me many questions. After that, they told me that I would be sharing a room with another female patient. They then showed me where my room was. Now, remember I always wore dress pants, a dressy top, knee highs, jewelry, make-up, and dressy shoes ever since I lost over 110 pounds. I looked like nobody else in the facility who wore everyday clothes.

A guy who was 20 years younger than me kept following me around. He would try to "pin" me in a corner and try to get sexual with me. He asked me if I would be his girlfriend. I told him, "No way!" I went into the dining area and sat down to read the Bible. This same guy came into the dining area and sat next to me. I tried to ignore him, but he kept talking to me. He told me to "Look at this." I looked at him, and he told me to look down. I looked down to see he had his pants unzipped with his private hanging out. I told him to zip his pants up and to get away from me. I then got up and went to the staff. I told the staff that this guy sat next to me, and unzipped his pants, and had his thing hanging out.

After that, this guy kept following me wherever I went. If I sat at the end of the couch where there was a wall blocking the view for the staff to see, this guy would purposely come toward me and say something like "Blah" with his face looking like a criminal. This continued to happen until one day, this guy told a male staff member after breakfast, "Do you guys have a counselor for RAPE victims? The male staff said, "No. Why do you ask?" The guy following me around told the male staff, "Oh, I was just wondering. I have a family member who needs to see a counselor for being raped."

I knew right then this guy was talking about raping me at the mental hospital. I went to the staff ASAP and told them about this guy following me all over and now asking the male staff about a rape counselor. I told them, "I know this guy is now planning to rape me!" After I talked to the staff, I went to other male patients and told them that this one male patient was talking about raping me. The other male patients were shocked to hear what I had to say. They told me that they would beat this guy up. I told the other male patients not to get themselves in trouble by beating him up. I told them to just watch him and stay close to him in case he did try to rape me.

Whenever I was in my room with the door shut, I felt somewhat safer being away from the so-called rapist. However, I came to realize otherwise. The door to my room stayed closed because of the so-called rapist. However, whenever I went to leave and open the door that I shared with another woman, I would see the "so-called rapist" leaning up against the wall next to my room. He had his hands on the zipper of his pants. When he saw me, he would "unzip his pants" and put his "private" out on me. I would tell the staff about this incident each time it happened to me.

In group meetings or activities, I had to always sit in the middle. I could never sit at the end of the couch or table. This guy plotting to rape me was going to try to rape me if he had a chance to without anybody witnessing it.

There was this one female patient there who was always crying. I asked her what was wrong. She told me how her family made fun of her and called her names. I comforted her by asking her if she had self-esteem. She told me, "Yes." I told her, "Well, your family, who calls you names and makes fun of you, has no self-esteem." I told her, "They *have* to make fun of you in order for them to be happy and have self-esteem." I then told her, "You have self-esteem. You don't have to make fun of anybody to make yourself happy." After I told this woman that, she stopped crying. Those words I said to her must have made sense to her because ever since then, this woman wasn't crying constantly anymore.

***

I was in the dining room with the other patients one day, waiting for breakfast to come. The guy who wanted to rape me always sat near me. I would say to him, "How are you doing, BOY?" This guy laughed at me and said, "Ha, guys, she's calling me a BOY." I told this guy, "That's right. You *are* a boy. A man wouldn't treat a woman the way you treat me. Only a boy would act the way you are acting toward me." After that, the guy stopped laughing at me. Now, all the patients there knew that he was trying to rape me if he got a chance. I continued to say to this so-called rapist every morning in the dining area, waiting for breakfast to come, "How are you feeling today, boy?" This so-called rapist would tell me, "That is what my mom used to say to me every morning."

There were a few wireless headsets to listen to the radio. I listened to music to keep me calm dealing with this rapist. I had the headset tuned into a country station. I was walking around the area listening to music when this one song came on titled "I will always love you" by Dolly Parton. I started singing this song while I was walking toward the big bay window. I was looking up in the sky, singing this song. I was dedicating this song to my dad (or is he my dad?). I didn't know how loud I was singing because I had the volume in the headset on high for this song. I was pouring out my feelings into this song, looking up into the sky. I got to a high pitch in the song. Right after the high pitch I sang, I heard commotion. I heard someone say, "What is going on?" I never paid any attention to the commotion. I was dedicating this song to my dad! After I was done singing this song, I turned the volume down on the headset. I then turned around and saw a crowd of people behind me (staff and patients). Suddenly, everybody applauded me for my singing. They all told me that I sang good. Everybody told me that I needed to go to Nashville. The patients told the staff, "Evelyn needs to get out of here and go to Nashville." Once again, I have had others notice how good I could sing. Just two years prior, my sister (who was married to my ex) told me, "Evelyn, I didn't know you could sing like that." Then she wanted me to go karaoke with her and her newest husband.

After the episodes with the rapist not only laughing at me when I called him a "boy" and then standing outside my room waiting for me to come out so he could unzip his pants and put his private out, the other male patients would always be around this so-called rapist who wanted to rape me. Then, one day, I went to place my tray that had food on it. This guy who wanted to rape me stared at my every movement. I told this guy, "Keep your eyes to yourself," and walked away. While I was walking away, I heard him say, "F… you, whore." That infuriated me. Nobody had ever called me a whore in my life. I was a virgin when I got married. I turned around and walked toward this guy who wanted to rape me. I stared right into his eyes with a furious look on my face and narrowed my eyes in a slit. When I was locked, staring into his eyes for a few minutes, this so-called wanna-be rapist got scared of me staring into his eyes. While I was staring into his eyes, I heard the staff tell me, "Evelyn, don't hurt him." I did not and do not believe in laying a hand on anybody. I was not going to be like my dysfunctional family. Once the so-called rapist unlocked his eyes from staring at me, I walked away.

It had only been about a week since I was admitted to this mental institution when the doctor and staff asked me questions about the reason I was admitted there. I told them what had happened. They had to make a few phone calls to see if what I had to say was the truth or not. After a few days, the doctor and staff told me that what I had told them was legit. They told me that the charges that got me put in the mental hospital were false charges. They told me that they could not keep me in the hospital with false charges and that I would be discharged from the hospital as soon as I got a ride to take me out of there.

The staff told me, "Evelyn, we don't know what we are going to do without you here. You know how to calm these patients down." They offered me a job working at the mental institution as an Advocate. I told them I didn't know what an Advocate was. They told me that they would teach me to be an Advocate. I told them I didn't have money to get a place to stay or have any furniture, dishes, etc., for an apartment. The staff told me that they would find me an apartment and get everything that I needed for it. I told them the patients here were a piece of cake. They were nothing compared to my family. I told them to take these patients out of the hospital and replace them with my dysfunctional family. Once they had my dysfunctional family there, they would beg for these patients to come back. The staff was stunned to know that there were worse people to deal with than the patients in their mental hospital.

During this time, somebody called the mental institution to tell them I needed to be told that my brother, who had had epilepsy for over 30 years, had died in the nursing home he had been in for two years. The mental institution staff never told me about my brother's death. The mental institution would not deliver bad news to a patient while they were in the hospital. They were there to improve the patients' lives, not to bring more drama into their lives.

Why did my brother go to the nursing home, you might be wondering. My brother purposely broke his foot to go into the nursing home. You see, men with epilepsy cannot get any Medicaid for themselves. It doesn't matter if the adult male has a medical issue or not, nor does it matter if he has kids. Men **do not** have any medical insurance for themselves unless it is from their employment. How is an epileptic going to get a good-paying job with good medical insurance? My brother needed his epileptic medication. He couldn't afford to buy his medication. An epileptic cannot go without their epileptic medication! If they do, they will have epileptic seizures! Well, the doctors at the nursing home told my brother that since he was not having any epileptic seizures, they were taking his epileptic seizure medication away from him! The epileptic medication kept the seizures under control for not only my brother but for all people with epilepsy taking the medication. Why take the seizure pills away because my brother isn't having a seizure? Do doctors treat diabetic patients like they do epileptics? Do they take their diabetic medication away from them because their diabetes gets in control and regulated? Why do diabetics get treated with more respect than epileptics? The doctors then claimed my brother to be psychotic instead of an epileptic.

I sat down and tried to figure out what respect stood for. Here is what I came up with:

RESPECT
R-Remember
E-Everyone's

S-Special
P-Personality
E-Eventually
C-Comes
T-Together

The staff at the hospital liked what I put up on the chalkboard about what RESPECT stands for. They kept it on the chalkboard for nearly a week for others to see.

The doctors drugged my brother up with psychosis medication. It wasn't long before my brother was having epileptic seizures. NONSTOP! The nursing home would take my brother to the hospital to be treated for his seizures. He would stay in the hospital for up to two weeks before he went back to the nursing home. My brother's ex-girlfriend called me and asked me to come help him. The nursing home would not let her talk to my brother anymore. I called the nursing home and talked to a staff member. They told me I could not talk to my brother. I demanded to talk to my brother. The staff member asked me who I was. I told her I was his sister. She told me that my brother didn't know he had any family anymore. She went on to say that my brother could not comprehend what they said to him anymore. Basically, my brother had severe brain damage due to the nursing home doctor taking his seizure pills away from him. Now, no seizure medication would help my brother. He needed brain surgery like I had done, but I couldn't help my brother since he lived in a different state.

Back to the mental hospital I was at. It had been ten days now since I was admitted to the mental hospital. On the tenth day there, there were two male patients standing by the guy who wanted to rape me. I walked past them when I heard the so-called rapist tell me, "You better get out of here. It is too tempting not to rape you." Now, I had confirmation that this guy really wanted to rape me ever since I came into the mental hospital. I called my friend, who took over the paper routes I used to have, to come pick me up. He told me he needed gas money. He was short on gas before he got paid again. I told him I had $20 to give him if he came to get me. He agreed to come and get me in the afternoon the next day.

Well, the next day, my friend came in the afternoon to pick me up to take me out of the mental hospital. I told him that I would not go back to Dad's house. I would stay with him overnight and leave with him in the morning when he delivered the newspapers. I told him to drop me off by my car early in the morning. When I went to my car, I noticed that my dad's porch light was on in the early morning. My dad never had the porch light on. I knew something was wrong, but I refused to go up to his house to find out. I just went to my car and left.

"I spent 11 days in the mental institution on false charges."

Well, I always told the dysfunctional family that I would leave for good when nobody knew I left. When my friend dropped me off by my car, I got in and went to have coffee at a restaurant. When the bank opened up, I took my money out of the bank. I went to the food pantry when they opened and got some nonperishable food. I then went to a second-hand store and bought some dress pants, dress shirts, and undergarments. I then went to the pharmacy and got my epilepsy medication. I hadn't had an epileptic seizure since my brain surgery 11 years ago, but I still took the epilepsy medication. I have taken epilepsy medication since I was an infant. I could not stop taking it after having taken it for over 40 years because it would change my body chemistry.

I then went to the department store to get shampoo, towels, washcloths, body soap, makeup, etc. After I had my basic needs in my car, I started driving out of state. I was determined to start a new chapter of my life elsewhere, away from the dysfunctional family and the dysfunctional community that I had lived in for over 40 years. My heart was racing while I was still in my state. Once I got two states away, I felt 100 pounds fall off my chest. I never got a hotel room; I slept in my car at night. I drove at least 2000 miles before I was determined to plant a new life elsewhere.

Well, when I went to get help to get a place to stay and get on my feet, the police ran my license plate number. They called my state to find out more about me. That was the worst thing that the police could have done to me. I was here to start a new life elsewhere, and I was being checked on by the police by the dysfunctional state that I left! I was told by the officers that my state had told them that I had two days to get back to my home state. I told them, "No way! This is a free country! Americans have the right to go and live wherever they want to. Nobody tells

Americans where they can and cannot live. Americans have the right to live wherever they want to live. This is a free country!"

The officers had a group of people who were going to help me get a place to live in their community. The group of people who were going to help me find a place to stay were in the room with me. They were more than willing to come to my aid. I was ready to leave with them when I was told by an officer that since I had driven for so long, they wanted to take me to the hospital to make sure I was medically fine. I believed their lie. The group of people who were willing to help me went with me to the hospital. When I got to the hospital, I was admitted and evaluated for the next 48 hours. After a few hours, the medical staff told the group of people to leave because I was going to be admitted. The group of people were stunned to hear that. There was nothing wrong with me leaving and starting a new life elsewhere without anybody knowing. When the wicked sister asked me in the past, "When are you leaving"? I told her I would leave when nobody knew I left. It was nobody's business where I went.

Well, I asked when I was going to leave the hospital, but the nurses wouldn't answer me. Within 24 hours, I was told that I was being admitted to a mental institution in this state!!! I had gotten discharged from the mental institution in my state just three days ago on false charges, and now I was being put back into a mental institution again!!!!

I found out later that my three siblings went to the courthouse in the state that I had left and filed charges to have me put into a mental institution 2000 miles away from them. This was where I was going to start my new life.

Why was I discharged from the mental institution on false charges to be admitted just three days later to a mental institution again a thousand miles away? This time, I was dealing with more dangerous mentally ill patients. The staff at the mental institution here told me that I had a court hearing to go to. I had no idea why I was going to the courthouse 2000 miles away, but I sure found out soon enough. The judge in this new state court ordered me to be put into a state mental hospital! There was no way I belonged in a state mental hospital.

A relative found out where I was and wanted to talk to the medical staff there. The staff asked me if they could talk to this person. I told them, "No way!!" Then, a few days later, my son called the mental hospital. They asked me if they could talk to my son. I told them, "Yes, but nobody else." My son flew to come and get me out of the mental hospital. I had to get a taxi to go and get my car out of impoundment. My car was parked in the mental hospital parking lot, but somebody had my car towed away. Once I got my car out of impoundment, my son started driving away. He told me that he was going to go see his brother on the way back. My two sons lived thousands of miles away from each other. I told my son not to drive through the state that I had left. My son told me I would be fine; he was with me. Once my son got to my dysfunctional state, I felt my heart racing again the whole time we were in this dysfunctional state I used to live in.

Once we were out of the dysfunctional state, my heart stopped racing. My sons went back to my dad's house in the dysfunctional state to get some of my belongings there. They drove my car there. When my sons parked my car by Dad's house, some cops pulled up to my car. The cops asked my sons, "Where is your mom at?" My sons told them that I was out of state at one of my sons' houses. Were the cops going to find a reason or way to put me away again, just like the last time? Once my sons got back to my son's house, we stayed for a little while before we left to drive several states away to my other son's place. It was a two-day drive to get to my son's place. Once we got there, I noticed that my son was renting a room that was apart from the house. It looked like a game room that my son was renting. There was no refrigerator, stove, or sink in this room. I knew my son was starting a new life of his own, but I never knew what his place looked like before this. It wasn't too much later that my son got his own home to rent.

I was new to this new state. I had no idea where anything was in this town. I did not have a cell phone or any other device to find out where anything was in this town. My son told me, "Mom, you took care of me when I was a kid. Now it is time that I took care of you." I told my son, "No way. You are grown up now. Now, it is time for me to have my own life." I lived with my son for about a month before his friend back in the dysfunctional state came to live with him and me at his home. Things didn't work out living with my son. I got in my car and started driving. I was going to figure out where I wanted to set my roots.

I knew I wanted to live in a big city to mingle in. Small communities liked to pass their time gossiping about people. I did not believe in gossip. Gossip leads to making a mountain out of a molehill. I finally decided to go to this large city in this new state. I had no idea how to get any resource help there, so I lived in my car. I went to a restaurant for breakfast every morning with a new, clean pair of dress pants, dress tops, knee highs, makeup, towels, shampoo, conditioner, a bar of soap, etc. I took a bird bath in the bathroom every morning. I put on my makeup and jewelry with my dressy clothes. Nobody knew that I was homeless. It wasn't too much later, after being homeless, that the cops took me to the hospital to be evaluated again. So, less than two months after my son got me out of the mental hospital and brought me back to his state, I was in the mental hospital again.

I was not talking to my son now. I was in the mental hospital for about 11 days before I got discharged. In the big city, there was no place that I could find to be alone and pray to Jesus and God, so I went by the river and looked up in the sky, and I prayed to God out loud. The citizens started freaking out that I was praying to God out loud. Everybody has their own way of how to pray to God and Jesus. There is no set pattern of how you talk to God or Jesus. I noticed that the citizens would come by me when I was looking up at the sky, praying to God and Jesus out loud. They would look up in the sky to see what I was looking at. I did not have my own

216

place to pray to God and Jesus in my own home. I was homeless. The only way I could pray and talk to God and Jesus was in public. However, the public saw me praying out loud as something different.

***

My car had now been stolen from me. All my epilepsy medication was in my car. Now, I had no epileptic medication. I had to walk a long distance to find a drugstore and tell them that I needed my epileptic medication. My medication was in my car, and my car was stolen. Now, I was sleeping in the streets. I tried to sleep on a park bench, but after a few hours, a cop would wake me up and tell me to get off the bench. Apparently, there was a curfew in the park. I told them I had no place to sleep. All night long, I would wake up every few hours to move on. It was getting so bad living outside that I had to always keep one eye open during the night.

I hadn't had a good night's sleep since my car was stolen. If a person does not get enough sleep, they become delusional. Since I was homeless and tried to sleep outside where it was unsafe to be, I was not getting my sleep. Worse yet, I took epileptic medication every day. The medication made me drowsy at night, and it was not good going without getting my sleep.

Sure enough, not even one week after I was discharged from the mental hospital, the cops took me away. They eventually put me back into the mental hospital. This was the fourth time that I had been put into the mental hospital in two months! Well, after a week or two in the hospital, I was taken to the courthouse for a hearing. *What this time?* I found out that I was at the courthouse so the judge could court order me into the state hospital! In two and a half months' time, I was put into the mental hospital five times!

I was in my room, upset with all the trauma that had happened to me. Did this all start because my wicked sister forced our 90-year-old Dad to put a restraining order on me against his will? Dad and I got along great. We never argued or fought. One day, I was on my bed looking up at the ceiling. I started praying to God out loud. A doctor came into my room and asked me, "Who are you talking to?" I told him I was talking to God. The doctor asked me "Where is God at?" I was surprised by his outrageous question. I pointed to the ceiling and said, "God is up there." How else was I supposed to answer such a weird question? The doctor looked around the ceiling and said, "I do not see God. You are seeing things. You are delusional!" I asked the doctor if he went to church. He told me yes. I told him, "Don't you pray to God?" He wouldn't answer the question. I told him I was in my room praying to God out loud. I knew God was not in the ceiling. God was everywhere. The doctor refused to listen to me.

Once I got to the state mental hospital, I had to deal with many different types of mentally ill people there. I had a female roommate who liked women. She came after me one day when I went to take a shower in our room. I screamed for help. The staff came and saw the female roommate coming after me. Ever since then, the woman couldn't be in the room when I took a shower. She would also urinate on my bed or on the floor by my bed. I had another female roommate who would throw all my stuff around on the floor. Then I had another female roommate who did a number two on the shower floor!

Then, 30 days after I was admitted to the state hospital, the staff had a meeting with me. They told me that they had evaluated me for the first 30 days that I had been here. They told me, "You do not belong in the state mental hospital. Now, we have to work on getting you out of the hospital." The person in charge of finding me a place to live tried to tell me she had found a group home for me to live in. I told her, "NO WAY! I will not live in a group home. I need my own apartment." The woman tried to also tell me that someone had to oversee my money. Once again, I told her, "No way. I manage my own money! Nobody tells me where to go, what to do, how to do it, when to do it, or why I should or shouldn't do something! This is my life. I have been controlled by my dysfunctional family all my life. I lived at home until I got married. Then I had kids. After I got divorced, I had to play the "mother and father" role to my kids. Then, after that, I moved in with my dad. I then lived with my son for a short time after that. I have never lived on my own in my whole life. This is my life. I have my own place. I pay my own bills. I buy my own groceries, get my own medication, etc."

She tried to tell me that I would have my own place and that I would only have to go to the nurse's station to get my medication. I told her, "No way! I take my own medication without anybody controlling my medication." I told her I had been put in the mental hospital five times in two and a half months. There were no more mental hospitals. Nobody would ever control my life again! I told her if I did not get my own apartment, take my own pills, buy my own groceries, pay my own bills, etc., then I would stay there in the mental hospital.

The woman knew I was bound and determined to have my freedom. She left to do some research to figure out where I could go. A few weeks later, the woman talked to me. She told me that there was this one counseling group she found for me. I told her I did not need counseling. She told me the only way I could get out was to have this counseling group. She told me that I would have my own apartment, pay my own bills, buy my own groceries, etc. The only thing was that they would come and see me at my apartment a few days a week. I told her I did not need anybody. She assured me that the counseling group would not control me or my life. She told me this was the highest anybody could get to be on their own without supervision with this counseling group. She told me they would stand up for me if anybody tried to say I needed to go to the mental hospital again. I agreed to have that counseling group help me.

While I was in the mental hospital, I called the neurology doctor to make an appointment to see him so I could get my epilepsy medication. I also made an appointment with a medical doctor on my own while in the mental hospital. I had made plans to have my doctors all set up prior to getting out of the mental hospital. The staff thought that they had made these appointments with the doctors. When I told them I had called the doctor's office to make these appointments, they told me I wasn't supposed to do that; that was their responsibility. I told them I was responsible for taking care of my medical issues and getting my doctors to prescribe my medication to the pharmacy. Oh, once I found out the area I was going to live in, I had the doctors prescribe my medications to this pharmacy. When I saw my doctors at the doctor's appointments while I was still in the mental hospital, I asked them to prescribe my medication at this pharmacy area.

I met up with a woman in the counseling group. She oversaw helping their clients get housing. I couldn't get out of the mental hospital until I had a place to live. After we met and she knew more about me, she left. Before she left, she told me she would be finding an apartment for me to move into. About one week later, she contacted me and told me that she would be picking me up on Friday to look at this studio apartment. Well, Friday came, and she never showed up. I was so excited to look at the apartment and then have my hopes in despair. The next week, the woman contacted me. She told me her boss had told her that I could not live in an unsupervised apartment. So, she found an apartment for me that was supervised by staff. I told her no way! I had to have my own apartment with no supervision. She told me her boss had stopped her from letting me go look at the studio apartment. She told me that she had another person look at the apartment instead of me. I was disappointed by that.

This woman took me to the supervised apartment that they wanted me to live in. I was dumbfounded! I would only be having a room there instead of my own apartment. All the tenants shared the living room, dining room, and kitchen. I saw the room that they wanted me to live in. I was very upset. The room looked like a hotel room. It had just a bed, a microwave oven, a small rack to hang a few clothes on, and a bathroom. I told the woman, "No way! I will go back and live at the mental hospital if I have to live here. I was promised the studio apartment, but you lied to me and let somebody else look at it instead of me." The woman saw that I wasn't going to budge. She took me back to the mental hospital. A few days later, this woman contacted me again. She told me that she had convinced her boss to agree to let me be in a studio apartment. She said the same apartment complex that had the one studio she showed the other person had a second studio for rent now. She took me to see the studio apartment. It was huge, over four hundred square feet. I agreed to move into this studio apartment.

On my discharge day, the counseling group had a different person pick me up. She took me to the studio and put what little belongings I had in the studio. She then took me to the store to buy silverware, towels, blankets, etc., that I needed. A company brought me some necessary items, such as furniture. I finally got my freedom! I was living alone in my own apartment! Nobody got to tell me what to do, how to do it, when to do it, why I should or shouldn't do it, where I could and couldn't go, etc. I could come and go as I pleased. I could finally have my new life.

I was receiving SSDI monthly, and I knew exactly what amount of money I was receiving. The counseling service agreed to be on my lease and pay $100 toward my rent every month. Every month, I got a piece of paper and wrote down what bills I had to pay. I then estimated what the bills would cost me. I added all the estimated bills and came to a total. I had put a small amount of money aside each month to save up to get my driver's license in this state. I deducted the amount of my SSDI from the total amount of my estimated bills. I then came up with what amount I had left. I then went through what items I would need for the month. Some examples are shampoo, conditioner, laundry soap, laundry money, vitamins, paper towels, etc. I then estimated what each item would cost and added them all up. I would take what I had left after I had paid my bills and see if I had enough money to buy those items. Sometimes, my estimated prices were higher than the estimated money I had left over for the month. I would then decide what I could do without and come up with enough money to purchase the items that I needed. I had just a little over $60 left over for the whole month for myself. I figured I would divide the $60 by four weeks. I came up with $15 I could splurge on myself each week.

Note: I do not smoke, drink, or do drugs. If I did, I wouldn't have been able to afford the studio apartment.

There was a secondhand store just a few blocks away. They had specials on Monday on color items that didn't sell half off the previous week. They priced all those colored items at 99 cents. I found a recliner there that never sold for half off the week before. I asked the manager if I could get the recliner for 99 cents. She told me yes. The furniture was also 99 cents if it had last week's color tag at half off. So, I purchased the recliner for 99 cents. I also bought lamps, an end table, pictures, and other things there for 99 cents.

I would go to a restaurant close to home and purchase something to eat or drink. It felt good to sit there and relax. I started walking around the area to find a church nearby and found one to go to. I decided to go there for Sunday Services. I was only at the church for about a month when I found out that they had a room filled from the floor to the ceiling with boxes and bags of clothes, shoes, belts, etc. They had so many boxes and bags of donated items that you couldn't open the door all the way. You could not get inside the room because the room was stuffed with boxes and bags. Only one or two people could be at the door to look through a box. Then, they had to move that box to look at a different box. I couldn't believe how horrible it looked.

I had saved up enough money to go to the DMV and get my new driver's license in this state. I took the Rules of the Road book home so I could read over the Rules of the Road in this state. Once I was confident I could take the written test, I went to the DMV office and asked to take the test. The woman looked at my driver's license from my previous state. She saw that my driver's license was still good. She told me, "The test is hard. You might not pass it the first time, but you can come back and retake the test again." I was dumbfounded by what she said. I told her I would pass the test. She told me many people could not pass the test the first time. I was going to prove her wrong. I would pass the test. After I turned in the driver's test paper, the woman looked it over. I heard her say to another woman, "I gave her the hardest test, and she passed it." Why did everybody assume I could not succeed in life?

My son came to my studio to give me a kitten. I told him I could not have any animals because this place did not allow animals. I told him that besides that, I would need a Companion Pet Letter from my counseling service. My son told me to get a Companion Pet Letter from my counseling service. He left my studio a short time later. I called the counseling service to tell them I needed a Companion Pet Letter. I finally got the counseling service convinced that I could take care of the kitten's needs, and they gave me a Companion Pet Letter. I still found a way to be able to manage to pay my bills and to get the necessities needed for my kitten and me.

At church, I asked around and found out a church member was in charge of getting those boxes and bags gone through so they could start up a clothes closet. I knew I could get this room up and ready to become a clothes closet in no time. I went to the pastor and asked him if I could go through the boxes and bags of donated items and get that room up and ready to become the clothes closet.

The pastor told me that this one woman was in charge; I would have to ask her if she would let me go through the boxes and bags that were donated. I went to the church lady and asked her if I could go through the boxes and bags to get the clothes closet up and running. She told me I could and wished me luck. "You will never get through *all* the stuff," she said.

I went to the pastor and told him the church lady had told me I could go through the boxes and bags. I asked him if I could come every day that either he or the secretary was here for me to go through all the bags and boxes. The pastor told me I could. I went to the store and purchased about ten packages of ten hangers in each package. I went to work at the To Be Up and Running Clothes Closet. In five days, I had gone through all those boxes and bags that were in the room. I had all the adult clothes hanging up on the racks. The children's clothing was in boxes until the day the clothes closet opened up. That was when the children's clothes would be put on tables.

I showed the pastor what the new clothes closet looks like now. He was astonished at how everything was in order and how I had gone through everything in just five days' time. Fifty bags of donated items were donated every week to the clothes closet. The pastor only wanted the clothes closet open once a month for the homeless people. I told the pastor there was no way once a month was good enough. I told him there were so many people barely getting by in an apartment or house. They had kids. We had children's clothes here; we needed to help the community as well as the homeless. I finally got the pastor to realize the need was greater than just for the homeless. I went to work to advertise the clothes closet to the community. I put flyers in laundromats and grocery stores and gave flyers to people I saw on the street.

When I opened the clothes closet for people to come in, the secretary agreed to make coffee and bring coffee cups with cream and sugar to the clothes closet. She also had a pitcher of water she brought up. I made five peanut butter and jelly sandwiches to take to the clothes closet. I cut each sandwich into four pieces so more people would be able to have a snack if they were hungry. The pastor made several signs that said, "Clothes Closet Open." I had a church member who came every day to the clothes closet opening to help me. She would iron the clothes to make them look nice.

One day, I saw a group of five homeless guys (one who was a teenager) in an area. I went to them and told them about the clothes closet. Then, one day, the homeless teenager came into the clothes closet and handed me some lilac flowers. He gave them to me and thanked me for letting him know about the clothes closet. He said he needed clothes. He started coming frequently to the clothes closet after that.

A few months later, this homeless teenager came to the clothes closet upset. He said that somebody had stolen all of his clothing and college paperwork. I was shocked when he told me about his college paperwork. He told me he was going to college. He got himself some new clothes and left. The next day, this same homeless teenager came to the clothes closet crying. He said he was afraid to be outside anymore. He then told me somebody had thrown a rock on his head when he was sleeping the previous night. He needed to find some place to live. He asked the pastor for help, but he was of no assistance. I told the homeless teenager that he could live with me in my studio apartment. He was stunned to hear that offer. I told him, "You are going to college. You need some place to live so you can go to college and come home and do your college work." He was hesitant at first. A week later, he told me he would look at my studio and see what it looked like. After he saw my studio apartment, he agreed to move in with me. I told him that when he got his financial aid money, he would give me some money to stay there. He agreed on an amount to give me for each term.

The homeless teenager had been living on the streets for three years before he moved in with me. He had a terrible smell to him. He hadn't taken a bath in so long, so when he moved in with me, he took several baths a day to try to get the smell off of him. I would go to the clothes closet and find him different clothes, shoes, underwear, etc., that he needed so badly and bring those items home for him to wear. He was looking much nicer but he still had a bad smell to him. It would take time for the body odor to go away.

One day, this homeless teenager went to church service with me. He sat next to me. The church people around us were saying, "He stinks. Get him out of here." I told them, "You do not push people away from church because they smell." One day, after church service was over, the homeless teenager and I were walking out of church. To my surprise, I heard a young woman say, "Matthew, is that you?" The homeless teenager said, "Yes." Now, all the church members were astonished that this teenage girl knew Matthew. Then the teenage girl said, "Matthew used to come to church here when he was a kid. I remember his Adam's apple." After that, the church members started treating Matthew differently.

It was summertime now. The homeless teenager who moved in with me kept telling me every day to go to college. I told him I could not go to college; I had had brain surgery. They had removed all of my front left temporal lobe brain, including my memory. That was no excuse for this homeless teenager living with me. Every day, he would tell me once again to go to college. I kept telling him I could not go to college. I didn't know how to say or write my ABCs, 1, 2, 3, read, write, etc., after brain surgery. Finally, one day, this homeless teenager told me to just go take the test. "You don't know if you cannot go to college unless you take the test." That sparked something in me. I always wondered where my IQ was. My IQ was in the 30th percentile two years after brain surgery. It was eleven years since I had had brain surgery. I wondered where I was that day.

My neurosurgeon saw I could only put a first-grade puzzle together after brain surgery. The neurosurgeon told me that I wouldn't advance much more than that in ten years. It was now eleven years since my brain surgery.

229

Since I didn't know where the college was, the homeless teenager took me on the bus to go to the college to take the test. The college test took a while to do. When I answered all the questions, I turned it in to the staff. I waited in despair of whether I would be laughed at like I was laughed at back in my dysfunctional state and with my relatives back there. The staff person came to me and told me the final score of my test. The college staff told me, "Evelyn, you passed the college test! You can go to college." Oh, my God! My heart was racing with excitement. I couldn't believe that I had passed the college test when my IQ was in the 30th percentile just nine years ago.

Going to the mental hospital five times in two and a half months, and nine months after getting out of the state mental hospital, I was going to college.

"Nothing is more beautiful than a real smile that has struggled through tears."

— *Unknown*

Chapter Twelve

I was still filled with excitement from passing the college test for the first time with 100% of my front left temporal lobe removed, which included removing my memory from my brain surgery eleven years ago. I remember my neurosurgeon (brain surgeon) told me 11 years ago that I wouldn't advance much more than putting a "first-grade puzzle" together ten years after my brain surgery. Well, 11 years later, I went much further than just being able to put a first-grade puzzle together.

I went to the college to ask them to help me apply for financial aid and grants. Once financial aid was granted to me, I went to the college to look at what I wanted to major in. I decided to major in Business Management. The college staff helped me figure out what classes to take for my first term. Since I had informed the college staff that I had never owned or used a computer, they told me I had to take a Beginner's Course in Computer Class for the first term. I also took a math class, an English class, and one other class for the first term of college. However, I went to talk to the college president to let him know that I needed more time to do the test than most of the other students in college due to the brain surgery I had.

This college had no disability department. Because of that, I had to see the college president.

The president told me that I needed to have a doctor's note to verify that I needed extra time to do a test. I decided to contact my neurology doctor, whom I had just started seeing. My neurology doctor had only seen me once since I moved to this state. This doctor had only known me for nine months. I saw this neurology doctor right before I got out of the state mental hospital nine months ago. Since I had a lot on my plate to get ready for my first term of college, I told my new neurology doctor to fax the letter to my college, saying that I needed extra time to take a test.

Well, when I went to see the president of the college, he looked scared of me! I asked him if he had received the fax from my neurology doctor saying that I needed extra time to do a test in college. He said yes with a scary look. I asked him what my neurology doctor had written. He told me my neurology doctor had stated that I had a "chronic mental illness." I was both shocked and furious that my new neurology doctor would write something like that. The neurology doctor was to write a statement about my brain surgery and how I needed extra time to take a test because of my brain surgery. The college president told me that he recommended that I take just two classes for the first term. I told him, "No way. I take four classes for the first term, or I will not go to college here!" The president kept trying to persuade me to just take two classes for the first term, but I refused to. I kept telling him I would take four classes in the first term or that I would not go to college there! The president gave in and allowed me to take four classes for the first term.

I never had cable or internet at my studio, so I needed to call the cable company and get cable and internet at my apartment. I would be paying my Cable and internet bills with my financial aid money. Since I had never had a computer my whole Life, I had the homeless teenager help me find a place to purchase a computer for college. He went with me and recommended what type of laptop I should purchase. I only had a house phone that I paid around $14 a month for prior to going to college. Since I was going to college now, I needed a cell phone. I found a cell phone company and got a plan with them.

Even though I was getting ready to go to college, I was still running the clothes closet twice a week for a few hours. I would go early in the morning to the church to prep to open the clothes closet with this guy who was willing to run the clothes closet for the whole four hours that it was open. I watched the clock for when I had to leave to take the city bus to go to college. I always left at least 30 minutes earlier than I should have. You never know what the traffic is going to be like going to college. I preferred to be early rather than late for class. I went to church on the weekends to go through the 50 bags of clothes for the clothes closet every weekend.

I started college, and it felt great going to college. However, I was afraid to ask questions in class since I had been treated horribly by my dysfunctional family. I will never forget the humiliation I received from my two adult nephews when I was trying to learn what a knife, fork, or spoon was, or that a chair had arms, legs, and a back, etc. That didn't include learning to speak, say my ABCs, or counting, etc. I had many questions to ask in class. Every time I raised my hand to ask a question, I always told the instructor, "I have a stupid question." The instructors would always tell me, "There is no such thing as a stupid question." You have no idea how relieved I felt being able to ask questions without being looked upon as a freak! I went to the college library to get help learning how to use the computer to do my college work. My instructors would even spend time after class explaining anything I had a question about.

My first term of college was over. I received my grades for those four classes. My grades for two of the College classes for the first term were both As, while my grades for the other two classes were both Bs! I had a 3.5 grade point average in college for my first term despite having 100% of my front left temporal lobe brain removed, which included removing my memory.

I noticed during my first term of college that I had to put some cleaning chores aside to focus on college. Now that I had a two-week break from college before my second term started, I decided to thoroughly clean my studio. I pulled out furniture, the stove, the refrigerator, etc., and cleaned. I also went through my cupboards and organized them. I went through all my college paperwork from the classes that I took for the first term. I decided that this would be my new tradition: I would thoroughly clean my studio after each term of college was over. I basically did spring cleaning every three months.

I signed up for my second term in college. I took four classes for the second term in college. The homeless teenager and I were both taking the bus to get to college. We got along great. He treated me as if I were his mom or aunt. He would not let anybody say anything bad about me. He had told me that some people would say bad things about me. He told me that he told them, "What you are saying about her is not true! I live with her; I know what she is like. She is not what you say she is." I finally had somebody who would stand up for me. I never had anybody stand up for me like that before.

I went to the college library to get help learning how to use the computer. The hardest part of learning on the computer was Copy and Paste. The college library staff showed me how to click Copy and then close that tab to go to Word. I was scared I had lost what I was going to print up. The library staff tried to tell me not to be so hard on myself. They would then click Paste, and what I was trying to save was now in Word. I was shocked! I would tell the staff, "It is like magic. It disappears and then reappears again." It took me two years not to fear copying and pasting.

When my second term of college was over, I received my grades for the second term. Again, my grades were all As and Bs. I was getting confidence in myself now. The thought came back now that I was in the college of my wicked sister, bragging about her having a nice home, nice cars, money in the bank, and a good-paying job. And then she would tell me, "Look at you, Evelyn. You are a nobody. You do not have a brain." I remember telling my wicked sister, "Whoopy ding. Big Deal. You passed a test to be in the medical field. If I wanted to go to college to be in the medical field, I could also pass the test, but I do not want to go in the medical field."

College was important for me. I wanted to learn as much as I could. Remember, just five days after I had my four brain surgeries in two weeks, I came home instead of getting rehabilitated. My state insurance would not let me be rehabilitated where I had my brain surgeries (out of state). My state insurance wanted me to be rehabilitated in a city in my state that was five hours away from my brain surgeon. I refused to be five hours away from my brain surgeon in case I needed to see him.

Back to the neurology doctor. What he wrote to the college never left my mind. I was not chronically mentally ill! Nobody knew that was a false accusation started by my dysfunctional state and dysfunctional family. But now I was out of that dysfunctional state and away from my dysfunctional family. I was bound and determined to get justice for what my neurology doctor wrote to my college. I made some phone calls to see what justice I could get out of this ordeal that the neurology doctor had put me through.

After a few phone calls, I was told that the HIPAA Law was broken by what the neurology doctor wrote about me to the college. I was told to contact the HIPAA office. I had never heard of the HIPAA Law before, but I sure was going to find out and get justice! I Googled where the HIPAA offices were near me. I found out that the HIPAA office was over in the next state. I called the HIPAA office and told them what happened. The woman at the HIPAA office asked me if the incident had occurred within the last six months. I told her yes; it had not been six months yet. She asked me to send her all the documents I had and the doctor's statement that was written to the college about my chronic mental illness. I got all the paperwork together and mailed it to the HIPAA office. I called in a few weeks to make sure the HIPAA office had received what I had mailed them. They said yes. I felt a sigh of relief. Now, I could focus on getting ready for my third term of college.

I decided that my financial aid money would go toward buying three months' supply of cleaning supplies (laundry soap, bath soap, paper towels, toilet paper, softener, shampoo, conditioner, etc.). I also decided to use my financial aid to put three months' worth of laundry money aside in a safe place. I also had to purchase college supplies for each term. I decided to stock up on school supplies in July/August when the stores have "Back to School" supplies on sale. I would purchase folders, tablets, a lot of pens, rulers, etc., for me to last one year in college. So I would purchase at least 16 folders, 16 tablets, three to four packs of ten pens (black, blue, and red), many different colors of highlighters, etc.

One day, I had taken the bus. At one of the bus stops, there was a group of kids who had just gotten out of school. Amongst these kids was a teenage girl who was lying on the sidewalk. One off-duty bus driver who was on the bus went out to check on the teenage girl. The off-duty bus driver said to the bus driver on duty, "She's breathing, and she has a pulse, but she will not wake up." The off-duty bus driver started shaking this teenager and slapping both sides of her cheeks, saying, "Wake up. Come on, wake up." I knew right away that the teenager was epileptic. I got off my bus seat and went to the bus drivers (on-duty and off-duty drivers) and said, "She is epileptic! You do not shake or slap her. She's having an epileptic seizure." The bus drivers listened to me and put the teenager on her side. Just a few minutes later, she was having a convulsion! I said once again, "She is epileptic." The people on the bus told me, "You already said that." I told them, "Yes, I told you she was epileptic when she was unconscious. Now that she is having a convulsion, I am reinstating the fact that she is an epileptic!"

The Fire Department came to the scene. I went to one of the firemen and told him, "I think she is epileptic." The fireman asked me if I knew her. I told him, "No. I am an epileptic. I know she is an epileptic." The fireman asked me what her name was. I told him I did not know. I told him to look in the school backpack and find out what her name was and then call her school; her school would know if she was an epileptic. The fireman then ran to the teenager's side. After a few minutes, the ambulance came. Once both bus drivers were on the bus, the off-duty bus driver sat near me. I told the off-duty bus driver, "She is EPILEPTIC." The off-duty bus driver told me, "No, she isn't. These kids nowadays are doing drugs." I was upset with his assumption. Then, just a few minutes later, the on-duty bus driver told the off-duty bus driver, "No. She *is* epileptic. They got her medical records."

Once again, an epileptic was treated miserably. People assume that an epileptic is a "Drug User"! People who do drugs are Mocking an Epileptic! A drug user thinks it is "COOL" to get this funny feeling like an Epileptic! Drug users are Endangering Epileptics' lives for being treated with respect! In today's world, it is dangerous to be an epileptic. Why? A Drug User can go to a "Safe Place" and get the "High Feeling" like the Epileptics experience, but Epileptics "Do Not" have control over being in a "Safe Place" to have an Epileptic Seizure! An Epileptic could be "Crossing" the street and go into a Convulsion!!! Because Epileptics have been Hidden, Ashamed to be around, and considered "Demonic" all this time, the community continues to "Shut Out" Epileptics. I have been told that the medical team doesn't know if the person is an epileptic or overdosed on drugs, so the medical staff give the epileptic "NARCAN"! If the person doesn't respond to NARCAN, then the medical team takes them to the ER. Epileptics have been treated unfairly since the beginning. First, they are considered as demonic. You have no idea how horrible epileptics are treated unless you are an epileptic! There are rights for all races, cultures, gays, lesbians, drug and alcohol users, etc., but why are EPILEPTICS treated like TRASH?

I have learned even more about how miserably epileptics have been treated and still are today to some degree. I was at the store talking to a customer about my plans to start a Re-

Learning Center for people with brain damage. I then told her about the four brain surgeries I had had in two weeks' time due to my epileptic seizures. I told her I had no family or community support, nor did I have any rehabilitation. I explained to her how horrific it was that epileptics were considered demonic and drug addicts today. Well, that was when the woman told me that when she was in medical school, she was told in class about epileptics. She told me that epileptics were put in the mental institution!! She was told the medical field didn't know how to treat epileptics, so they put EPILEPTICS in a MENTAL INSTITUTION!!! She said she and her other classmates wanted to go visit this mental institution that the epileptics were put in, but they were told that that "part" of the mental institution was "CLOSED DOWN." She said nobody, not even the medical students, could go into the area where the epileptics were put in the mental institution! Why put an EPILEPTIC in a mental institution because they are EPILEPTICS?

What living conditions were epileptics living in? Were epileptics tortured in the mental institution? Were they put on psychiatric medication and not taking epileptic medications? *Was that why I was put in the mental institution five times in two and a half months?* Remember, my brother had epilepsy and was in the nursing home. The doctors at the nursing home told my brother he was psychotic, and the doctor took his epileptic medications away from him and drugged him up with psychosis medication! Not too long afterward, my brother had nonstop epileptic seizures!! It is too late now. My brother lost his memory due to the seizures. Every time a person has an epileptic seizure, part of their brain dies!!!

Oh! Did you know that the neurology doctors who see epileptic patients who haven't had an epileptic seizure for at least one year are told by their neurology doctor that they, the epileptic, are being ordered to "go off" their epileptic medications?! Why?? Every time an epileptic has an epileptic seizure, part of their brain DIES!! The more seizures an epileptic has, the more their brain dies!! Look at what happened to my brother. The nursing home doctor took him off his seizure medications and drugged him up with psychosis medication!! My brother then had nonstop epileptic seizures. My brother's brain was so DESTROYED by having those seizures that he couldn't comprehend what anybody said to him! He didn't even know he had family anymore (a nurse at the nursing home told me that).

Why don't diabetics and heart patients who "are not" having either a diabetic attack or a heart attack go off their medications??? Why is it more important for diabetics and heart patients to stay on their medications but epileptics are told they must go off their medications because they are not having an epileptic attack??? Once again, I will reinstate that whenever an epileptic has a seizure, another part of their brain DIES!!! A person who is dying of a heart attack is still alive. Their brain is still alive. However, if an epileptic has an epileptic seizure, they have a higher risk of dying because they will be BRAIN

DEAD!!! A heart patient is not brain dead if they die from a heart attack. There are no brain transplants for epileptics like heart patients having heart transplants!!! I had a neurology doctor in the past tell me that there are over "100" different types of epileptic seizures. I had four different types of epileptic seizures prior to my brain surgery!!!

Epileptics have been considered demonic, crazy, drug users, etc.!! It is time that people stand up for EPILEPTIC RIGHTS!!!

All epileptics must have the following free to them:

1. *Free medical visits to the neurology doctors and any other doctors they need*
2. *Free medications! Epileptics need their epileptic medications. One prescription of epileptic medication will cost around $400-$600 per month just for one medication!!*
3. *Free EEG test*
4. *Free CAT scans*
5. *Free MRI test done*
6. *Free blood work done to see where their medication levels are at*
7. *Free brain surgery!!!*
8. *Etc.!!!*

Once again, I will reinstate: why does every culture, race, gays, lesbians, bisexuals, drag queens, etc. have rights but

EPILEPTICS are put on the back burner, not to be seen? Where are epileptics' right????

I kept in touch with the HIPAA lady about my case with my neurology doctor, who broke the HIPAA law on me. In a few months, the HIPAA lady told me that the person in charge of all the medical staff there told her that "they" (the medical staff) broke their policy. The HIPAA woman told me she told the person, "No, you did not break your policy; you broke the federal policy." This person in charge of the medical staff there was confused, I guess. Everybody in the medical field seemed to think that they could broadcast to anybody anything about the patients they saw. The HIPAA woman sent me the paperwork after her findings were done. I got justice for the torture that the doctor had put me through, but I wasn't finished there. The HIPAA law was not being enforced in any of the medical fields. I had a few more encounters I had to endure to make sure that this HIPAA law was enforced at all times!

My next encounter for justice for the doctor breaking the HIPAA law on me was contacting an attorney. Every attorney I spoke to told me they would not represent me. They said that the doctors always won when they broke the HIPAA law. Finally, one attorney told me to contact this one attorney; he represented people who had had the HIPAA law broken. I called this attorney and made an appointment. I went there with all my paperwork, from the doctor's statement to all the forms I had from the HIPAA office. I told the attorney that the HIPAA office found that the doctor had broken the HIPAA law. My attorney wanted to make a copy of all the paperwork. He said he never knew that the HIPAA office would enforce the HIPAA law.

After my attorney had looked over all the paperwork, he told me that the doctor had been found guilty by the HIPAA office. He said he didn't have to prove anything. He told me that I would win the lawsuit against the doctor for breaking the HIPAA law when we went to court.

I decided to settle for a smaller amount out of court so I could focus on college. Even though I had won this battle, I wasn't finished with broadcasting the HIPAA law. I went to the website and looked up all the HIPAA offices in the U.S. I wrote down all the addresses of the HIPAA offices (over 20 different offices in the U.S back then). There was one HIPAA office for every three to four states. I put all these HIPAA addresses and the states they represented in a Word document. I printed it up and saved it.

Not long after I won the lawsuit, I had this class in college for which I had to do a speech on something for the final term. I knew exactly what my speech was going to be on: the HIPAA Law. Well, I gave my speech in class about it. Absolutely nobody knew anything about the HIPAA law. I told the class that the HIPAA law was a federal law. After my speech, I handed out a sheet of paper with all the HIPAA offices in the U.S, their addresses, and the states they represented. Students in class all had stories to tell of the HIPAA law being broken on either them or one of their family members or friends. I reinstated the HIPAA law is a Federal Law. I wasn't done talking about the HIPAA law there. I spread the word about it being a federal law. I explained to them what the HIPAA law was if they asked me.

I had more copies of the HIPAA offices and their addresses with me. When I went to the doctor's office and witnessed or overheard somebody talking about the doctor or medical team saying this or that about them or someone else without their permission, I would give them information on the HIPAA law. I explained that the HIPAA law was a federal law. The doctor/medical team was breaking the HIPAA law, and we needed to keep contacting the Federal HIPAA Office to get the doctors and the medical team to stop breaking the HIPAA law. Well, nowadays, every time you go to the doctor's office, they ask you (supposed to) if you want a "copy" of the HIPAA law. I have been told that everybody in the medical field today must take a class on HIPAA law every so often. Did my boldness in spreading the word of the HIPAA law to so many people bring it to all medical offices to inform you of your HIPAA rights and ask you if you want a copy of the HIPAA law?

***

Coming back to college, I took a math class for one term. This math class was not a basic math class. I had already taken basic math and Algebra classes. I received As and Bs in these classes. Now, however, I was taking a more serious math class called

"Business Math." I knew I had to be serious with this class. To my surprise, I never had to take any Business Math homework home with me to work on. The day that there was a test in Business Math, I would just browse through the book and look it over (just like I did in Algebra class in high school). After browsing through the chapter quickly, the instructor handed out the test papers to work on. To my astonishment, I received an A on my test paper. For the whole term, I never had to take any homework home for Business Math, and on every test I took, I received an A. My final grade for Business Math for the term was an A. My other classes were also As and Bs. I had one term in college when I was on the Dean's List. I had an IQ in the 30th percentile two years after brain surgery, and ten years later (12 years since my four brain surgeries), I received an A in Business Math and got on the Dean's List. What an accomplishment! I went to college because I allowed a homeless teenager (going to college) to move in with me so he could be safe. This homeless teenager had confidence in me. He also kept encouraging me to go to college until I finally took the college test and passed it the first time.

A different class I took at college was a business class. I learned many things about managing a business. The instructor told us to design our own business cards and have a "20-second" elevator speech that we would tell people we encountered about the business we planned to start up. You start up the conversation about your business plan with people who could be on an elevator stairwell, bump into somebody at the store, doctor's office, etc.

The instructor told us that before we walked away from these people, we needed to give them one of our business cards.

For the final assignment for the term, students were to write a business plan for themselves or for a job that they worked at. I took into consideration that I was going to write a business plan for my "own business." After taking time to think about what business I would want to start up, I came up with starting up a Re-Learning Center for people with brain damage. I had hands-on experience having the mentality of a young child (not knowing how to speak, count, add or subtract, say my ABCs, etc.) to be in college with over a 3.5 GPA. I even got on the Dean's List at college. I wrote up my business plan and presented it to the class. I told the class my Re- Learning Center would be a non-profit. I explained that people with brain damage couldn't afford to pay to attend the Re-Learning Center otherwise. The instructor liked my presentation for the Re-Learning Center. I received a high score for my final presentation.

Note: I still plan on starting up a Re-Learning Center for people with brain damage.

The homeless teenager was starting to skip college classes. He finally dropped out of college. He went back to his old ways prior to moving in with me. I told him he had to leave if he didn't go to college. He kept finding ways to sell me stuff so he had money. I told him no. That was his; I did not want it. I went to get the manager and let her know I was having issues with the homeless teenager. I told her I had asked him to move out, but he would not.

I told her I would not let him cause issues here while he was living with me. The manager talked to the homeless teenager. After he talked with the manager, he agreed to move out, but he wanted money from me. I refused to give him any money. He hadn't been paying any rent for a few months now. The manager told me that if I wanted him out, I should just give him $100. Since I had just received my financial aid money, I gave the homeless teenager $100. The homeless teenager said he found somewhere else to move to, got his stuff, and left.

The college I had been attending for a few years was raising the tuition fee very high to go to college there. I was left with very little money after the college tuition fees were paid. Many college students left this college due to the high tuition fees. I finally decided to find a different college due to the high tuition fees. This college had been a college for over 100 years. Why was this college becoming greedy with the high rise in tuition fees? I finally found a different college to go to. I gave this new college my sealed envelope with my grades inside it. I got help applying for financial aid and signing up for classes there. This college charged way less than the college I left. This college was also closer to my home. I wouldn't have to leave the house as early as I did with the other college I left. I was now going to my new college for the first time there. I was still going to the clothes closet to prep to open the place in the morning for about one hour before I had to leave to get on the bus to go to college.

Back to the clothes closet, one day, when I was working in the clothes closet, this guy threatened me. I went to the pastor and told him the guy helping me at the clothes closet was threatening me. Both the pastor and I knew that this guy had made threats before. He had told me at the clothes closet several times that he was going to "burn" the church down. I would go to the pastor and tell him about the threats this guy would make to our church. I told the pastor that this guy did not go to our church, and he was threatening to burn the church down. The pastor would take him aside and talk to him, then bring him back to the clothes closet, and he would be calmed down. So now that this guy was threatening me, I went to the pastor and told him this guy was threatening me, and then I left the clothes closet until the next week. When I returned the next week, I saw the pastor walking out of the church building. I asked him if the guy was in the clothes closet. The pastor told me yes. He said he had talked to the guy and that everything was fine. After the pastor said that, he left the church. Nobody else was in the church except for this guy and me.

One of the many rolling clothes racks that I had purchased to put the baby clothes, men's and women's tank tops and shorts on, etc., was broken by this guy. He decided to throw all the clothes off the other clothes rack to put the clothes that were on the rack that he broke. I told him not to throw those clothes off the rack; they belonged there. He insisted he needed the rack because he had broken the other rack. He started getting a temper with me. He threatened me again. After that, he took a large coffee pumper (to keep the coffee hot) and put it on top of his head. He was looking right at me, huffing and puffing with the coffee warmer above his head, still looking meaningful. I told him, "You do not hit me in the head with that coffee pumper."

He finally put the coffee pumper down. He then, out of nowhere, started assaulting me! I had my arms down at my sides when he grabbed me and did a tight bear hug. He squeezed tight with his bear hug tight assault. I couldn't get my arms out to defend myself. I kept trying to get my arms out of the tight bear hug. I finally got one arm out, and I squeezed his cheeks tightly. He then squeezed my sides even tighter. My sides were hurting badly. I kept squeezing his cheeks until he finally let go. He started throwing things all over the place and having a temper. I called the police. The police came when the secretary was coming inside the church. She told the cops she would take care of it, so the police left.

The pastor came back. He heard I had called the police. The pastor first got rid of the guy, and then he came to me and said, "Evelyn, since you called the police, you have to leave too." The pastor kicked me out of the church. He knew the guy had threatened me the previous week, and yet he had done nothing about it. Now, this week, the guy assaulted me, and the pastor threw me out of church. I went home, hurting severely. I called the police when I got home. I told them how my sides hurt severely and that I had an injured finger from the guy assaulting me. The officer took pictures of the injury. I told the officer I knew where this guy lived because I had taken him home before. I gave the officer the address where he lived. I went to the ER and told them of my injury. The ER doctor refused to take X-rays. He told me even if I had broken ribs, there was nothing that could be done for broken ribs. I was hurting severely, and the doctor couldn't care less about the serious assault I had encountered.

I went home in severe pain. I thought that I could talk to the church members and let them know about the assault when I went to church on Sunday. When I told the church members about the guy assaulting me in the clothes closet, and I was hurting severely, all the church members told me was, "Forgive him for what he did to you." I was stunned by the church members' response. I used to go out for breakfast with these church ladies once a month prior to the assault I had encountered by this guy. How could absolutely nobody care less about the severe assault this guy did to me? Was it because it did not happen to them?

After not even the church members could care less about the severe assault I had encountered by this guy at the clothes closet, I no longer went to that church anymore! After the assault, I had nightmares every night of this church. The nightmares of this church was so severe that I would wet myself while I was in the nightmare. I would wake up to my night clothes being severely wet from urine. My nightmares of the church continued every night. I had to start wearing adult diapers in bed because I would wet myself every night because of my regular nightmares of the church.

After being assaulted at the church by this guy, I knew if I didn't find somewhere else to volunteer to work very soon, I would be scared to work again. I heard my neighbors talking about this one second-hand store that had many volunteers. I asked the neighbors where this store was. They told me where this second-hand store was. I drove there and applied to volunteer there. I was hired to be a volunteer there. They told me I would be hanging clothes up, pricing the clothes, etc. I told the manager that I had just left a place where I volunteered because I was assaulted by a guy who volunteered there. The manager assured me that I would be safe here to volunteer.

I noticed that I could only work for about 20 minutes before my sides started hurting severely. I told the manager I had to go sit down and rest due to the injury I received from the assault. The manager told me that was fine. Every 20 minutes, I had to go sit down and take a break for nearly half an hour before the pain subsided enough to go out and hang up clothes again. One day, a customer approached me and said to me, "You look like you are mad at the clothes."

I told her I was not mad. I then explained to her that I was in severe pain from the assault I received from the clothes closet that I volunteered at by another volunteer.

The customer looked concerned and said, "Oh no, I am sorry. I shouldn't have said anything to you."

I told her I was glad she asked me. "If you hadn't asked me, you would have left the store thinking I was mad."

She told me to continue talking about the trauma I encountered from this guy. "The more you talk about it, the better off you will be," she said.

I told her, "Okay, thank you."

I was still going to college while I was dealing with these nightmares. I was fine during the day while I was awake if I stayed away from everybody from this church. I would get justice for the neglect from the pastor and the church. Absolutely nobody cared about my injuries. I was kicked out of church for calling the police. Then, I was told to forgive him for what he did to me. How cold-hearted could this church be toward any church member? I made some phone calls to find an attorney and eventually found one. I gave the attorney the police report and the medical records I had and told him of my nonstop nightmares of the church. I told the attorney that my nightmares of the church were so bad that I wet myself in bed every night! I went into detail with the attorney about what happened and how the pastor kicked me out of church for calling the police. This attorney took my case.

Well, I went to the nearby grocery store one day and saw one of the church members. She came toward me and said very loudly, "So, you think you can sue the church?" I asked her how she knew. She told me the pastor had broadcasted that I was suing the church at church service. Then she said while pointing her finger at me,

"Ha, guys (saying loudly for all customers to hear her); she thinks she can sue the church."

This church woman wouldn't leave me alone in the grocery store. I finally got out of the grocery store. I went home and called my attorney. I told him of the encounter I had had at the grocery store with one of the church members. My attorney was very upset. He told me the pastor was not allowed to talk about the lawsuit I had against them. He told me he was going to call the church's attorney ASAP! The pastor kept refusing to settle the lawsuit. He thought I was suing because I wanted to get paid for working at the clothes closet. I was not suing because I worked without pay; I was suing because of the neglect and assault I encountered. I wouldn't give in. I was going to win this battle I had encountered. Finally, the church's attorney and my attorney agreed on a settlement.

I had just enough settlement money to move to a different area and purchase the used furniture that I needed for this apartment. One of those furniture items was a bed. You see, while I lived in the studio apartment, I slept on the recliner. I refused to have my studio look like a hotel room because I never had a bedroom. So, I needed to purchase a bed for my bedroom now. I needed to move far away from where I was living to stop having these terrible nightmares of the church every night. I had to be far enough away from this church and the church members. I found a two-bedroom apartment that was about five miles away in this city. I went to the furniture store to purchase a bed, dresser, couch, end tables, coffee table, etc., with my settlement money for my two-bedroom apartment. The furniture store delivered the furniture to my new two-bedroom apartment. My son helped with one of the moves. Other than that, I had found some people to help me move the rest of my stuff to my two-bedroom apartment. I found some people who were willing to help me finish moving. Of course, I paid them to help me move.

This new apartment had a swimming pool, activity room, and a sauna for women and another for men. My rent would only be $25 more a month for this two-bedroom apartment than the studio I had been living in. You see, my studio rent was jumping up $300 more per month the next month. Of course, given that my rent had jumped up $300 while living in the studio apartment with the new rent increase or an extra $25 more (than the new studio apartment) while living in the two-bedroom apartment, I was tighter on my finances. I had just $25 left over from my Social Security check every month after paying my rent.

I now had to figure out how to pay all my bills and get all the supplies I needed for three months with my financial assistance. I was shocked when I received a notice of how much financial assistance I was going to receive after all my tuition was paid. I had more than enough money left over from financial assistance to pay three months of bills for all my Cable/internet, utilities, phone service, etc. I roughly estimated how much my utility bill would be for three months, and then I would pay for three months for my utility bill. The same went for my cable/internet, phone, etc. I even went to the bank and got three months' worth of laundry coins so

I could do my laundry for the next three months. After I had paid all my bills for three months, I went through my house and wrote down what items I needed to purchase to last for three months. I then went to the stores and purchased the items that I would need to purchase to last for the next three months.

Now that I had figured out how to manage to pay my bills with my rent jumping up $300 more per month (if I lived in the studio or a two-bedroom apartment), I could rest assured that I could focus on college once again. I only had $25 left over every month after paying my rent with my Social Security check, but where there is a need, there is a way to thanks to be God. Now that I had time and everything was managed, I decided to meet and spend time with my new neighbors. I made friends living in this apartment complex. We were like family. Everybody looked out for everybody. If one of us had a need, there usually was a neighbor who was there to either talk to us or help us out.

Back to college. I received mostly As and Bs in my classes; I had just one or two Cs since I had enrolled in college. I noticed something with each first day of the term in this new college. I had a college bag on wheels that I rolled to each class. When I walked toward the door to my new class on the first day, I encountered a few students standing there asking me, "Are you the instructor?" I was surprised by them thinking I was the instructor. I would tell them, "No, I am not the instructor. I am just a student here like you." Here, I had gone a long way from having 100% of my front left temporal lobe brain removed 14 years ago to now being asked if I was an instructor for the class in college. I was told by my Neurosurgeon that I would not advance much more than putting a "First Grade Puzzle" together in ten years to 14 years later when I was asked if I was an instructor. It was through the grace of God that I had accomplished so much thus far after 100% of my front left temporal lobe brain was removed.

"Let your light shine before others, so that they may see your good works and give glory to your Father in heaven."

— Matthew 5:16

Chapter Thirteen

While I was still living in the studio apartment, I took the bus to go to the store. I was at the traffic lights with other pedestrians. When the "Walk" sign came on, everybody started crossing the street. Since I had had six ankle surgeries so far, I walked slower when crossing the street. Prior to crossing the street, I looked at the cars at the red light to make sure they were stopping. There was a car about one block away. I knew this car would see the red light and stop. I had just gotten on the crosswalk a few feet when the car hit me hard on the outer left side of my leg. I fell on the hood of the car. I screamed, "Oh my GOD!" I saw stars. My legs were hanging down near the tires of the car. I tried to keep my legs up in the air so they didn't get caught in the tires of this car.

The car kept moving. The driver wanted to take a right turn on red. How could she not hear me fall on the hood of her car? The car kept moving with me on top of the car's hood. I was looking inside the windshield of her car (still seeing stars). She was looking to her left while I was on the right side of her car. I screamed loudly, "You f….. b….!" The woman looked out her windshield and saw me on the hood of her car. Once she saw me on the hood of her car, she stopped her car.

I was hurting badly. Nobody (other drivers or pedestrians) came to see how injured I was. I needed to get off the car. My leg and back were hurting me badly. I was on the hood of the car for several minutes. I couldn't take the pain anymore. Nobody came to my aid, nor did the driver come out of her car and see how I was! The driver just looked at me while I was on the hood of her car. I was scared. I decided to just try to get myself off the hood of the car myself since nobody, not even the driver who hit me, came to my aid. I finally got out of the car by myself, hurting badly.

Now, I was terrified of crossing the street to go to the store. When I got the courage to try to cross the street, I double-checked to make sure no cars were moving. I started walking across the street, limping. The woman who had hit me with her car put her head out of the car window and said, "I am sorry," and then drove off! About five minutes later, four cop cars with sirens roaring came to the scene. I was across the street by then. I was scared and terrified. The cops never really looked for the injured victim – me. They stayed on the other side of the street. I was scared to speak up. I had nearly gotten killed!

I went to sit down at a restaurant and get off my legs. I called the police station. I told them that I got hit by a car. I told them the driver had driven off and I was hurting badly. I told the dispatcher where I was. The dispatcher said she would get an officer to come to the restaurant and talk to me. I waited and waited for nearly an hour, but no cop or ambulance came to my aid. For the next two years, I had severe pain in my upper leg constantly.

I decided to work at the same restaurant that I worked in prior to moving away. I was still going to college while I was working part-time at this restaurant. I had ten years of experience in this restaurant. I knew every aspect of this restaurant and how it ran. Remember, I helped the restaurant that failed inspection three times to pass the final inspection without the managers telling me what to do. Remember, the managers failed the inspections three times in a row. The final inspection score, for which I did all the cleaning, organizing, co-dating, etc., scored 96 out of 100.

Well, I found out soon enough that this restaurant in this other state was way different. Every employee in the kitchen had a different culture than me. They spoke their language constantly in the kitchen. When any food needed to be cooked, sandwiches made, or any food needed for the dressing table, it was all spoken in "their language"! How could I be part of the team when they would not speak English? I had a difficult time re-learning English after brain surgery. Now, I was around the crew that I worked with who refused to speak English in the kitchen. They knew English; they just "preferred" to speak their language! When I told them I did not know their language and needed them to speak English, they told me in English, "Then you will have to learn to speak our language." How? I was in college learning. I couldn't overload my brain by learning their language. I had a very hard time just relearning my own language – English – after brain surgery.

In no time, I realized that speaking their language wasn't the only issue there. The dishwasher was broken, and the owner refused to get it fixed. I then realized that the sink that the dishes were to be done in, since the dishwasher was broken, had hardly any hot water coming out of the water faucet. I found out you had to get the hot water from where the mop bucket got its hot water. You had to use a bucket to fill up with hot water and then pour that bucket of hot water into the sink. Oh, wait! Do you think that was bad? There was even worse. When you emptied the sinks after doing the dishes, you had to let the water go out very slowly. Why? Because there was a hole in the "grease trap." If the water got up too high in the grease trap while draining, the grease trap leaked out the greasy water onto the floor. Now, you had a flood on the floor of greasy water. The owner refused to fix the hole in the grease trap either.

Then, one night, one of the employees who spoke a different language was cleaning the grill with a liquid cleaner. You lay a grill towel on the grill and poured water on top of the grill towel. Once you were done with the scraper cleaning the grill, you used a squeegee to take all the cleaner off the grill. You then put a small amount of oil on the grill. You were then to take the squeegee and the scrapper back to the sink and clean it. After that, you were to get new grill towels so you could lay the scraper on them. Well, none of the tools nor grill towels were being taken away to be cleaned and replaced with clean utensils and grill towels. Once the employee was done cleaning the grill with the grill cleaner, she put the squeegee and scraper back in their resting place without cleaning the utensils! That meant that the grill cleaner was still on the utensils. Now, they were cooking meat on the clean grill but using the utensils with some grill cleaner on the utensils. There was a very high risk that the grill cleaner was on the meat that was being served to the customers!

I went to the manager and told her what this employee had done. The manager approached this employee. The employee said to the manager, "I have been here for three years. I know what I am doing. Evelyn is new. She hasn't been here very long. She doesn't know things here yet." I wanted to jump in and tell this employee I had "ten years of experience" working in this restaurant.

I have heard from citizens in the city that they will never go back to that restaurant again. They said they got sick eating there. I heard this same complaint from many citizens in this city about this one restaurant.

One day, in one of my business classes, the instructor was talking about how when you run a business, you must have a certain percentage of different cultures, sexes, disability employees, etc., working at your business. It was the law. After I heard this from my instructor, I went to work and told an employee who was not the same race as the group in the kitchen that this restaurant was breaking the law. They were to have a certain percentage of each culture. I told him the employees here were over 95% of one culture. I told him they all spoke their own language in the kitchen instead of speaking English. I told him, "This is America. You speak English at work."

One of the workers who spoke the other language was in the breakroom listening to what I said. She ran to the manager, complaining that I was biased. I was confronted by the manager and the supervisor. I told them I had told the one employee what I had learned at college. The supervisor told me to keep what I learned at college out of the work. I told him, "You are breaking the law, having around 95% of the employees in this one culture. There is to be a certain percentage of all different cultures, races, and disabilities." After that, the supervisor threatened to press charges against me for being biased. I told him I was not biased! I had brain surgery. I had to re-learn everything all over again. I didn't even know my own language – English. I explained to him that I had had brain surgery, and they had removed 100% of my front left temporal lobe brain, including my memory. However, it was of no importance to him that the other culture employees knew English but refused to speak English at work. They preferred to speak their own language.

Once again, I was being discriminated against.

The business class I took taught me to make up a business plan and business cards. The instructor told us to have an elevator speech prepared for when you bump into somebody. I now had an elevator speech with my business cards made up for the re-learning center I planned to start up. I wanted to get this business plan up and running. I thought of who I could go to to help me get my re-learning center up and running. I decided to go to a Brain Rehabilitation Centre at the University Hospital where I now lived.

I took my business plan to the Brain Rehabilitation Centre at the University Hospital and spoke to the manager there. I explained to him my business plan. After I presented my business plan to him, he asked me, "Can I make a copy of your business plan?" I asked him, "Why?" The manager told me he wanted to make a copy and take it to the big shots at the University Hospital. I asked him if I would be involved. He told me, "No." I told him, "No way! You are not taking my business plan from me. I have gone through this. I know what it takes to get back to normal. I know now that I have a good business plan if the Brain Rehabilitation Center likes it."

I was walking downtown when I came across a place where they did IQ tests. It caught my eye. I wanted to know where my IQ was since the last IQ test, which I had two years after my brain surgery, was in the 30th percentile. I went in and took the IQ test. They came to me and gave me my IQ score. My IQ score was now 96th percentile. My IQ had jumped nearly 70 points.

I had been living in this two-bedroom apartment for about one year now. I lived on the first floor. There was an apartment above me. In the fall, it started raining a lot. I started noticing the carpet was soaked and that the ceiling was leaking. There were no pipes in this area. The ceiling never leaked unless it rained. I had to get a restaurant pickle bucket to catch the water leak when it rained. The pickle bucket would fill up fast. I went to the apartment manager, but she wouldn't do anything. The leak was so bad that the ceiling was sinking in. I noticed that I had black mold on the carpet now. I went to the higher-up in the apartment management

– still nothing. I then said I wanted to move to a different apartment. They told me I had to wait until my lease was up. I was very upset. I was living in black mold! Finally, my lease was up. There was a different two-bedroom apartment I could move into. I had to get help packing my belongings and moving. Once I had moved out, I found out the owner of the apartment complexes came to see the damage to my apartment. The owner fired this management company ASAP. There were a lot of repairs to be done now that management refused to do them in the beginning.

The new management team let me be on a non-lease for two months to see if I liked this new apartment. Well, it was nearly two months, and I got a phone call from a low-income housing manager. I had been on the waiting list for several years to move into low-income housing. The low-income apartment was only a one-bedroom apartment. I told them I would let them know if I would take it. Then, about a week later, I received a notice from the apartment complex where I lived. The notice stated that they were raising the rent by $400 more per month! There was no way I could afford to stay there. I only had $25 left over every month after I paid my rent now. My new rent would be about $400 more than the Social Security I received. My financial aid at college had been keeping me afloat this far. I let the low-income housing know that I would take the apartment after all. When I saw the apartment at the low-income housing, I was not happy. This one-bedroom apartment was smaller than my studio apartment, but rent was jumping up everywhere, and I was on a fixed income. The low-income housing was a high-rise apartment complex.

I had to find some people to help me move. I had to get rid of a lot of my belongings. One of the things I had to get rid of was my bed. I had to go back to sleep on my recliner. Then, one day, the secondhand store where I volunteered had a hospital bed for sale. It was 75% off due to the color change discount. I bought the hospital bed for under $40. I needed a bed that was elevated so I could elevate my head and feet. I needed my head elevated due to a sleep disorder. I also needed to raise my feet to elevate them because of all of the surgeries I had had on my feet.

It didn't take long for me to start to realize that this place was neither a healthy environment nor a safe place to live. People were smoking cigarettes and doing drugs in their apartments, hallways, elevators, and stairwells. My respiratory system shut down around smoke. I had to learn to hold my breath or cover my face with my shirt. Then, the bedbugs started up. I had never heard of bedbugs before here. The bedbugs were in a lot of apartments. I told the person who sprayed bugs that these bedbugs were coming from out in the hallway and heading to tenants' apartments. I told her I knew these bedbugs were in the baseboards; I had seen the bedbugs crawling in the baseboards. I kept telling her to take the baseboards off and look for herself. She finally took the baseboards off and used her flashlight to see if I was correct. She saw that the bedbugs were traveling just like a group of ants would. She saw the bedbugs traveling under the baseboards, up and down the doorframe, and back into the baseboards. Now, the lady realized that she had a more serious issue. There was a notice for the tenants to "bag up" everything in plastic bags (dishes, knick-knacks, clothes, etc.).

Everybody had to wash all their clothes, towels, blankets, etc., and then put them in garbage bags. We could only keep out a few days' worth of clothing, towels, and washcloths. I had to keep all my bagged stuff in the bathtub! I even had garbage bags of clothes on the bathroom floor that I was wearing every day. I had to live like that for several months.

I found out that my next-door neighbor was living in filth before the bedbug issue. His apartment was filled with bedbugs. He smoked and drank a lot; he was always drunk. He also did drugs. He was basically in a "frail" condition. He used a porta-potty. The health department came and dumped his porta-potty just once a week! His apartment stank horribly! I knew the bedbugs must have started from his apartment.

Just a few months of living there were so horrific that I couldn't focus on finishing college. I had to stop going to college with more than enough credits to graduate, but I needed five mandatory credits to graduate! When I quit college, I got a sealed envelope with my grades in it. I had to stop college with a 3.2 Grade Point Average (GPA) with 100% of my front left temporal lobe brain removed, including my memory.

Back to my dysfunctional family. I was informed by a relative that my wicked sister's husband had left her. She couldn't handle her husband leaving her for another woman. She started drinking. One day, she drank so much that she was drunk! She drove her car while she was legally drunk and crashed into another car. The driver of the car that my wicked sister crashed into died from her crashing her car into this other driver's car! I heard my wicked sister put a lien on her house about this time without her ex-husband being aware! Did my wicked sister borrow money and put it on the house loan to pay off the dead driver's family?

It was not too much longer that I was told my Dad had been in a nursing home for years. I was told that Dad was no longer eating or drinking. They were waiting for him to die! Dad stayed alive for several months without eating or drinking. I never went back to this dysfunctional family or dysfunctional state to go to Dad's funeral. I was told that my dead brother (who died from severe brain damage caused by his seizures) had been sitting at the funeral parlor until Dad died! The dysfunctional family refused to give my brother a funeral service or burial. They planned that my brother would be put in Dad's coffin once Dad died. Well, I found out that my dead brother, who died from severe brain damage caused by epilepsy, was in Dad's coffin without his name on Dad's tombstone! The future generations would never know where my dead brother was buried, let alone his birth date and death date.

Now, my wicked sister had never spent any prison time for killing another driver because of her driving drunk! I then found out that this wicked sister hurried up and sold everything she had because she was moving over 1,000 miles away from the dysfunctional state she lived in. Did my wicked sister sell everything and move at least 1,000 miles away because she was going to go to court for killing a driver because she was driving drunk?

Ever since I started college, I had continued to stay stocked up with my basic supplies (toilet paper, Lysol, food, etc.) to last for three months. Then COVID came. Not too much later, grocery stores, department stores (e.g., Walmart), and convenience stores ran out of food and basic needs like paper products, Lysol, etc. Since I had stocked up for three months of food, toilet paper, Lysol, and other basic needs, I wasn't in a rush to grab the last toilet paper, paper towels, etc. For years, people had asked me, "Why do you have so much toilet paper, paper towels, food, etc.?" I always told them I did not know if I could afford the stuff next month or if I got sick or injured and would not be able to go shopping for these items. I would rather be prepared. I told them I had been doing this ever since I started college. I told them that I still thoroughly cleaned my apartment every three months like I did when I was in college. I refused to break myself from these good habits. I basically "spring cleaned" every three months – I still do today.

It was just several months into the COVID, and my hips were hurting me severely! Those lipoma tumors on my hips that I had had since my brain surgery were very large and hurting severely. Doctors told me that my insurance would not pay to have them removed from both of my hips. Since my doctor would not listen to me, I called my insurance and told them how chronic my pain was from these lipoma tumors on each hip. I told them that I had had these lipoma tumors on my hips for over 20 years now. I could not lay on either one of my sides or on my stomach. I told them I could only lay on my back. I told them that since I had had epilepsy all my life but was seizure-free since my brain surgery, if I ever had a seizure and I was lying on my back, it would be dangerous! I explained that epileptics shouldn't lay on their backs when they sleep. If they do and go into a seizure, the epileptic seizure would last much longer. After I explained my issue to my insurance company, they finally approved me to have surgery on the lipoma tumors on each hip.

I saw the surgeon, and there was a surgery date planned to remove the very large lipoma tumors that were on both of my hips. I started planning what I would need to cook ahead of time and put it in the freezer. This way, all I had to do was microwave the food. I went to the grocery store and found some other food and basic needs I would need during my recovery. I called around and talked to people to see if they would help me out with things like taking my garbage out, going to the store for me if I needed it, getting my medications at the pharmacy, etc. I even had church ladies who planned to bring me dinner to my apartment every day while I was recovering. I then contacted the doctor and told him I needed him to order a home health care nurse to come and see me during my recovery after my hip surgery. The doctor ordered a healthcare nurse to come and see me the day after I came home from my surgery.

Well, it was the day I went into the hospital (during COVID) to have the surgery done. The surgeon told me that I would go home the same day. I tried to tell the doctor that I could not go home the same day; I needed to stay in the hospital overnight to recover from the surgery. The doctor told me, "No. You will go home after the surgery is performed." After I came to from the surgery, the surgeon told me that I had two lipomas on each hip. They told me that the lipomas on one side of my hip measured 12 inches across. He then said the other lipomas on the other side measured 14 inches across. I had four lipoma tumors on my hips that totaled "26" inches across laying on my hips. That was over two feet of lipomas lying on my hips! I hadn't eaten all day, and the hospital didn't check if I had some food to eat before I was discharged! A church member brought me home from the hospital. He left after a little while. I kept my door unlocked.

I tried to get up to go to the kitchen to get something to eat. When I stood up, I had blood rushing to my face! I sat back down. A short while later, I tried to get up to get something to eat, and I had the blood rushing to my face again. I decided to try to get to the refrigerator and get something to eat ASAP. I went to the refrigerator, and I was feeling lightheaded. The next thing I knew, I woke up on the floor. I had wet myself and threw up a little bit. My cell phone was across the room. I was very weak, and I couldn't get off the floor. How could I get to my cell phone and dial 911 with surgery done on both of my hips? I figured I had to try to crawl like a paralyzed person on the floor to the other side of the room to get to the cell phone to call 911. I dragged myself by keeping my body on the floor and using my hands to pull myself forward to the cell phone. I finally got to my cell phone. I dialed

911. The ambulance came and took me to a different hospital. I told the ambulance I had just come home from having surgery a few hours ago. I needed to go back to the hospital where I had my surgery just hours ago. The ambulance refused for me to go back to the hospital where I had the surgery performed.

The ambulance took me to another hospital. I told the ER that I hadn't eaten all day and needed something to eat. One of the medical staff gave me a turkey sandwich. I told the medical staff that I could not have turkey! Turkey raised my potassium over the borderline high. The medical staff looked at my blood work and told me my potassium was fine in the blood work that they did. I told him that it was because I did not eat turkey, tomatoes, bananas, etc., that were high in potassium. The guy refused to listen to me. I had no other choice but to eat the turkey sandwich!

I was admitted to the hospital. In the early morning, a medical staff came to draw blood from me. The doctor came later and told me that my sodium was very low. She then told me that my potassium was very high. The doctor blamed me for drinking too much water. I told her it was not the water. I then told her that my potassium was normal after they had done blood work last night, but one of the ER staff had given me a turkey sandwich. I tried to tell him I could not eat turkey, which would raise my potassium over the borderline high. The doctor looked at my blood work from the previous night and saw that my potassium was normal then.

The doctor told me that my sodium level was dangerously low. She had ordered me to have two bags of IV fluid sodium to be put in me to raise my sodium. The doctor ordered me to have only a "few ounces" of water a day. I had to get my sodium to rise back up. I told her my blood work showed that I was dehydrated. It was not the water causing my sodium to go down. I asked her, "Why would I be dehydrated if I drank too much water?" She had no answer to that. She ordered me to start drinking V8 juices. I tried to tell her I could not have V8 juice. It had tomatoes in it – tomatoes are high in potassium. My potassium would go over the borderline high! She refused to listen to me and left.

The next day, the doctor came to me and told me, "Evelyn, you are getting older now. You are not able to take care of yourself anymore." I told her, "Bull. I am not that old. You are just about fifteen years younger than me. So, fifteen years from now, will you be too old to take care of yourself, and will you be put in a facility?" I told her I had planned my surgery. I had lined up neighbors to help me with my daily needs, the church ladies were going to bring me dinner every night, and I had gotten a home health care nurse to come to see me at my apartment. I told her the home health care nurse was going to come the day after my surgery, but I came to the ER because I was unconscious. The doctor told me that people didn't usually plan for their surgeries. I told her I had planned for my surgery. I told her how I had four brain surgeries in two weeks, and I went home with no rehabilitation.

I got the doctor to see that I was more than capable of taking care of myself. She told me that I could go home the next day, but I needed to stay away from water and drink a lot of V8 juice. Well, ever since I was put in the hospital, the medical staff had an alarm cushion on the chair I sat on during the day. They didn't want me to go to the bathroom by myself in case I would fall or go unconscious. I always had to buzz the button to let the nurse know I was going off the chair. But now that I was being discharged the next day, I thought they would take the alarm cushion away.

Well, the next day arrived. A different nurse came in to see me that morning. She told me that the doctor had decided for me to stay another day in the hospital. The doctor wanted to see how I did when I drank more water. I told her, "No way! I was told that I was going home today. I am going home. I am not spending another day in the hospital." The nurse told me that a different doctor was taking my case that day. This new doctor wanted me to spend another day there. I told her to tell the doctor to come in here and talk to me. The doctor refused to come in and see me. I decided enough was enough! I got off the chair with the alarm on it. Once I got off the chair, the alarm went off! I got my clothes and went into the bathroom to change into my own clothes! The nurse came in and asked me what I was doing. I told her, "I am leaving! I was told by the doctor yesterday that I was being discharged today! I am leaving. I am out of here!" The nurse told me that it would be better if the doctor discharged me instead. I told the nurse I didn't care what the doctor had to say. I was out of there.

Not too much later, the doctor came in and discharged me. I called a neighbor to come and pick me up at the hospital. I was leaving. I told the neighbor of the ordeal I was going through. I told him to come into my room and get me. "I am walking out with you. I will not have anybody put me in a wheelchair and take me out. God only knows where they might take me," I told him. The neighbor came, and I walked out of the hospital with him.

When I got home, I decided to do some research on the medications and vitamins that I was taking. I wanted to see if any of the medications would cause my sodium to go down. After about an hour, I found that one of my medications prescribed to me caused you to LOWER your SODIUM! I found the answer. Why wouldn't the doctors do the research? The medication that caused my sodium to go down was ZOLOFT! I had been taking Zoloft for nearly ten years. My sodium had been going low for the last six years. For the last six years, the doctors had been trying to tell me to stop drinking so much water. I always told them I was not drinking too much water. For the last six years, the doctors had accused me of drinking too much water, which caused my sodium to keep going down. Why didn't the doctors look at all of my medications to see if it was the medication that I was taking?

Well, the home health care nurse was coming to see me on a regular basis. The church ladies would only drop off the food for me at dinnertime. They didn't want to go inside anybody's apartment because of COVID! My hips were large because of the swelling due to the surgery. There was a group of neighbors who saw me wearing sweatpants, and my hips were huge. This group of neighbors would start laughing at me, pointing at my hips and saying, "Look at that. That is FAT!" Then, they would continue laughing at me while I was going inside the apartment complex.

The incisions on my hips were draining out. I took a shower before the home health care nurse came. Once I took a shower, I had a funny color of fluid coming out of my incision. The nurse came not much later and looked at my incisions. She told me that I needed to call 911 and get to the hospital ASAP. She told me my blood was "brown." She bandaged my incisions up well. I dialed 911. The ambulance came. I told the ambulance, "I am going to the hospital where I had the hip surgery done. You do not take me to the other hospital again." I told the ambulance I had called the hospital where I had the surgery, and they told me to come to their hospital. After the ambulance disagreed with me, they took me to the hospital where I had the hip surgery done. Once I got to the ER, there were a lot of people in the waiting room. Everybody was wearing face masks because it was still the beginning of COVID-19. The ER was full of patients in the emergency room, so I had to stay in the waiting room until they had a room for me.

It was about ten hours later before the ER put me back in a room. They had doctors look at my incisions and saw the brown blood coming out of my incisions. After about six hours, I was admitted to the hospital. I was on three different types of IV antibiotics. The IV antibiotics weren't the cure for my brown blood; these antibiotics were stopping me from getting sicker. The medical staff had draining tubes put in both of my hips where the incisions were to drain out all the fluids. The medical staff took a sample of the brown blood to the lab to see what type of infection I had in my blood. While the blood sample was in the lab, I tried to stay focused on getting healthy again. I focused my mind on the Re-Learning Center that I was planning to start up.

When the nurses came in, I told them about my brain surgery. I then told them that ten years later, I had gone to college. I told them of my grades in college. I also told them about the Re-Learning Center that I planned to start up. The nurses told me that I needed to get my Re-Learning Center up and running after COVID-19 was over. I showed them my business card. I told them I had met a woman on the bus who had memory issues. I gave a few suggestions of what she needed to do to help with her memory. I told them I showed her my business card, and she told me she would draw me a logo for my business. I told the nurses that this logo was from the woman who drew it for me. The nurses loved the logo drawing. Once again, they told me I needed to get my Re-Learning up and running after COVID was over.

In a few days, the medical team figured out what antibiotic I needed to kill the infection in my blood! After six days in the hospital, I was discharged. However, before I was discharged, the doctors wanted to make sure I knew how to read the measurements of how much fluid came out of my incisions. They told me I had to keep track of the measurements on this chart. I understood how to read the measurements of the fluid in the tubes when I drained them. I was now going home. A church member picked me up and took me home. Once again, the home health care nurse started to come back to check on me. I was on the recovery path now. After over one month of draining the tubes of fluid, there was no more fluid coming out. Now, the drain tubes were removed at the doctor's office. I had to keep bandages on for a while until the incisions were closed completely.

The low-income housing high-rise was getting ever more dangerous to live in. There were a lot of homeless people sneaking into the high-rise apartment whenever the electric doors opened or if the basement door was left open by a tenant. Now, there were homeless people sleeping in the hallways, stairwells, etc. There were cigarette butts in the hallways, elevators, stairwells, etc. This place had become too risky to live in anymore. There were more problems happening every day. There was always yelling, screaming, slamming of doors, fights, etc. It was so bad that the police were called there a lot. I had a neighbor who was stalking me on top of this. He was a prior boyfriend for about six months before I broke up with him. He had never lived in this apartment back then, but now, this ex-boyfriend was a next-door neighbor of mine. His door was just four feet away from my door! He kept knocking at my door, asking for food or money. I told him, "No!" Whenever somebody knocked at my door, he would open his door to see who was at my door.

Whenever I left my apartment, he would come out of his apartment and be walking right behind me. I caught him taking a picture of my rear because I heard somebody and turned around real fast. I saw his cell phone aimed at my rear end. Worse yet, one day, he saw me in the hallway. He told me, "I found out you do not have a boyfriend." He then put his hand by the zipper of his pants, saying, "I am going to get some of this." He put his hand (closed hand position) by the zipper of his pants, making an outward and inward motion while he said that to me. I told him, "No, you aren't." He then put his hand forward and pointed his finger at me, saying, "Oh, yes, I will"!!!

I got a restraining order, but the apartment manager wouldn't make this ex-boyfriend move out of his apartment due to the restraining order. The cops told me they couldn't do anything because the landlord had to do it. Then the landlord said cops must tell her that my ex-boyfriend, who I had a restraining order on, needed to move out of his apartment.

I'd had enough! I got a hold of the apartment manager's boss. I kept bothering them until I got to move to a different apartment complex that low-income housing had. I contacted the YWCA to help me with my move. Being in low-income housing, the YWCA helps people who have domestic issues and need to move. The YWCA told me they would get a moving company and move all my belongings to my new apartment. I found a new low-income housing complex. It was not a high-rise apartment; it was a normal apartment complex. I looked at the new apartment that I would be moving into. This new one-bedroom apartment was double the size of the tiny one-bedroom apartment I was living in.

It was the dead of winter when I moved into this new apartment. I had a lot of boxes, milk crates, totes, and furniture that the movers had to move for me. Before the movers loaded up anything to put in the moving truck, I told them to put all the boxes, totes, and milk crates in first and put the furniture in the truck last. This way, unloading would be much smoother. The movers listened and put all boxes, totes, and milk crates in the truck first. Once we got to the new apartment, it was a breeze for the movers to unload everything. It took half the time to unload the truck than it did to load it up.

I felt a sigh of relief that I was in an apartment complex rather than a high-rise apartment. I put away all the refrigerated food and a few other items this day before I called it a night. The next day, I started going through my boxes, totes, and milk crates. I finally went through all of them. Everything was put away. I even had all the pictures hung up on the wall. All the furniture was in order, and the knick-knacks were put in their places. It took me only seven days to go through all those boxes, totes, and milkcrates. I counted the boxes, totes, and milk crates I had. I had gone through over 80 boxes, 30 totes, and 20 milk crates in just seven days. I had my apartment looking like I lived there for a while within seven days! I went to tell my next-door neighbor to come and see my apartment. I had finished going through all my stuff and had it put away in seven days. The neighbor didn't believe me. I insisted she come and see my apartment. She came over and looked at my apartment. Her eyes popped open when she saw my apartment. She told me, "It looks like you've lived here for a while, Evelyn. You did this in just seven days?" I told her, "Yes. All by myself."

***

Now, I was at ease living in my new apartment. Things were going well so far. I received a phone call from a relative. They told me that one of my cousins had died. I looked up this cousin's obituary, which was out of state. While looking at his picture, I wondered what he had ever done for me when we were kids. I was drawing into my childhood life. Then suddenly, the missing puzzle to what happened to me when I was nine years old came back to me! I was visualizing the episodes that took place when I was nine years old. It was scary! What really happened to me when I was nine years old was becoming clearer now. What happened? Why did it happen? Well, brace yourself for a frightening time that I experienced. Here it goes:

It was Vietnam War time. My brothers were in the Vietnam War when this happened. They had no idea what happened when they were fighting the Vietnam War, nor did they ever find out what happened when they came back from the War. What happened? Well, I was still looking at the picture of my dead cousin while I was going back into the time of my trauma. Here it is:

Nobody was to be in the kitchen until after the food was all cooked for supper. Nobody could put what food they wanted on their own dinner plates. You had to eat what was put on your dinner plate. My mom and my two older sisters (then teenagers) were putting the food on the dinner plates at the stove. I would sit on the kitchen chair and wait for the food to be put on the table. Dad was the only one who had an assigned seat to sit in. Everybody else could sit at any seat. Once the food (potatoes, meat, and vegetables) was on the first plate, Mom told my older sisters (teenagers):

"Make sure you put arsenic in Dad's food!!!!!!"

I said in a scared voice, "You are not killing Dad, are you?" My mom told me, "No." I let it be at that, but I watched my dad start coughing and choking on the food. After that, I knew they were putting poison in Dad's food! I decided to continue sitting on a kitchen chair next to Dad's chair while my mom and two older sisters served up the food onto the plates. Just like yesterday, Mom told my sisters, **"Make sure you put arsenic in Dad's food."** My sisters would tell mom, "OK." I saw my sisters sprinkle stuff on the food that was on the plate. Then, one sister would place that plate of food in the spot where Dad would sit to eat his dinner. Then, the rest of the plates of food that were served on the plate were normal plates. However, when the second plate of food (not arsenic) was put on the table, I would say, "I want that plate. I am hungry." My sister would give me the second plate of food. Then, when everybody's back was turned, I would take my plate of food and put it in Dad's spot. I would then take the arsenic plate of food and put it where I was sitting. Then, when one of the sisters brought over the third plate of food to place on the kitchen table, I would watch them and make sure they had all their backs turned so I could take the arsenic food I had and switch it to the spot the third plate of food was placed. There were times when one of the sisters would turn around and bring the fourth plate of food, so I couldn't switch my arsenic plate of food, which I had now, but I always got to switch my arsenic plate of food to either the third or fourth plate of food. Once in a while, one of my sisters would catch me switching my arsenic plate of food to either the third or fourth plate of food. They would ask me, "What are you doing?" I would tell them, "This plate of food has more potatoes." Once mom heard that, she would tell my sisters to give me more potatoes. I would then get another spoonful of potatoes. I made sure that Dad, my baby sister, and I never got arsenic food. Sometimes, my baby sister would sit in the spot where the arsenic plate of food was. I would tell my baby sister, "Don't sit there; sit over here." My baby sister listened to me.

Now that all the plates of food were on the table, everybody was called to come out to eat. Once everybody was eating, my mom and older sisters would "stare" at Dad eating his food. My dad didn't cough or choke on his food anymore. My mom said, "Why isn't he getting sick? We need to put more arsenic in his food!" Once Dad was done eating, he wiped his face and started to leave when my mom asked Dad, "How was your supper?" Dad grinned and said, "That was good. Thank you." While Dad walked away, Mom and my older sisters kept wondering why Dad never got sick from his food. But while they watched Dad eating his food, everybody, even my mom and older sisters, would eat. One of them would have the arsenic plate of food that they never knew they had and would start eating the food. Whichever one got the arsenic food (neither my Dad, baby sister, or I got it) would take a few bites before they started coughing and choking. My mom would always tell the person coughing and choking on their food to "not put so much pepper in your food." My mom even got arsenic food. After they coughed or choked on their arsenic food, they would throw their food in the garbage and say, "I will get something later to eat."

This continued to happen. I needed it to stop before they found out I was trading arsenic food for somebody else to eat other than Dad. I decided to go to my uncle. I went to my uncle crying and told him, "Uncle", please don't let Mom kill Dad." My cousin was standing near his dad when I told his dad (my uncle) that Mom was putting arsenic in Dad's food. My uncle was dumbfounded. I told my uncle how I was switching the arsenic food so Dad never got it. I told the uncle that whoever got the arsenic food would be coughing and choking while eating it. They would then throw the food in the garbage, thinking they put too much pepper in their food.

My uncle came to the house and confronted my mom about the arsenic in Dad's food. I walked away. I was happy that my uncle was helping me save Dad's life. After my uncle left, my mom went to my older sister and told her, "When you go to school tomorrow, you ask your cousin who told his dad about the arsenic." I was scared. I was hoping that my sister would never find out that I had told the uncle. Well, school was out, and we all came home. My wicked sister looked at me and then looked at Mom. She then told Mom, "Evelyn told the uncle about the arsenic." My mom came after me and said to me, "You ruined my life. I will make your life miserable!" I started screaming, "No! No!" My mom said, "Oh yes, I will. You just wait and see!!!" I went to my uncle and told him that his son, my cousin, had told my wicked sister that I had come to him and told him about the arsenic being put in Dad's food. My uncle confronted my cousin, his son, and scolded him. The cousin told my uncle that my wicked sister had asked him, so he told her the truth.

I came out of focusing on this event of my life when I was nine years old. I saw the picture of my deceased cousin and said to my dead cousin, "You tattled on me and ruined my life for saving my dad's life." After that, every night around dinner time (between 4 pm to 6 pm), I started getting severe panic attacks. I knew the panic attacks were from reliving that torturous life when I was nine years old. It took a few months of me having severe panic attacks before they went away for good.

I now know why I had such a miserable life and a very rotten family. I saved my Dad (is he?) from being killed by my mom and two older sisters. If I hadn't saved Dad's life, he would have never seen his kids graduate from high school or get married. Dad would have never seen any of his grandchildren or great-grandchildren, nor would any of Dad's grandchildren have ever gotten to know their Grandpa because he would have been killed by arsenic during the Vietnam War time.

Is Dad really my Dad, or isn't he?

"Maturity is not when we start speaking about big things. It is when we start understanding small things."

- *Unknown*

Chapter Fourteen

Now that I had found the "missing puzzle" of why my life had been so miserable, I was dawning back on the drama. I was realizing the episodes that had occurred. There was so much drama in my life, but I believed I had found the real reason why (besides saving my dad's life from arsenic) my life was miserable. I recalled that whenever I would say something to somebody (be it a relative or visitor), my mom would tell them, "Do not 'listen' to Evelyn. She does not know what she is talking about. She is epileptic!" This became a usual saying, like a "skip record." I remember how my mom would always say this, so much so that the other family members started believing that I didn't know what I was talking about because I was epileptic. Did this start because I went to my uncle about Mom and my two older siblings put arsenic in Dad's food? Was this why the community started believing that I was not all there?

I knew I had Jesus, God, the Holy Spirit, and the angels watching over me. I knew there was a reason why they protected me. I had been through so much and had to deal with so many issues and trauma in my life. I mean life-or-death issues that were not medically involved. Let me tell you several of the life-or-death issues I have experienced on my own.

You see when I lived in the studio apartment, there was a laundry room on site. The apartment manager was on site 24/7 as well. One evening, I put my laundry in the washer and started it up. The water was leaking all over the floor in the laundry room.

I went and knocked at the apartment manager's door to let her know that the laundry room was getting flooded. Nobody (the apartment manager or her boyfriend) answered the door at first, nor did anyone look out the window to see who was knocking at the door or ask, "Who is there?" Then suddenly, the door opened, and the manager's boyfriend took his rifle and aimed it at my head. He clicked the rifle and was ready to shoot me with his rifle! Then he saw that it was me, and he put his rifle down. The manager saw what her boyfriend did to me, but she said nothing. She just turned her head and didn't want to see me get shot dead. I had trauma after that whenever the 4th of July came around. I subconsciously had the memory of the rifle aimed at my head when fireworks went off. When the fireworks did go off, I would jolt out of my seat with my heart racing. I can imagine other people who have had a gun put to their faces going through this same trauma during the fireworks on the 4th of July. It took years before I got over the trauma of the fireworks going off on the 4th of July.

Oh, a few more life-or-death issues were when I was using the crosswalk to cross the street at a traffic light. I lived in high-rise, low-income housing then. I waited for the walk sign to come on before I crossed the street. I was in the middle of the crosswalk when a ¾-ton pick-up truck wanted to take a left turn when the traffic light was green. I looked at my surroundings all the time; I never took anything for granted. I saw the ¾-ton pick-up truck put on the gas and start making the left turn. The truck was aiming right at me. I stood frozen and screamed very loudly and cussed at him in a very loud voice. The pick-up truck driver slammed on his brakes. Jesus and the Holy Spirit must have intervened because I was so close to being run over by this pick-up truck that both of my hands were on the hood of the pick-up truck, and my chest was barely touching the front end of it. I stared into the windshield, staring at the driver. I refused to move until he backed up so I could continue crossing the crosswalk. People nearby heard me scream and witnessed me nearly being killed.

Oh, at this same intersection, I had another issue with another driver who wanted to take a left turn on the green. She started turning without looking at me on the crosswalk. I had to scream at this driver as well to get her to stop running over me. That was when I heard from many neighbors that this was an ongoing issue at this traffic stop. I was told that a person in a wheelchair was on the crosswalk when a car wanted to take a right turn on red and hit the wheelchair. The wheelchair flipped over with the handicapped person in the wheelchair. That was when I decided to contact the city. I complained that the traffic light at this intersection needed to have all the traffic lights red when the crosswalk sign was on for the pedestrians to cross the street. The person in charge of the traffic lights would have people come out and watch that traffic intersection. I told them this intersection was just one block away from a high-rise apartment with many people in wheelchairs and using walkers. I also told them that this was the city limits where the freeway traffic came to a head over the bridge.

I had had enough of the close calls at this intersection, so I started carrying an air horn. Not even a few days after I had contacted the city, I went to cross the street when the crosswalk came on. I looked to see if the traffic which had the red light was stopping at the red light before I started crossing the street. There was a semi-truck. I had just started crossing the street when I noticed the semi-truck wasn't slowing down. I then used my air horn at the semi-truck (which was half a block away)! The semi-truck started slamming on its brakes. You could hear the loud noise of the semi-truck slamming on the brakes. The surveyors were across the street when they heard this noise. I heard them say, "What is that?" The semi-truck was getting too close to me before stopping, so I had to walk backward to the sidewalk so the semi-truck didn't run over me. I then heard the surveyors say, "Did you see that?"

I returned to my apartment, and a few hours later, I went back to this traffic light to see if the surveyors did anything about the crosswalk sign being on, all the traffic lights were red! Well, sure enough, once the crosswalk sign came on for me to cross the street, all the traffic lights were red! I had finally accomplished this dangerous dilemma. Nobody would have to worry as much about using the crosswalk and worrying about whether they would be the next one to be hit by a vehicle.

Back to my life at this new apartment, I had been living in for about a year. One day, I was going to a neighbor's house when I saw a neighbor walking past me. She didn't look good, so I asked her, "What's wrong? You do not look good." She told me that she had headaches every morning and had memory issues.

She told me that she kept forgetting things. I told her I knew what she needed to do for her headaches and her memory. I then told her to do this every morning for her headaches. I explained why and then told her she needed to do this for her memory. I then left her and went to see the neighbor I was going to go see before I bumped into her. A few months later, I saw this same neighbor, and she looked much healthier. I told her, "You look so much better." She told me she did this every morning for her headaches. Then she said she does this other thing all the time for her memory. I told her, "I told you that." I helped somebody with memory issues remember things once again.

When I was in college, one of my business instructors told me that his sister-in-law was in a car accident. I was stunned He said she had rehabilitation, but she never recovered. He then told me his sister-in-law's husband put her in a facility where he paid over $6,000 per month for her to be there. This is when I told my instructor I believe my Re-Learning Center will be a success for people who had memory issues or a low IQ. I then told him people who have a GED, High School Diploma, or a college degree, even a master's degree, get brain damage after their degree there is no place for them to go to learn. I told him of my experience of trying to take a GED class and was refused to take the GED class because I had a High School Diploma 20 years ago.

I then told him my Re-Learning Center would be a nonprofit. People with brain damage cannot afford to get rehabilitated. Then, one day, the instructor asked me a question about his sister-in-law. He said that when her husband came to see her, she just stared at the ceiling and didn't say anything. He asked me why she just stared. I told my instructor that it was an easy question. I explained to him, "Do you know what it's like when you need time to yourself and tell people to leave you alone because you need time for yourself?" My instructor replied, "Yes." I told him, "Well, your sister-in-law is weak, and she cannot tell anybody that she needs time for herself, so she just stares at something and makes believe you are not there." This was when the instructor told me that her husband was always at her side. I reinstated, "She needs time for herself."

I had worked at a few temp jobs. For each temp job I worked at, the employer liked my performance, but the temp jobs only lasted one to three days. I did temp jobs on top of volunteering at the secondhand store. One of the temp jobs had hired me. This store that hired me was an organic grocery store. I had was at an organic grocery store. There, I cooked rotisserie chicken, made pizza, worked in the deli, and did the dishes. The employees and manager told me that the employees who did my work on my days off couldn't keep up with the work as I could. I told them, "Thank you. I was told by a manager in the past that I do work of three people." I worked there for nearly two years before I had to move to a different apartment because the apartment was being renovated. I gave the manager a six-week notice that I was leaving. I told them I would stay that long so they could not only find someone to take over my job, but so I could train them as well. The manager hired someone to take over my job. I started training her the way that I believed a person should be trained. I gave the new employee a few jobs to do while I did the other jobs. I wanted her to be comfortable doing one task before learning a new one. The new employee was now comfortable doing all the tasks by herself before I left. Before I left, the manager told me, "Evelyn, you are a great trainer." I told the manager, "Thank you." My six weeks were up, and I left the job for good. The store manager wrote me a "Letter of Reccommendation" before I left.

At my last temp job, I had to clean and organize the store. I impressed the manager with my cleaning. I then noticed that the store's stock room shelves just had everything on top of everything else. I got one storage rack (four shelves high) organized when I went to do the other storage rack. I saw this box was very large (in width). This box was on top of the drinking straws that the store would need for orders. I climbed up the ladder (like I did the other storage rack) and started grabbing this box. That was when the box fell on top of me, making me fall off the ladder backward. I landed in a "sitting" position. My hands were in a position like somebody sitting at the beach with their hands on the sand. There was nobody around me when I fell. That was when I screamed in pain. People came running to me. I told them I could not get up. My hand was hurting; I thought I had broken my hand. I was in a different town than where I lived. I wasn't going to have the ambulance take me to the hospital and leave my car there. I told them I would drive myself to the emergency room in my city.

Long story short, I broke a large bone completely off my hand/wrist area. The temp agency wouldn't help me by contacting workman comp for me. I needed them to contact them. I couldn't use my one hand; it was broken. I couldn't use my cell phone with my good hand because it made my broken hand hurt. I never realized how much people use both their hands to do simple things. I couldn't hold the cell phone with one hand and dial the phone numbers with my broken hand. After nearly one week of my complaining, they contacted workman comp for me. I couldn't get medical treatment without the workman comp giving me a "case number" to give to the medical staff I saw. I finally got to see the surgeon. They told me the large bone in my wrist/hand was completely broken off and that I needed surgery on my hand.

I tried to tell the temp agency that I needed somebody at my place to help me with my daily activities like taking garbage out, opening anything up, breaking ice cubes, doing dishes, doing laundry, etc. The temp agency told me they would not help. I asked them to have a temp worker come to my place every day and help me with my needs. I needed help doing things since I couldn't because my hand was broken. Once again, the temp office told me, "No." I had to find neighbors to help me.

At the hospital, I was put in a room prior to surgery. I had my broken hand wrapped up, and the nurse put a needle on my other hand so I could get IV fluids. The nurse left the room and closed the curtain. I was lying with my eyes closed, trying to meditate to calm myself down before I had the surgery.

I had several anesthesia people come into my room and tell me that they would be giving me "numbing medicine" before I came out of the surgery to keep the pain level down. I told them I could not have the numbing medicine; I had nerve damage. I had to use my upper muscles to do anything because I did not have hand muscles. I had had surgery years ago to remove excess tissue in my elbow, which was causing me to have severe shakes before the surgery. I told them I could not have my nerves numbed. The anesthesia people tried to tell me that I would be in severe pain if I did not have the numbing medication. They kept pestering me until I agreed and said, Okay. When I come to and I am in a lot of pain, I will let you. They wanted me to have enough numbing medication in me to last three days. I told them, "No Way! I wanted just enough for 24 hours."

I was wheeled into surgery. When the surgery was done, I was still out of it. The anesthesia person asked me while I was still coming out of it if I wanted the numbing medication. I guess I said yes. It was late evening when I was finally discharged from the hospital.

I got a ride home after I was discharged from the hospital. My hand was hurting me worse than I had expected it to. Having the numbing medicine in me was worse pain than the broken hand surgery. It felt like I had sat on my hand way too long. It was very numb and tingly. It felt like my hand was going to burst open with that numbing medicine in it. It was a long recovery from my broken hand surgery. The physical therapy I had several days a week was making my hand worse. I needed to rest my broken hand. I couldn't open anything with my broken hand. I couldn't do dishes, use any utensils to cook with, etc. I never realized how much I used both of my hands to do things with. To this day, I have permanent damage to my hand in the thumb and palm area.

It had been a few months since my broken hand surgery when my breast started hurting, and I felt a lump. I told my medical doctor I needed a mammogram done. My medical doctor told me I was not due for one yet; I had a few months before the medical insurance would pay for the mammogram.

Well, I was having loose stools constantly. Anything I ate or drank went right through me, and I had diarrhea. I went to the doctor, and they scheduled a colonoscopy for me. It was close to Christmas time, and on top of dealing with my medical issues, my companion pet, a cat, was very sick. The vet informed me that my companion cat had double lung cancer! I was terrified. I had had my companion cat since she was four weeks old. Now, she was eleven years old and dying. It was exactly one week before Christmas when my lovely cat started vomiting blood! I got a towel to wrap her up with. I tried to get her in the pet cage. It was a struggle to get her in there. It was about midnight when I had a neighbor go with me to the emergency vet hospital. When I got to the emergency vet hospital, they took my cat right back. Just a few minutes later, one of the staff came out and told me, "I am sorry. Your cat is dead. She was dead before we got her out of the cage." It felt like I had lost my child. I never knew how close I was to my companion cat until she became sick. She meant the world to me. She would always want to give me love and lay next to me, and she would never let me go to sleep at night until she gave me her nightly love.

I needed my cat to be cremated. I needed her with me, even if it meant to be in a container with her ashes. Remember, it was seven days before Christmas when my cat died. I took my dead cat to a humane society to have her cremated. I got a call a few days later telling me that I could pick up my cat's ashes. I went to my car to go to the humane society, but I could not see my car in my parking spot! I was even more terrified now. I was on a fixed income. I just had liability insurance on my car. I looked all over for my car, but it was nowhere to be found. My car was stolen! It was stolen from me just three days before Christmas. So, not only did my cat die seven days before Christmas, but my car was stolen just four days after my cat died! I called the police and told them that my car had been stolen. I gave the dispatcher my information. What a horrific Christmas year.

It was the evening time of New Year's Day when I received a phone call from a police officer about 50 miles away. They told me that my car had been found in a private neighborhood there. I told the officer I had AAA insurance to pay for the towing. I asked him to have it towed to my son's house. I notified my son and told him the tow company was bringing my stolen car to his place. I asked him to please check out my car. I took the bus to the city that my son lived in. My son told me that the battery was dead and the ignition was messed up. He said he got it fixed so I could drive it home.

My life had been torn upside down since my car was stolen. I felt like nothing that belonged to me was mine anymore. The ignition and the gear column of my car had been destroyed by car thieves. My car insurance wouldn't pay for the auto theft damage due to the type of liability insurance I had. I had to find a different car at a used auto dealer. I also had to find an auto dealer who would do financing since I didn't have the money to pay upfront. I found a car dealership that did financing. I put the car I had on Facebook Market for sale. I had offers right away. I sold my car within two days. I wrote up on a blank paper a bill of sale. I used this money for a down payment for the used car at the used car dealership. Right after I got this new car, I went to an auto parts store and got a lock to put on my steering wheel. I then went to an auto store where they put in stereos, speakers, and car alarms in your automobiles.

I told the auto store I needed an alarm put in my car. I told them how my other car was stolen and the damage done to the car. They put an alarm in my car. I told them I needed the alarm to be loud; I did not want to have my car stolen from me again. They agreed and set the alarm for me.

Well, not too long after I brought my newer car home, my car alarm went off. When I got out there, the thieves disappeared but left behind damage to my passenger side door. My passenger side door would not lock anymore. They had ruined my car lock. Now they could get into my car. I had full coverage in my auto insurance now. I had to get my car fixed. This neighborhood had become very dangerous to live in now. I had noticed that there were homeless people hiding in all the trees across the parking lot where I lived. The homeless people had caused many large bonfires. Their bonfires had caused the fire department to be called out to put out the fire. One time, the bonfire was too close to a neighbor's fence and led to the neighbor's fence catching fire!!

Now, back to my medical issues. Just a week or two after I got my stolen car back, I had a colonoscopy done. After the procedure, the doctor told me that I had a bleeding ulcer in my colon! I was told I needed another colonoscopy done in a few months.

Well, I was now going to have my mammogram done. About one week after the mammogram was done, I received a phone call from the mammogram office. They said I needed to come in and have a biopsy done on my breast tissue. About ten days later, they called me and told me they needed to do some more biopsies of my breast. After that biopsy, I was scheduled to see a surgeon. I saw the surgeon, and she told me that I had BREAST CANCER! I was terrified of what the breast surgeon had just told me. I went home crying and calling everybody about my diagnosis of breast cancer.

In nine months' time, I went from having surgery on my broken hand to my cat dying of lung cancer. Then, I went from having a bleeding ulcer in my colon to breast cancer! Oh! That doesn't include the drama of having my car stolen from me in this time frame.

My sons came to my house and took me to the hospital on the day of my breast cancer surgery. My sons stayed with me during the surgery. After I came to from the breast cancer surgery, the breast surgeon came in and told me I had "three" different types of cancer in my breast. She told me she was going to put me on a cancer pill. She said I must take the cancer pill for the next five years! My sons were terrified to hear I had three different types of cancer in my breast that the breast surgeon had taken out of me. My sons had to go back to their cities/towns to take care of their families. I spent the night at the hospital and called an old neighbor friend to see if he knew of someone who could drive my car home from the hospital when I was discharged the next day. He told me he and this woman would come and get me.

The woman drove me to my place and brought my belongings to my apartment. She gave me her phone number in case I needed anything. The church ladies at the church I went to started bringing me dinner every night when I came home from my breast cancer surgery. I was very thankful for their help.

After all, I had gone through in just nine months (broken hand surgery, bleeding ulcer in my colon, and now breast cancer), I drove my car back home after having a doctor's appointment. I was in my apartment for just two minutes when I heard my car alarm go off!! I dropped everything and went outside to see who was in my car. I saw two pickup trucks. One pickup truck had a bunch of junk in the tailgate with the driver inside the truck. The other pickup truck had nothing in the back tailgate and no driver. I was walking closer to my car, yelling, "Who is at my car?" The guy who was in his pickup truck drove off fast when he saw me heading toward my car. I then got to the passenger front of my car when I saw a guy lying on the pavement under my car. I started yelling and cussing at this guy. The guy got out from being under my car and ran to his pickup truck and drove off fast!!

Back to my medical issues. I was supposed to set appointments to see the cancer doctor and the radiation doctor soon afterward, but that never happened. You see, I was allergic to a lot of things. The bandage the surgeon put on my incision was making the skin turn very red. The surgeon saw that my skin was very red, so she took off the bandages. A few of the incisions came off when the doctor tried to take off the bandages. Now, I was leaking out of my opened incision. I had difficulty with the fluid bursting out of my breast constantly. I had to go to the emergency room several times because of that. That doesn't include all the visits to the breast surgeon's office to help me with the fluid coming out of me. She tried sealing it several times, but the fluid would burst open the sealing. I kept complaining to the staff and surgeon to have the excess fluid drained out of me. I requested the surgeon to put a draining tube in my breast when she was performing my breast cancer surgery. She refused to do it. I kept requesting it, but she never listened to me.

I only had three months after my breast cancer surgery to get my chemo or radiation done. If I did not have the chemo or radiation started within the three-month period, then it would be too late to have my chemo or radiation treatments. It had been going on for two months now, and no treatment yet. My incision kept leaking out fluid. I had been complaining about the poor treatment I had received. After I complained enough, I had an appointment to go to the clinic, and they would drain fluid out of my breast. I had about three different appointments to drain the excess fluid out of my breast. I had a total of about **260 cc** worth of fluid taken out of my breast!!

I was done with this horrible treatment here. I called a different cancer facility and asked to see the cancer doctor for a "second opinion." I told them I needed to be treated as a person instead of a "number"! I had an appointment with the new cancer doctor. She got some of my cancer tissue from the other hospital where I had my breast cancer surgery. She had my cancer tissue taken to her lab to be examined closely. When I saw the cancer doctor again, she told me that I had a 95% chance I would never get cancer again, so I did not need chemotherapy. She then told me that my HER2 cancer was in a low range. She told me that the HER2 cancer had to be at this certain range or higher before I could have HER2 cancer treatment. She told me that since my HER2 was so low, I did not need HER2 cancer treatment. Then my new cancer doctor told me all I needed to have done was radiation treatments.

Now, I was stunned. I had the old cancer doctor telling me that I needed chemo, radiation, and HER2 treatment. Then, my new cancer doctor told me I did not need chemo or HER2 treatment. Which way should I go? I was confused. I needed a third party to break the tie. Who could I contact? Who could I know for sure would tell me the truth? I needed an outside party to help me decide which doctor was more precise. I was thinking about my cancer when I saw a commercial for the American

Cancer Society! I knew right then that I needed to find the American Cancer Society phone number and call them. I needed to talk to them. I found the phone number and called the American Cancer Society. The person I talked to knew so much about cancer, but the operator didn't know about the HER2 treatments or chemo. They asked for my phone number and then an oncology nurse would call me from the American Cancer Society. I received a phone call from the oncology nurse from the American Cancer Society. I told her I needed her opinion on having or not having chemo and HER2 cancer treatment. The nurse told me the new doctor was right about not needing chemo treatment if I had a 95% chance of not getting cancer again. Then, she told me she had never heard of not doing HER2 treatment. I insisted that the new cancer doctor explain it had to be at a certain level or higher to have HER2 treatment or else it would do me more harm than good. That was when the oncology nurse told me to hold on; she was going to look up on the website to see if there were any new breakthroughs in treating HER2 cancer. The oncology nurse got back on the phone with me, all excited! She told me in excitement, "You tell your new cancer doctor thank you!! Your new cancer doctor just educated us!" She then told me with even more excitement that she was going to go tell all the other oncology nurses at the American Cancer Society the good news of HER2 Treatment.

I knew then that my new cancer doctor was the right doctor for me. When I saw my new cancer doctor at my next appointment, I told her I had called the American Cancer Society and asked them for their opinion. My cancer doctor looked a little upset at first until I told her what the American Cancer Society said. I told her they never knew of the new treatment for HER2 cancer until I called them, and they looked it up on the website. I then told my cancer doctor the American Cancer Society told me to tell you, "Thank you." You had just educated them. My cancer doctor smiled happily.

Now, my cancer doctor had me see the radiation doctor. The doctor there told me that I did not have much time left before it was too late to have my radiation treatment done. They told me that since I only had about two weeks left before the deadline was up for radiation treatment, I would have to have triple doses of radiation treatment at each appointment. They said I would have to have the triple doses five days in a row, and then I would be done. I drove myself to have my radiation treatments for five days. After all the radiation treatments were completed, I only had about five days left before it would have been too late to have my radiation treatments!

Thank God I had gotten a second opinion for my cancer. It was just like when I had to go to six different doctors before the last doctor (neurology doctor) did an MRI test on my brain. I had made it just in time to have my brain surgery. As you remember, I died on the operating table. That was when the neurosurgeon realized that the oxygen going to my brain was clogged! I was basically brain-dead until the neurosurgeon unclogged the airway so oxygen could go to my brain again. Oddly enough, the neurosurgeon had only been a surgeon for three years before he did my brain surgery. The same goes for my cancer doctor. She had specialized in breast cancer for about three years before seeing me.

Since I had been having issues where I lived in this low-income housing, I started requesting to get an emergency Section 8 to get away from this city. Not only that, but my doctors wanted me to live near my sons and their families. I finally got an emergency Section 8. I still had to wait to heal from my breast cancer. I was slowly packing up with a neighbor's help. I explained to my neighbor how I needed my belongings packed and marked. I told her if I packed my stuff the correct way, then I could unpack much faster. I then explained to her that when I had moved into this apartment, it only took me seven days to unpack all the boxes, milkcrates, and totes. I told her I even had all the pictures hung up, and all the knick-knacks put away.

I was looking for a much safer neighborhood to live in the area where my sons lived. I found this just newly built (two years old) apartment complex. It had a washer/dryer in the apartment. It also had a dishwasher, built-in microwave, and central air. I applied for this apartment and was approved. Since I had an emergency Section 8, the YWCA helped me find a way to move my belongings to this new city. I made a few trips to this new apartment prior to moving there to bring down some of the items with my neighbor. I had to figure out how I would put the furniture in this apartment ahead of time. After making a few trips and coming back from the new apartment I would be moving into, my car was starting to stall out when I drove too far or stopped at traffic lights or stop signs. The car was running, but it would not move. It took a few minutes before the car got back into gear to move. I knew from that day forward that I couldn't drive my car to my new city. It would be too dangerous to drive if the car was stalling/locking up when driving. I knew then that I had to use my AAA insurance to have my car towed to my new apartment in the new city.

On the day of the move, AAA Insurance got a towing company to come and tow my car to this new address in this new city. I also had this one neighbor of mine in this low-income housing whom I had had issues with in the past who was now harassing my movers. She spit on the movers. I had to call the police to get them to stop her from harassing my movers. I told the police that I had had issues with this neighbor in the past. The officer confronted the woman and told her to leave my movers and me alone. When the movers got everything in the truck, and I went with them in the moving truck, they told me they were happy I was moving away from this dangerous neighborhood. I told them, "I have been dealing with these types of neighborhoods for about seven years." The movers told me that they were going to contact the person at the YWCA and let them know that I really was in a dangerous living situation. When the movers got to my new apartment in the new city, they told me they could tell me this was going to be a safe neighborhood to live in. They told me that they knew this area and that it was a safe neighborhood.

Note: I moved to this new apartment in this new city just seven months after my breast cancer surgery!

When I got to my new apartment with the movers, my son and my grandchild were there waiting for the movers to come with me. There were also church people in my new city there to help the movers. Even though I had downsized before I moved here, I realized I still had too much stuff. After everything was brought in, I had to make a pathway to walk. I had no idea where anything was. The movers wouldn't load up the truck the way the other movers did in the past. These movers wanted to load my things up their way. Because of that, I had to work on unpacking much longer than usual. On top of that, I could only do so much since I had just had my breast cancer surgery seven months ago!

There was a church lady who came and picked me up for church the next morning. I had just moved in not even 12 hours ago. I never had time to unpack and find any clean clothes. I had to wear the dirty clothes I wore yesterday to church, but in due time, I started unpacking and going through stuff. In a few weeks, it would be Thanksgiving. I had to get my apartment to look decent enough for my sons and their families to come over. I got my living room and kitchen done up. I just had to do my bedroom and the balcony. I made Thanksgiving dinner for my sons to come over with their families. My one son and grandchild came over and were there for a while. The other son always went to his in-laws' house for every occasion. After he was done with the in-laws, he came over for a little while and talked.

Now, it had been about two months since I had been living here. My breast (the side where I had breast cancer) was hurting me badly. It got so bad that it hurt to move my arm. Then, one evening, I felt like I was having a stroke. I called 911. The ambulance came and checked my blood pressure. They said I needed to get to the emergency room. My blood pressure was high. When the doctor saw me, I informed him I had had breast cancer surgery and that my breast had been hurting. The doctor told me he wasn't going to check my breasts; he said he was checking to see if I had a stroke. The nurse put an IV in me without any fluid going in me. I had an MRI done on my brain to see if I had a stroke. I was still in the ER. I hadn't had any IV fluid or anything to drink for nearly 14 hours now. I asked for something to drink, and they kept saying they had to talk to the doctor. Then, a doctor came into my room and basically yelled at me for faking a stroke. I told him I wasn't faking a stroke. He continued to put me down for no reason. He wasn't my doctor. He told me he was told by a different doctor to come into my room and talk to me. You have no idea of the slandering words that were said to me by this doctor.

I found out after I left the ER and saw my cancer doctor that the fluid on my breast that they said I had was all gone. The doctor said the fluid must have found a way out of my breast, and that was why I felt like I was having a stroke!!

I started seeing a physical therapist who specialized in breast cancer fluid build-up. I saw this specialist a few days a week. It took me months before the fluid in my breast subsided, and I didn't build up excessive fluid anymore. I continued to see my cancer doctor every four months for check-ups. I was now on my two-year anniversary of being cancer-free, so my cancer doctor told me I should see her every six months.

Dealing with having epilepsy all my life and becoming seizure-free since my brain surgery over 25 years ago was amazing. However, what the Epileptics must face every day by society is outrageous and uncalled for!! Epileptics are not demonic, crazy, or drug users! When an epileptic has a seizure in public, aren't they considered a danger to society? That's right! Epileptics who have a seizure in public are considered a danger to society! Why do I say this? I witnessed this happening to an epileptic at a medical clinic. A woman had an epileptic seizure at the medical clinic waiting room. The medical team went to her and basically treated her like trash instead of helping her come out of the seizure. What they did next made me very furious!! They called the ambulance for her to go to the hospital. The woman coming out of the epileptic seizure refused the ambulance to take her to the hospital. It gets even worse. It was making me really mad at what they said next!

The medical team told this epileptic woman that if she did not go by ambulance to the hospital, they would call the police on her and press charges that she was trespassing on their property! What?! Did I hear the medical staff was going to call the police on the epileptic? Because she had an epileptic seizure and refused to go by ambulance to the hospital, the medical staff called the police on her. The Police went toward the epileptic woman. The woman was frantic about having the police called on her because she had an epileptic seizure and refused the ambulance.

That was when I went to the police officers and told them

this woman had done nothing wrong! She had an epileptic seizure. It takes a while for an epileptic to come out of the seizure. I told the officers that you do not go by an epileptic when they are coming out of a seizure. It is like coming out of a coma where you are trying to figure out where you are and what happened. Once the epileptic comes out of it completely, they are normal again. I told the officer, "You do not arrest an epileptic because they had an epileptic seizure!!!" After I was done talking to the officers, they left the woman alone. A guy in the waiting room let this epileptic woman call someone to come and pick her up from this medical clinic. This woman doctor appointment was basically cancelled because she had an Epileptic Seizure!

Well, I was at a physical clinic, and I told this person how horrible this woman was treated at this medical clinic. When I told him about the clinic calling the police on the epileptic because she had a seizure, this medical staff told me something that shocked me! He told me that they were taught in the medical school that if you encounter an epileptic having an epileptic seizure, you are to consider that epileptic as a "danger to society"!! He said they teach you that if an epileptic refuses medical treatment, then you are to call the police and get them arrested!!!

How sick is the medical field teaching Epileptics are a danger to society!! Epileptics have absolutely no rights!! It is time that people come together to fight for epileptic rights!! Epileptics are no longer to be considered a:

- a danger to society,

- demonic,
- crazy,
- drug user, etc.

Society Should Not Automatically give a person Narcan when they see someone knocked out or having a seizure in public. You have No idea if this person is having an Epileptic Seizure or a Drug Overdose!! Because of the Assumption of a person knocked out or having a Seizure in public that person is Overdosed on Drugs Only! They do not take into consideration that this person could be an Epileptic having an Epileptic Seizure!! Like I said Society brush "Us" Epileptics aside and treat Us as a Nobody!! I am sure CPR classes Does Not teach the people about the signs of an Epileptic Seizure and how to treat the Epileptic. Why teach so much about Drug Overdose and helping the drug users but push the Epileptic aside and treat "US" as a Freak, Demonic, Crazy, etc. As far as society is concerned Epileptics are everything but a human being with a medical issue! Epileptics Did Not Choose to be an Epileptic but the Drug User had a chose to use or not use the drugs. Like I said earlier Drug Users are Mocking an Epileptic! Because of Drug Users, Epileptics has to live with the assumption as being a Drug User!!!!

Why should every culture, race, gays, lesbians, bisexuals, and drag queens be considered "he, she, or it" if the person wants to be called that? The list goes on of rights for all medical rights for everybody who is diabetic, has a heart condition, etc., and needs to take daily medication. However, Epileptics are taken off their medications if they haven't had a seizure in at least one year!! Why are Epileptics pushed aside? My epilepsy was caused by having a brain infection!! So, because I am epileptic due to having a brain infection, I am considered a "danger to society" if

311

I have an epileptic seizure?

Drug users are ruining Epileptics' Rights. Why do drug users have more rights than Epileptics? When are we all going to stand up for epileptic rights? It is time we stand together and fight for epileptic rights!! All Epileptics should be paid for restitution for all the trauma that they have suffered from not only society but also the medical field and the government not seeing Epileptics as Human Beings.

It's now time to form the Epileptic Rights to be Formed!!

"Help the weak when you're strong. One day, you might be weak."

Unknown Author

Chapter Fifteen

I started volunteering at a secondhand store. I had had my breast cancer surgery just ten months prior to volunteering here. I only volunteered about two days a week for a few hours. I wanted to slowly get back on my feet after having the breast cancer surgery. I stayed there for a while, but then there was another person who worked there that was fine at first. However, then she started tattling to the manager over every little thing I said or did. When the manager would call me in the office and talk to me with that woman there, I heard of the issue. I then told the manager the truth about what happened. I told the manager how everything happened. The manager looked at the employee and asked her if that was true. The employee would look down and say yes. After that, I could not handle working around somebody who wanted to make a "mountain out of a molehill."

I went to Vocational Rehab to see if they would help me find a place to work. I had many meetings with them. They wanted me to work with people with disabilities. I told them that was what I wanted to do. I told them about the Re-Learning Center that I planned to start up. I told them everything about my brain surgery, from not knowing anything to going to college. I was not getting very far with Vocational Rehab. Somebody told me about going to Easter Seals and that they would find me a place to work. I Googled to find Easter Seals in my city. I met up with the woman there and did all the paperwork. I told her my story of the brain surgery, from having to learn all over again to go to college.

I told her that I wanted to start up a Re-Learning Center for people with brain damage. I told her it didn't matter if they had the mentality of a two-year-old; I believed I could get them back to normal. I also told her I wondered if I could help people with Alzheimer's and Dementia. I told her my memory was removed during my brain surgery. I told her that Alzheimer's and Dementia deal with memory loss.

Well, Easter seals found me a place to work. I started working at an adult daycare for people with disabilities. Before I was hired by this adult daycare, the manager asked me what I could bring to the table there. I told him, "I used to be like these people out there." The manager was stunned. I told him about my brain surgery and all. I told him I wanted to start a Re-Learning Center for people with brain damage. I then told him I went to college ten years after my brain surgery. I showed him my certificate of being on the dean's list in college one term with my IQ in the 30th percentile two years after brain surgery.

On my first day at work, I saw how the disabled people were being treated was not the way that I believed they should be treated. On my first day there, I sat down and worked with these people. I encouraged them to try to do things. After the other workers saw me working with these disabled people, they asked me, "Are you a teacher?" I told them, "No. I used to be like one of these people." I then told them I had brain surgery and that my IQ was in the 30th percentile two years after brain surgery. I am now seeing these disabled people are doing much better now. This is the experience I need to produce more when I would start my RE-Learning Center.

***

Oh, back to the issue of "Is my dad really my dad, or is he not my dad"?

I decided to have a DNA test done to find out who my biological mother and father really were. In my opinion, the mom who raised me treated me as if I were her stepchild instead of her own daughter. Like I said earlier in the book, my life is a simile of Cinderella. Cinderella had an evil stepmother and two cruel and selfish stepsisters. Every time I watched this movie growing up, I saw myself in it. I always wondered when a prince would come to rescue me from this dysfunctional family. I wanted to find out the truth about who my real biological father was. The question of whether Dad was or wasn't my dad was stirring up in me. Why wouldn't it? After over half a century, I was told I had a different father. To top it off, my siblings, nieces, and nephews always told my kids that they had a different grandpa than they did.

I received the DNA test kit in the mail. I did the DNA test at home and mailed the DNA samples to the DNA lab to be done. I made sure I had insurance on the DNA samples that I had mailed off so my DNA reached the correct company. I was waiting impatiently for my DNA results to come back to me. I wanted to find out the truth about who my dad really was. Mom did nothing but state the fact that Dad wasn't my dad without any proof. I sent off the DNA and waited for the results. I finally got the email from the company that did my DNA. My eyes were in shock when the DNA results came back of my real biological father and mother. Oh my God, was this person really my father? No way! I waited so long to find out the truth about who my biological father and mother were. Of course, my real biological mother is the mother who treated me horribly and has told me I had a different dad. But who is my real biological father? My eyes are focused on the results who my real biological father is. Oh my God! Am I reading the results correctly of who my real biological father is? No way! I waited so long to find out the truth about who my real biological father is."

The DNA results stated that my dad was the man that I was told all my life "was not" my dad! My dad sheltered me, taught me how to use pliers, screwdrivers, how to use a hammer and nail, helped me understand words I didn't know, helped me learn the rules of the road before taking the driver's permit test, taught me to write cursively again, etc. This was my real biological father!

My mom told me when she found out I went to my uncle, about the arsenic being put in my dad's food that she was going to make my life miserable. Well, she did! My children and I were considered outcasts. How many times had I heard my siblings say to me, "He is not your dad! So and so is your dad!" This was said to me over and repeatedly all my life. Mom and Dad's house was supposed to go to me when they both died (according to their will). Well, my wicked sister saw that it got changed when Dad was around 90 years old. She made Dad go to the lawyer and courthouse to have it sealed so that Dad's house went to my wicked sister's daughter. You see, my wicked sister had power of attorney over Dad. She had threatened Dad around this time, saying to him, "Dad, if you do not get rid of Evelyn, I will sell the house from you." That was when my wicked sister and her husband took Dad out for lunch supposedly, but it turned out that they were persuading Dad (who was around 90 years old) to put a restraining order on me to get me out of his house.

I had been called every name you could imagine in the book by my family and the citizens in town. I will not forget how many times I had told somebody something with my relatives there, and my dysfunctional family would always say, "Don't listen to Evelyn. She doesn't know what she's talking about." No matter how right I was, I was always wrong in their eyes. Why could other people say or do the same things that I did, and it was okay for them to do it, according to my family? But if I said or did the same thing, I was considered "crazy, an idiot," etc.? No matter what I said or did, it was wrong in other people's eyes, even today.

****

I always look outside the box and find solutions that other people cannot figure out. One example was writing up the step-by-step how to "Prep to Close" the restaurant and giving it to the owner of the restaurant. The assistant manager went by my step-by-step prep-to-close sheet of paper until she knew how to prep-to-close without my list.

Oh, how about the restaurant that failed inspection three times? If they had failed the next inspection, the restaurant would have closed. I asked the supervisor if I could go there and get it to pass inspection without the managers telling me what to do. I told her the managers had failed the last three inspections. I asked her take a chance on me to prove to her that I could get the restaurant to pass inspection. She agreed to let me go there, and I got the store to pass inspection without the managers telling me what to do. Well, sure enough, after I got the restaurant up to par, the inspectors came. The restaurant scored 96 points out of 100. Remember, this was after I had brain surgery.

Oh, how about working at a meat packing plant after my brain surgery? I worked next to the FDA employees. The FDA employees liked how I worked with them. They wanted me to be trained to be an FDA employee. I told them I was going to leave the state and live elsewhere.

Then how about the one Christmas Eve I drove out of town? I had an appointment with a doctor the day after Christmas, but the weather forecasted one foot of snow on Christmas day. I prayed to God to please help me find this church that would help me find a place to stay on Christmas Eve and have my first Christian Christmas. I drove for over one hour before the Holy Spirit told me to stop there; I found the church in this small town on Christmas Eve. This church paid for me to stay in a motel on Christmas Eve. Then, on Christmas Day, a lady at the church invited me to go with her and her husband to her daughter's house for Christmas. This was when I had my first Christian

Christmas.

Oh, then, about seven months later, this community had a massive flood. Houses were deemed severely damaged. Everyone had to wear a special face mask, high boots, long raincoats, Playtex gloves to touch anything in this area, etc. I went there with some church people to help members affected by the massive flood. I went back home to let the large city in the next town from me know how bad off this community was. I told them there were over 20,000 people who had become homeless due to this massive flood. I told them what this community needed desperately. This lady from the large city told me that she wanted to help this community but didn't know what they needed. Well, sure enough, there were three semi-loads of necessities that later went to this community. There were large donation boxes for school supplies for this community in desperate need as well.

Then, there was this guy walking on the highway with a military duffle bag, and the Holy Spirit told me to pick him up. I asked the Holy Spirit if He was sure. That was when I heard a loud "Yes" in my car. It was so loud that it made me jolt. As you remember, I told the Holy Spirit I only had a "quarter of a tank of gas" and had no money to put in my gas tank. I told the Holy Spirit I couldn't do much for him. Well, long story short, I drove this hitchhiker through four towns before I stopped at a convenience store and told him I could not take him to the next town. That was when I saw a construction guy outside the convenience store and told him about the hitchhiker. The construction guy worked for the state. He talked to the hitchhiker and asked him if he smoked, drank, or did drugs. The hitchhiker said he didn't smoke or do drugs, and he only drank occasionally. If you remember, the construction guy told the hitchhiker to come with him. He was getting him a hotel room, new clothes, and taking him out to eat that night. He then told the hitchhiker that he would take him to his job site tomorrow and would ask his boss if he would hire him. That was when I gave the hitchhiker a hug and went back to my car and looked at my gas tank. To my surprise, my gas tank was still at a quarter of a tank of gas, even though I went through four towns.

Then, there was the time when I was delivering for five different newspaper companies to stores, machines, and homes in several different towns. I made around $3,000 per month delivering all those newspapers to the stores and homes. I then prayed to God to help me find a newer home to rent for my two children and me. I told God not an apartment or duplex but a newer home with a nice big yard for my kids and me. I then took a ten-minute nap. In that ten-minute nap, I dreamt I was walking on the road when I heard a man say, "Come here. I want to show you something." Here was a man dressed all in white like Colonel Sanders. This man dressed all in white took me inside this ranch home. He gave me a grand tour of the ranch home. He asked me how I liked it. After I told him I loved it, he told me the rent price. I remember saying in excitement, "I'll take it. I'll take it." I then woke up. Then, three weeks later, I received a phone call from a woman out of town. She said she had a home out in the country for rent. I went to the home out of town to find out where this home was. To my amazement, the home I saw at this address was the same house that I had seen in my dreams with the man dressed all in white. I signed the lease and moved into a double-lot, three-bedroom ranch home out in the country!

Oh, how about the dream I had that I had a serious accident? There was nothing left but the steering wheel and me. I had glass in my eyes with cars driving fast in every direction. I felt like I was dying. I then felt someone shaking me and slapping my face, saying, "Evelyn, you are okay. Wake up! Come on, Evelyn, wake up." I felt someone shaking me and slapping my face constantly. I woke up to find nobody around me, and I had no marks on my face. I knew the Holy Spirit was warning me of being in a serious accident. My dreams usually come true between three days to one month. Well, on the third day, I was on a street driving at the top of a hill in town. I put my brakes on when I started going down the hilly street, and that was when I realized that I had no brakes! I screamed for Jesus and God for help all the way down. My van stopped just a few inches before the stop sign. The intersection was the highway leading out of town. If I never stopped at the stop sign, I would have been hit by oncoming traffic. I drove ¼ mile to the mechanics shop and they said that both of my brake hoses were dry-rotted. He said I lost all my brake fluid. I had to have the brake hoses replaced before I went back on my paper route.

Oh, how about the church clothes closet still in all the boxes and bags that had not gone through? The woman in charge of getting the clothes closet up and running never did it. There were so many bags and boxes of clothes, shoes, belts, etc., in all these boxes and bags that needed to be gone through. I got the pastor to allow me to try to go through all those boxes and bags that were from the floor to the ceiling up to the door. I went to the church during the week when the pastor or secretary was there. To everybody's amazement, I had gone through all those boxes and bags of clothes, shoes, etc., in five days. I had the room organized and ready to start opening up the clothes closet for others in need of clothes, shoes, etc.

Do you remember a homeless teenager who came to the clothes closet? He had all his clothes and college paperwork stolen from him. Then, the next day, he became upset and scared because someone had thrown a rock at his head when he slept outside at night. I let this homeless teenager move in with me. Long story short, this homeless teenager living with me convinced me to go to college even though I told him I had brain surgery, and all of my front left temporal lobe brain was removed from this brain surgery. It didn't even matter that I told him my memory was removed. I took the college test and passed it the first time. I was so excited that I had actually passed a college test even though my wicked sister told me, "Look at you, Evelyn. You are a nobody. You don't have a brain."

Then, I made up a business plan for a Nonprofit Re-Learning Center that I plan to start up once I find the right people to be on board with me. I know my Re-Learning Center will be a success. I have already helped a few people who had memory issues. I just gave them a few tips they needed to do to help them with their memory problems. That was why I wondered if my Re-Learning

Center could help people with Alzheimer's and Dementia. I had my memory removed, and Alzheimer's and Dementia deal with memory loss.

How about the brain rehabilitation center at the university hospital that wanted to make a copy of my business plan for my Re-Learning Center? I went through this. I have the rights to my business plan!! I had had so many things taken away from me that I would not have anybody take anything away from me again.

Remember that my IQ score was in the 30th percentile two years after my four brain surgeries in two weeks? Well, I recently had an IQ test done (three months ago). I scored an overall score of 115 percentile!! My math IQ was over the 120th percentile. Get this! My memory IQ score was 112 percentile! This was a huge success for me because I did this without any rehabilitation, family, or community support, nor did I have any speech therapy!

Remember how I didn't know how to drive, and the DMV laughed at me when I asked to have a driver's permit test done?

How about trying to re-learn what I forgot by taking a GED class? I was told that I had a high school diploma, so I couldn't take the GED class.

Oh, how about the woman who drove drunk and became paralyzed during the time I had my four brain surgeries in two weeks? All the different churches in town got together and raised over $60,000 to build this drunk driver who became paralyzed because of driving drunk a brand-new handicapped accessible home for her. She was young and living with her parents with no children. Here I had four brain surgeries in two weeks and I have two children at home. I never got rehabilitated after my brain surgeries. I came home after having four brain surgeries in two weeks. surgeries in two weeks and came straight home after my four brain surgeries. I asked the churches for financial help to pay my rent, and they all refused to help me.

Do you remember how my mom oversaw my checking account while I was in the hospital with brain surgery? She never wrote down any checks she wrote out; she just wrote down the deposits. My checking account went over, and I had a dilemma with the bank not willing to help me out. It didn't matter that I had just had brain surgery.

Remember my one brother had epilepsy since his late teens? Because he is a man, he could not get any medical insurance unless he got it from his job? My brother needed his epileptic medication desperately, so he purposely broke his foot several times which got him in the nursing home to recover. I will never forget my brother calling me at dad's house and telling me that the nursing home is a luxury. He told me he has free tv, food, room and board, and most importantly his medication. Well, because my brother didn't have any epileptic seizures in over one year in the nursing home, the doctors took him completely off his epileptic medication and drugged him up with psychosis medication! Not too long afterwards my brother was having nonstop seizures. My brothers' seizures got so bad he couldn't comprehend what anybody said to him anymore. His brain is destroyed from having these nonstop seizures because the doctors at the nursing home took him off his epileptic medication!!! My brother Died from his Epileptic Seizures. I have known other people who have died from

324

their Epilepsy at a young age because they are not being medicated with their seizure medications. Like I said, men with Epilepsy cannot get any Medicare or Medicaid insurance, even if they have children. Woman can only get Medicaid insurance if they have children and are earning poverty level income.

All Epileptics must be covered by either Medicaid or Medicare no matter how much money they make! Also, doctors need to Stop taking Epileptics Medication away from us Epileptics because we are not having an Epileptic Seizure! Why do Diabetics, Heart patients, etc. continue taking their medications even though they are not having a diabetic or heart attack? Like I said before Epileptics are Outcasted from society for way Too Long!!

I will finish this book with the success I have achieved today. I have more than enough credits to graduate from college. I just need to take five mandatory classes to graduate. I still sing along to music on the radio, my phone, or my record or CD player. Don't forget about the time when I got a call from Nashville Recording Studios. They wanted me. They said they were working with Reba McEntire and that I had this voice that they had never heard of before. They told me that I would be up there with Reba, but I needed $2,000 to get into the recording studio. They offered to help me out, but I told them my mom would help me. Lo and behold, was I wrong? Would Nashville Recording Studio still want me today?

Oh, by the way, let us stand up for the Epileptic Rights!! Do not let another epileptic be:

- Drugged up with Narcan
- Considered crazy
- Considered a danger to society
- Taken off their epileptic medication if they haven't had a seizure in at least one year
- Denied employment
- Denied government medical insurance.
- Put in a Mental Institution

Every Epileptic must have government-paid medical insurance, regardless of whether they make more than the poverty level. Epileptic medications are expensive! That doesn't include the blood work needed to see where their medication levels are at. Oh, what about the EEG, CAT SCAN, and MRI tests that need to be done for Epileptics? That doesn't include having brain surgery if their seizures get out of control. Remember, I was braindead on the operating table when I had my brain surgery. I had no oxygen going to my brain. The surgeon had to stop the brain surgery to unclog the airway so oxygen could go to my brain again. This is when my neurosurgeon realized I had Brain Infection.

Do not forget a Neurosurgeon Student who saw me at the E. R. 10 years after my Brain Surgeries. Remember he asked me what this & that is, count, add, say a,b,c's, count backwards 100 minus 7 & I counted backwards 93, 86, 79, 72,…..That's when the Neurosurgeon Student told me I was not to be where I am today. He told me I only had a 3 percent chance to be where I am today. He then said he was going back and watch the video of my brain surgery and see how my Neurosurgeon did my brain surgery.

"Is Jesus Calling You Out?

Let Us Now Stand-Up and Form

"EPILEPTIC RIGHTS FOUNDATION"

"Dream it. Believe It. Build it."

— Unknown Author

Short Stories

When an Egg Blossoms

David, a second-grade student, often wishes he could visit his maternal great-grandma Rosemary out on the farm since his great-grandpa Joe passed away. David loved his great-grandpa. He used to spend weekends with him and great-grandma Rosemary, helping to feed the animals and plow the fields. He even got to sit on great-grandpa's lap while he drove the tractor.

At lunchtime, David would notice his great-grandpa looking at a *Farm and Field* magazine. He would ask, "What magazine is that, Grandpa Joe?" Grandpa Joe would grin and answer, "It's a farm magazine." David enjoyed looking at those magazines with his great-grandpa Joe every lunchtime. Seeing how fond David was of the magazine, Grandpa Joe started collecting them for him, planning to give them as a gift someday. In a year, he had collected a box full of them.

One fall afternoon, while driving the tractor, Rosemary's husband had a stroke and passed away instantly. David cried for weeks over great-grandpa Joe's death. It hurt him the most on weekends, the time he would normally spend with his great-grandpa. Whenever he thought about going to the farm, he remembered that Grandpa Joe was gone.

Since his great-grandpa's death, David has found comfort in the *Farm and Field* magazines he was given. Looking at them brought him a sense of calm and made him feel as though he could smell the fresh farm air. His mind would wander back to the good old days with great-grandpa Joe. Inspired by these memories, David began to dream of becoming a farmer himself someday.

David doesn't have a father figure to look up to since his father passed away in a car accident due to drunk driving when David was just two years old. His father's car had wrecked on a bridge and plunged into a river. Now, David lives with his mom in an old, rundown duplex in town.

Nine months after his great-grandpa's passing, David's mother told him that they would be going to great-grandma Rosemary's farm for Easter. David's eyes lit up with excitement. "We are?" he asked eagerly. His mother smiled and confirmed it. David then went off to find his best and oldest clothes, wanting to wear his best for his great-grandma, but also bringing an old pair so he could play on the farm.

David's mother bought groceries to cook at great-grandma Rosemary's house on Easter Sunday. While she prepared the meal, David and great-grandma Rosemary looked through the *Farm and Field* magazines he had brought. When it was time for dinner, David eagerly held his great-grandma's hand and asked, "Which chair would you like to sit at?" When Rosemary pointed, David pulled the chair out for her, then sat beside her for the meal. Afterward, he helped his mother clear the table.

"Now, David, you can go out on the porch with great-grandma Rosemary while I do the dishes," his mother said. David quickly changed into his old clothes and joined his great-grandma on the porch swing. As they sat, enjoying the sounds of nature, Rosemary shared a story about her own grandfather's experiment with a chicken egg.

"You see, David," she began, "my grandpa had a summer assignment from school to plant something and keep a weekly chart of its growth. But instead of a plant, he used a chicken egg. He cracked a hole in the top, added an aspirin, and buried it in an abandoned field in June 1928. Soon, a 'white stem' started sprouting from the ground. He watered it weekly, adding more aspirin each time."

Curious, David listened as his great-grandma continued. She explained how her grandpa's father was shocked to see the egg grow a four-foot-tall plant with orange leaves. Birds were drawn to it, and soon, bubbles began forming on the leaves. These bubbles turned into eggs, which fell into bird nests below. The birds laid on these eggs, and one day, a shorebird hatched from one.

David's great-grandma then showed him a picture of a shorebird. Just then, David's mom came out with a tray of drinks, and they all sat quietly, enjoying the sounds of the farm. David's mom remarked on how peaceful it was and suggested they visit more often. Great-grandma Rosemary eagerly agreed, inviting them to come every other weekend. "David is growing fast. He belongs here on the farm," she said with a smile.

With his great-grandma's encouragement, David announced, "I'm going to be a farmer just like great-grandpa Joe!" His mother and great-grandma exchanged smiles as David ran off to explore the fields. He looked up at the sky and whispered, "I love you, great-grandpa Joe."

Before they left, David went into the chicken coop, carefully wrapped an egg in paper, and put it in his bag. As it grew late, his mother called him to gather his things. He gave his great-grandma a big hug and promised to visit in two weeks. She reminded him to keep looking at the *Farm and Field* magazines whenever he missed his great-grandpa Joe.

On the car ride home, David gazed out at the countryside. Once back at the duplex, he went to bed, clutching his egg. The next morning, while his babysitter was there, he snuck outside with a spoon, an aspirin, and his egg, ready to plant it and see what it would become.

Now, only time will tell what David's egg will blossom into.

Airline Flight on Christmas Eve

On Christmas Eve, a pilot named Oscar was heading to work, preparing for his upcoming airline flight. The airplane was in Atlanta, Georgia, with a destination of Madison, Wisconsin. With Christmas Day just hours away, he still hadn't bought any presents for his girlfriend, but he had some ideas about what to get.

One by one, passengers began boarding the airplane, taking their seats, and settling in. Everyone was filled with holiday cheer, excited to spend Christmas with their families. The crew was also in high spirits, enjoying the festive atmosphere. Soft violin and piano music played holiday tunes, filling the air with the spirit of Bethlehem.

But little did anyone know, a group of crickets had secretly boarded the plane. They marched two-by-two, carrying ants to eat in their tiny mouths. Some crickets stumbled, losing their ants on the way. Outside, a crow flew toward the plane, hoping to feast on the crickets. Just as the crow reached the door, it shut, trapping the bird's beak. Now, the crow was stuck to the airplane door for the entire journey to Madison.

The crickets made their way to the front of the plane, loudly chirping in unison. Passengers jumped at the sudden noise, reminded of the tragic events of 9/11. Panic spread as people wondered if it was the sound of a ticking time bomb. Frantically, they began calling their loved ones, fearing the worst. The pilot, Oscar, knew he had to act quickly. He searched for a safe landing spot and found an abandoned cornfield nearby. Carefully, he glided the plane down.

Nearby farmers heard the approaching airplane and started honking their vehicle horns to alert others. Soon, people from surrounding areas joined in, honking their car horns as they followed the plane's descent. Animals on the farm scattered in fear, some jumping fences to escape.

As the plane descended, a ghostly figure appeared, floating around the aircraft. The figure touched the brake line, causing the plane to slow down. Oscar saw the apparition and thought of his priest, realizing he hadn't been to church in a while. He began praying to Jesus for guidance. Suddenly, he heard a familiar song playing in the cockpit:

"Jesus loves me, this I know,
For the Bible tells me so.
Little ones to Him belong,
They are weak, but He is strong..."

Oscar turned up the volume, letting the passengers hear the soothing melody. The familiar hymn brought a sense of calm, and everyone breathed a sigh of relief.

Finally, the airplane came to a halt, and the doors opened for the passengers to disembark. But as they prepared to leave, a group of birds outside the plane squawked in alarm. The trapped crow fell to the ground when the door opened, shaking its head before joining the other birds. The flock angrily squawked at Oscar, who watched as the crickets hopped off the plane two-by-two, only to be eaten by the birds. The injured crow was given extra crickets as a reward.

Once the birds moved away, the passengers eagerly exited, grateful to be safely on the ground. Oscar stepped out, looked up at the sky, and whispered, "Thank you, Jesus."

Shuttles arrived to transport everyone to a new plane bound for Madison. When the press asked about the incident, Oscar shared his story, promising to attend Christmas Eve Mass before resuming his flight duties. The bomb squad inspected the plane for any explosive devices but found none. To this day, no one knows what caused the strange noise. Oscar believes it was Jesus reminding him to return to church.

Outside, the birds gathered in a nearby tree decorated with lights, their bellies full from the cricket feast. They had enjoyed their Christmas dinner on Christmas Eve.

Poems

Our Choice to Choose

We three are transparent
Floating in the air effortlessly
We chose one person to see us
She will understand
We know she will

She sees us now
We will not leave until she knows the scheme
There is only Ten minutes left
She must pay attention to the formula
She figured us out
She knows the plan

She goes to the store
Dot-dot-dot
She preferred us three
Now there are more instructions
Go home and watch TV

Seconds remain
She designates to the right station
We are live on TV
A-a...R-r...O-o...U-u...N-n...D-d...
One of us shows up first
A-r...R-r...O-o...U-u...N-n...D-d...
Instantly comes the second one of us
A-a...R-r...O-o...U-u...N-n...D-d...
Wow! She has her eyes glued to us on TV
A-a...R-r...O-o...U-u...N-n...D-d...
She sees the last one of us show up
She jumps for joy we were the true ones

We now fall back into our dark cages
We take a beating being tossed around like dice
Until next time we stay blended in with the others
It was an exciting day for us

Maybe our team will go to someone else someday
But will they know our scheme
Will they understand our formula
Only time will tell

<u>Where is Home</u>

I stray from place to place
I walk, run, and climb trees
I even drag along when I am exhausted

I search for food and shelter
I will eat anything
I need something to drink

Why do you treat me as a misfit
Why not look at me
Why do my eyes cry for you
Why do I have no place to call home

Too little to late
You will not see me tag along anymore
I have no other choice

You see I am scared
I am dying from being hit
I will leave but I will not be mad you ignored me

I am used to being ignored
Why now
Do
You
Have
Tears
In
Your
Eyes
For
Me

I walk Twelve Miles a Day

I walk twelve miles a day
Five days a week
I owned a car, but my husband would not let me drive it

I walk twelve miles a day
Five days a week
I am pregnant now

I walk twelve miles a day
Five days a week
My baby is kicking in my stomach now

I walk twelve miles a day
Five days a week
My big stomach is wobbling back and forth and back again

At eight and one-half months pregnant, I take a leave of absence
from work
One month later, I am in contractions
I have gained sixty pounds with my baby

I never knew pain like this before
My husband takes me to the hospital
My water is bursting open, and the baby's feet is coming out first

It is just past midnight, and the doctor is sleeping in the next room
Hurry I say the baby is coming
An hour later, the doctor is awake and tends to my baby and I

The hour felt like eternity
I am having a C-Section
Good thing; the cord is wrapped around the baby's neck

It is a baby boy the nurse says
He weighs a whopping twelve-pounds four-ounces
He is the attraction for all visitors to see

I used to walk twelve miles a day
Five days a week
Oh WOW! That equals sixty miles a week

My baby weighs in at over twelve pounds
I also gained sixty pounds while pregnant with my baby
Did I walk one mile per pound for my baby's weight
Or did I gain sixty pounds for the sixty mile I walked a week to
work

Who is My Father

I am being treated as an outsider
I was told I have a different father than my siblings
I have heard this since I was a young child at nine-years-old

Why treat me as a nobody
Why not accept me as your sister
Why do I have to cry

Even four decades later I am told I have a different father by my
siblings
But now my nieces and nephews continue this dilemma
I now have my nieces and nephews tell my children they have a
different grandpa than they do

You have no idea how torturous these accusations are
I did a DNA test
I am shocked of the DNA results

Why-My-Father
Is
The
Man
I
Was
Told
Wasn't
My
Father

Standing in the Clouds

I just came home from having my four brain surgeries in two weeks
I cling to the cross of Jesus on my chest
I listen to the songs of Jesus nonstop
I feel uplifted doing this

One evening I am lying on the couch taking a nap
The next thing I realize I am floating in the clouds
There is someone very-very tall in the clouds with me
This person is at least 100 feet tall
My eyes slowly look up to see who this person is

Oh; NO WAY!!
I am floating in the clouds with Jesus
He never moved or talked to me
I wake up on the couch

Ten years later I go to a bible study
The church people read a part in the bible that made me understand
"Why Jesus Why?"
Jesus causes the blind to see, death to hear, cripple to walk, etc.

I had four very serious brain surgeries in two weeks
I even died during one of the surgeries
I had a long road to travel to be healed
Jesus made the road easier for me to do it

Who is My Guardian Angle

I prayed to God after my sister died to be my guardian angle
I have had a rough journey before and after I prayed for her to be
my Guardian Angel
After six years of this, I prayed to God to give me different
Guardian Angels
I prayed to God to have my aunt and uncle who had a lot of friends
be my Guardian Angels

One night after the prayer for my aunt and uncle to be my Guardian
Angels, I had a dream
I heard a voice ask me in my dream, Who is the man 6 feet 2 inches
tall that my mom had an affair with
I thought the person was asking about the man my mom had an
affair and became pregnant with me
The Spirit in my dream said No, they know about this man
They don't know who the man is who 6 feet 2 inches tall that my
mom had an affair with

It came to me of the man that my mom had an affair with the Spirit
is asking about
I told the Spirit his name
Just like that, the Spirit that asked the question left and let me
continue my sleep
The next day I remembered this dream

I got to thinking of why the Spirit asked me this question
I was told by a Spiritual person that God is keeping my dead
siblings away from my dead mom
This person said God is having trouble having my siblings interfere
with my mom being judged by God

I got to realize why the Spirit asked me this question in my dream
The man my mom had an affair with on earth molested me when I

was 12 years old
My mom dropped the charges on this man
She said she doesn't want to see him go to prison for 10 years over molesting me

How a mom could let her lover molest her daughter and get away with it
I got to thinking of my dead aunt and uncle I asked God to be my Guardian Angels
Are they getting to the root of the trauma my mom put me through
Are they getting the answers that the judges in heaven need to know
Or are they swiping my plate clean from bad karma spirits

It feels good to have things turn around that I sit, and think is this for real
I lived half a century in torture with my mom, siblings, nieces, nephews, etc.
I always wish my aunt and uncle were my parents
They strayed away from me because of my mom in their lifetime
I ached for their attention while I was growing up
No such luck; my mom kept me away from everybody while I was growing up

I had never felt the feeling of having any friends growing up in school
I don't know what it is like to have a best friend
I was isolated from everybody
I wasn't allowed to learn to ride a bike or swim
I couldn't even play with neighbor kids

My mom had to talk to the man's mom who I was marring to discuss if it's o.k. for us to get married
Mom said she would have stopped me from getting married if she didn't said o.k.
My mom tried to stop me from letting my kids learn to swim, ride a bike, etc.
I fought back on her trying to stop my kids learning to swim, ride a

bike, having friends…
She managed to destroy my life though

Why was my mom so mean to me
I hope my dead aunt and uncle get to the bottom of that answer for
the judges in heaven
I hope I answered the question the Spirit asked me of my mom's
other lover
Does this mean justice in heaven will be done to my mom and her
"lover" who molested me

Living a Rough Road Journey

My older sister has full blown cancer
It is at Stage Four now
It is hard for her to eat or drink
She takes a fall in the bathroom one evening
She busted her tongue wide open
Her husband didn't tend to her
She swallowed blood all night long

The next day she is in a coma
Then her husband calls 9-1-1
That's when I received a phone call that she is in a coma being
airlifted to a hospital
My dad and I rush to her side

We see her gurgling in her own blood
Her teeth are stained in blood
Now visitors start to flood to see her
They leave in fear
For they know her life is coming to an end

I stayed with her until midnight
I go in a room and pray to Jesus to not let her suffer
Minutes later, the crying started
My sister silently parts into the other world
She now looks over me being unnoticed